Archives & Manuscripts: Conservation

A Manual on Physical Care and Management

Mary Lynn Ritzenthaler

BASIC MANUAL SERIES

Society of American Archivists   Chicago, 1983

Library of Congress catalog card #83-050878
ISBN #0-931828-58-9

Foreword

This manual, *Archives & Manuscripts: Conservation,* is a product of the Basic Archival Conservation Program sponsored by the Society of American Archivists. The guiding philosophy of the program has been the necessity of incorporating conservation principles into all phases of archival administration. A primary goal has been to encourage archivists to consider conservation as an ongoing archival function on an equal footing with such tasks as field work, accessioning, arrangement and description, and reference service. This philosophy of conservation management—along with practical means of its implementation—has been considered, discussed, and refined through a series of regional conservation workshops and a conservation consultant service. The Society wishes to express thanks to all of those individuals and institutions who participated in the Basic Archival Conservation Program and contributed to its success.

The conservation principles presented here provide a capstone to the core of archival literature previously published by the Society of American Archivists in its basic manual series. The encouragement and generous support of the National Endowment for the Humanities, which made this publication possible, is hereby gratefully acknowledged.

J. Frank Cook, *President*
Society of American Archivists

Mary Lynn Ritzenthaler is Director of the Basic Archival Conservation Program. She was formerly Assistant Manuscript Librarian/Associate Professor at the University of Illinois at Chicago. She received training in archival administration at Wayne State University, studied conservation at the Newberry Library and through numerous other courses and seminars, and has been studying hand bookbinding since 1972.

Contents

Introduction

Conservation is a management function, and archivists and manuscript curators, as custodians of historical records of enduring value, have primary responsibility for the preservation of collections under their charge. To date, conservation principles and techniques have not been accorded much attention either in academic archival and library training programs, or in actual practice within repositories. While this omission is now generally acknowledged, difficulties persist because there are few qualified instructors in this field, and there is often little opportunity for working archivists to pursue continuing education. Within tightly drawn parameters, this manual will address problems and issues--and propose some solutions to assist archivists in caring for their collections from a sound conservation perspective. It must be emphasized that conservation should be considered not as a new program element, but as an integral part of existing archival and curatorial functions.

The degree to which an archival conservation program will be successful will depend largely upon acceptance of four principles:

(1) Conservation is a management responsibility of the highest administrative level.

(2) An appropriate share of each annual budget must be allocated to the conservation program.

(3) A conservation program is diverse. It consists of actions and activities that include storage and handling, temperature and humidity control, security, and disaster preparedness as well as routine in-house preservation treatments and such other conservation procedures that may require special facilities and high technical competence. Acquisition, processing, research use, and exhibition are also integral components.

(4) Conservation must be the legitimate concern of all members of the staff at every level; it is not merely a technical matter to be relegated to a workshop or some remote specialist.[1]

Beyond attitudes, however, archivists and curators must have a reasonable understanding of the material nature of their collections and why these materials deteriorate, and must develop a working knowledge of appropriate control and treatment techniques suitable for in-house use, including their hazards and limitations.

This manual is directed toward persons having curatorial or administrative responsibility for archival and manuscript collections. Information will be conveyed from an archival perspective, assuming a prior understanding of archival theory and practice on the part of the reader. The convergence points between archival functions and sound conservation practice will be addressed from a nontechnical point of view. Preventive maintenance and practical means of building conservation programs within archival settings will be stressed. The focus will thus relate more to the basic and everyday aspects of archival activity than to the possibilities for highly sophisticated restoration techniques. Of practical necessity, the emphasis will be on means of preserving masses of material rather than unique items.

Textual records on a paper base are still the largest category of archival record materials and will be the primary focus. The conservation of paper records in a variety of formats—single sheets, bound into volumes, affixed to scrapbook pages, and oversized—will be discussed in the context of archival processing and preventive maintenance. A number of other archival record formats—including microforms and photographic materials, sound recordings, and videotapes—will be considered from the perspective of proper storage, handling, and environmental controls. Due, however, to the complexity of such record formats and, in some cases, a rather limited state-of-the-art knowledge of their treatment needs, complete coverage of these materials must await future research and development. References for further study are cited in the bibliography.

---

[1] Edward R. Gilbert. "A Conservation Primer: The Preservation of Library Materials in Tropical Climates." *Bulletin of the Florida Chapter, Special Libraries Association* 14:110 (July, 1982).

1 Definition of Conservation

The term "conservation" implies various meanings to audiences ranging from the general public to paper conservators, and from archivists to historic preservationists. The definition offered by *Webster's Third New International Dictionary* highlights preservation, a major sphere of activity that has come to be associated with archival conservation: "deliberate, planned or thoughtful preserving, guarding, or protecting: a keeping in a safe or entire state."[2] In the context of conserving cultural property the National Conservation Advisory Council (NCAC) has defined conservation as encompassing the three explicit functions of examination, preservation, and restoration:

Examination is the preliminary procedure taken to determine the original structure and materials comprising an artifact and the extent of its deterioration, alteration, and loss.

Preservation is action taken to retard or prevent deterioration or damage in cultural properties by control of their environment and/or treatment of their structure in order to maintain them as nearly as possible in an unchanging state.

Restoration is action taken to return a deteriorated or damaged artifact as nearly as is feasible to its original form, design, color, and function with minimal further sacrifice of aesthetic and historic integrity.[3]

This three-function approach represents a logical sequence in addressing conservation problems. A thorough understanding of the material nature of an item is required before any decision can be made regarding preventive maintenance. In fact, unless the chemical and physical makeup of an item is known, it cannot even be handled or stored properly. Restoration, the third element of this definition, is generally applicable in archival contexts only with highly unique or valuable items, and should be undertaken only by skilled professionals after consultation with the archivist or curator. From a broad conservation perspective, NCAC defines personnel directly involved in conservation as:

Conservation Scientists—scientific specialists in one or more of the associated areas of examination, preservation, and restoration.

Conservation Technicians—artisans trained in specialized skills but not in the theoretical concepts of conservation nor in a broad range of materials and techniques.

Conservators—specialists with advanced training in the arts and sciences relating to the theoretical and practical aspects of conservation who are capable of supervising and advising in the three functions of conservation.

Curators—custodians responsible for cultural properties who are expert in the identity, origin, significance, and cultural quality of the objects in their care.[4]

The NCAC definitions provide a common understanding of terms and necessary insights into the field of conservation. There are, however, limitations in their universal applicability to archival collections. In part, the definitions reflect a perspective pertaining more to unique items, such as museum objects or works of art, than to archival or library materials. While some archival materials are highly unique and warrant the same type of individual specialized treatment accorded works of art on paper, problems of archival conservation are more commonly described by the concept of volume or massive accumulations of single items which gain significance not solely on individual merit, but through their relationship to a greater whole. Thus, while much of the knowledge and many of the approaches being applied to the problems of archival conservation have been taken directly from collective experience gained in art conservation, they must be adapted to fit specific archival needs and problems.

For the purposes of this manual, the NCAC definition will serve as the touchstone for the understanding and usage of the term "conservation" and the functions it incorporates. The philosophy underlying this definition emphasizes a division of both labor and technical understanding as well as the training required for conservation personnel. Archival conservation, under optimal conditions, would be a responsibility shared by the scientist/researcher, conservator, and archivist/curator, each contributing specialized knowledge to solve the problem at hand. Realistically, however, in most archival settings it is the archivist alone who must make informed decisions regarding the material nature of collection items and their proper storage environment, as well as establish treatment options and priorities. Much of this decision making must be done without the guidance of trained conservation personnel, making it necessary for the archivist to acquire new knowledge and develop new points of view. It should be obvious,

---

[2] *Webster's Third New International Dictionary of the English Language Unabridged,* s.v. "conservation."

[3] National Conservation Advisory Council. *Conservation of Cultural Property in the United States.* (Washington, D.C.: National Conservation Advisory Council, 1976), p.31.

[4] *Ibid.,* p.31.

however, that the archivist's conservation activity should be centered around the functions of *examination* and *preservation*—not restoration. Effective conservation is largely intelligent housekeeping, the provision of a sympathetic physical environment, and the routine curatorial care of collection materials.

The relatively new emphasis on archival and library conservation has spawned a new discipline that unites many of the concerns and practices of the professional conservator with those of the archivist, librarian, and curator. Often termed conservation administration or conservation management, this developing field has many advocates but few professionally trained practitioners. While it may be unlikely that many institutions will be able to hire conservation administrators in the immediate future, all can take up the mantle, and custodians of collections, archivists and administrators alike, can begin to consider their collections from a conservation viewpoint.

2   Conservation Philosophy

An understanding of conservation philosophy is necessary before proceeding to evaluate or develop a conservation treatment program. The principles that comprise the generally accepted tenets of conservation have developed out of the world of art conservation but are applicable to archival concerns. While especially pertinent in treatment situations, this philosophy also provides the foundation for an overall conservation program that includes storage, handling, and preventive maintenance. The following principles should serve as guidelines in implementing broad archival conservation programs and procedures.

Rule of Reversibility

No procedure or treatment should be undertaken that cannot later be undone if necessary. Unfortunately, not all treatments or new materials withstand the test of time. If, a number of years after treatment, it is found that a particular procedure or material is causing damage or accelerating the rate of a document's deterioration rather than protecting it, it should be possible to reverse the procedure (i.e., return the document to its pretreatment state). It is thus important to know the physical nature of all materials involved (both collection items and treatment supplies) and how they may react together under various conditions. For example, will a given adhesive form a permanent bond over time, thus making future removal difficult or impossi-

ble? It is important to have specific knowledge regarding the method of removing or reversing a treatment. If the reversal process involves the use of water or other solvents, will these have any adverse effect on the paper or inks? It is necessary to test for possible reactions before treatment to ensure that reversal is both possible and safe.

With ongoing research and the passage of time, which allows for critical observation, techniques that once were considered acceptable may go out of favor. Silking, an early method of reinforcement that provided support to paper records by backing or lining them with silk, is an example. Once it was determined that the silk backing would break down much sooner than the paper it was meant to support, this practice went out of favor. Fortunately, most silking is reversible, since water-soluble adhesives were used.

Compatibility of Problem and Solution

It is inappropriate to apply a treatment greater or weaker than the problem to be remedied. The particular problem must be weighed against a range of possible solutions; that chosen should be most compatible in terms of like strength and material. In repair work, for example, the mending material should closely approximate the strength and character of the document to be repaired. A mending tissue that is weaker or lighter in weight than the document will not effect a strong, lasting repair. Conversely, a mending material that is much stronger than the surface to which it is to be applied will just as readily break down, essentially overpowering the problem and causing the weakened area to further break down or deteriorate. A strip of cellophane tape placed across a tear on a brittle piece of paper is an example of an inappropriate remedy. The tape (adhesive and plastic carrier) is much stronger than the paper, which may break off or tear further as it is flexed over time against the hard cutting edge of the tape. Beyond this example, pressure-sensitive tape is an inappropriate mending material in *any* archival context because of the nature of the adhesive, which is not easily reversible and which leaves permanent stains on paper (see Figure 2-1).

The principle of compatibility also may be applied to treatment systems or technologies. There is the tendency on occasion to apply a given technology just because the ability to do so exists, whether or not it represents an appropriate solution in a particular situation. The factors of existing equipment, staff expertise in a given technique, or the weight of tradition should not influence or mandate the choice of treatments that are inappropriate. Cellulose acetate lamination, an acceptable solution in some instances, is an example of a procedure that may be misapplied if individual decision making is

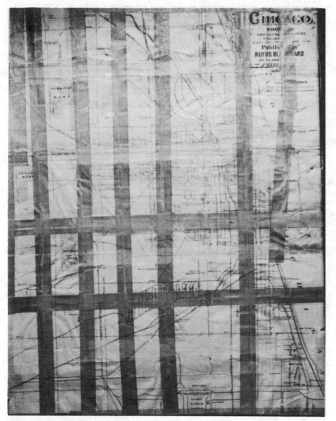

Figure 2-1. This map was repaired with several kinds of pressure-sensitive tape. As a result, information is obscured and the map is structurally unsound because the weak paper cannot adequately support the strong rigid pieces of tape. Permanent stains also will result from the adhesives. Reproduced with permission from the Newberry Library Conservation Laboratory Slide Collection.

not employed, considering such factors as the value and condition of the material as well as its use and expected life. It is necessary to evaluate unique problems against the range of possible solutions, perhaps rejecting all if they are incompatible or inappropriate. Treatment procedures that are routinely applied may require special scrutiny to ensure that proper decisions are made and no single procedure becomes nothing more than a rote activity.

It is important to accept the fact that in some instances it may be best to do nothing at all. There may be no currently acceptable treatment solutions for the problem, or the possibilities available may be simply out of reach due to technical or financial limitations. In such cases, it is better to provide optimum storage and handling for the material than to impose the wrong solution, which could cause serious problems over time. Much less damage will be incurred by waiting until suitable treatment can be undertaken than by applying potentially harmful half-steps or having technically demanding work done by well-meaning but unqualified personnel.

Adherence to conservation ethics mandates the use of sympathetic materials and treatments in any preservation or restoration work. It is important to select treatments that will minimize the chemical and physical trauma to the document, and to choose mending or support materials, such as mat board or Japanese mending tissue, that will be appropriate to the character of the original document or artifact. Thus, one would consider the age or historical period of a given document, as well as its physical and chemical stability, in evaluating the suitability of potential treatments and materials. The materials used in any treatment must be safe and must not hasten the deterioration of the original document, and they must not appear in jarring contrast to its historical period.

Restoration

A primary ethical consideration in any type of work that would qualify as restoration relates to the issue of just how far reconstruction of an historical document should be taken. There are a number of highly sophisticated techniques available that, though expensive, are capable not only of replacing lost textual or image areas, but also of replicating antique paper and such charactertistics as watermarks. A highly skilled craftsman can easily "fool the eye," making new additions appear aged and timeworn, even going so far as to create watermarks or laid and chain lines in additions to match the original paper. *Archival considerations must be imposed to assure that the historical, legal, and evidentiary values of a document are not lost or diminished.* The primary aim in most archival restoration is to ensure that the materiall is physically intact and as chemically stable as possible to assure long-term availability and use. While neat work using compatible materials is always desirable, with most archival records cosmetic improvements are less a concern than physical and chemical stability. When the importance of an archival document warrants restoration, it must be done with great care to ensure that its integrity and authenticity are not put into doubt. The aim is not to make the document appear pristine and new; and evidence of any restoration work, including additions, should be discernible to the practiced eye.

Documentation

Strict adherence to the philosophy of conservation requires the complete documentation of all treatments. The principle of documentation is doubly important in an archival context because of the necessity of maintaining a complete and accurate record of the provenance of the material. For legal purposes, it may be necessary to record any alteration of a document to assure its

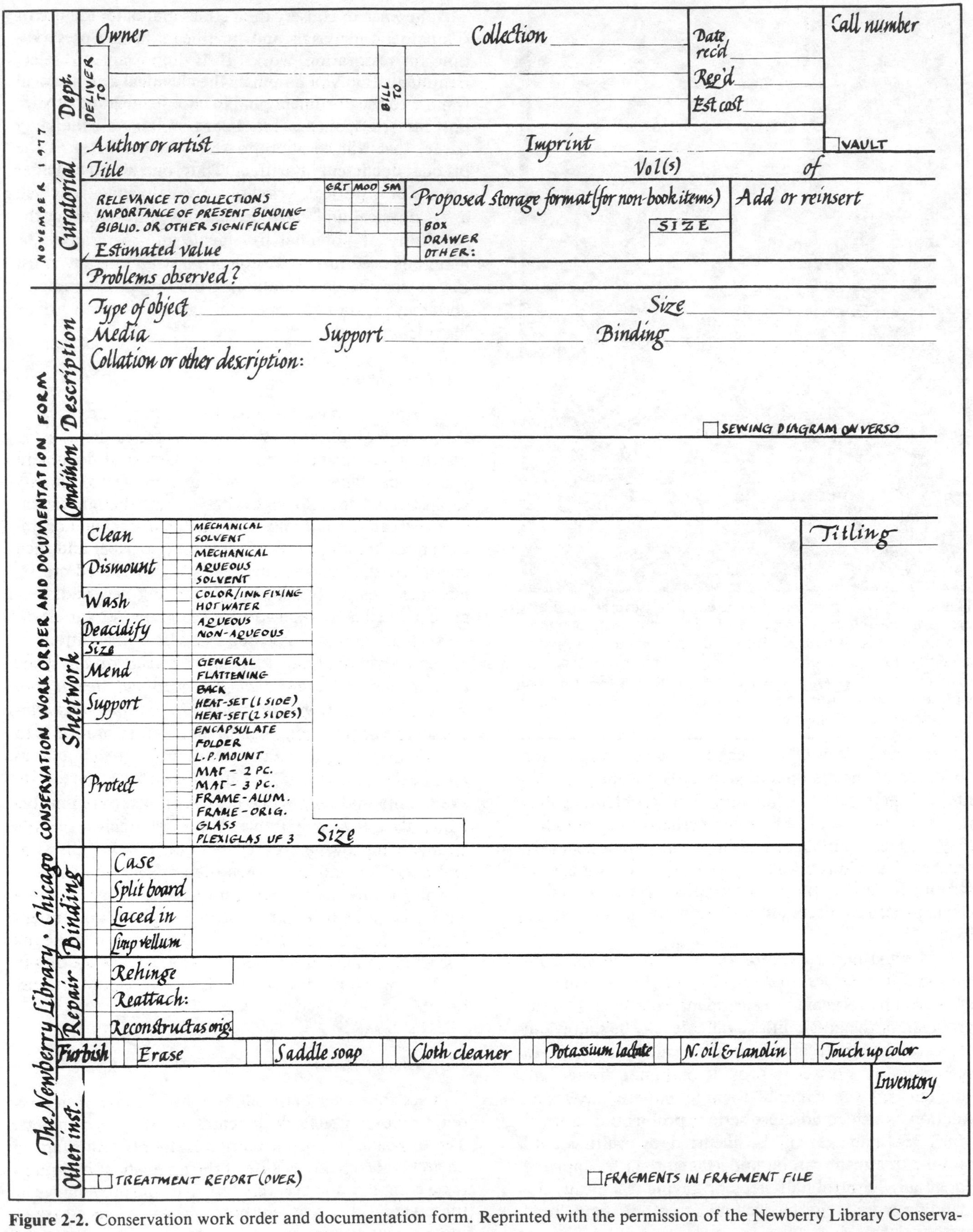

The Newberry Library · Chicago CONSERVATION WORK ORDER AND DOCUMENTATION FORM

NOVEMBER 1977

Dept.

Owner
Collection
Date rec'd
Req'd
Est cost
Call number
DELIVER TO
BILL TO

Curatorial

Author or artist
Imprint
VAULT
Title
Vol(s) of
RELEVANCE TO COLLECTIONS
IMPORTANCE OF PRESENT BINDING
BIBLIO. OR OTHER SIGNIFICANCE
GRT MOD SM
Proposed storage format (for non-book items)
BOX
DRAWER
OTHER:
SIZE
Add or reinsert
Estimated value
Problems observed?

Description

Type of object
Size
Media
Support
Binding
Collation or other description:
SEWING DIAGRAM ON VERSO

Condition

Sheetwork

Clean: MECHANICAL, SOLVENT
Dismount: MECHANICAL, AQUEOUS, SOLVENT
Wash: COLOR/INK FIXING, HOT WATER
Deacidify: AQUEOUS, NON-AQUEOUS
Size
Mend: GENERAL, FLATTENING
Support: BACK, HEAT-SET (1 SIDE), HEAT-SET (2 SIDES)
Protect: ENCAPSULATE, FOLDER, L.P. MOUNT, MAT - 2 PC., MAT - 3 PC., FRAME - ALUM., FRAME - ORIG., GLASS, PLEXIGLAS UF 3
Size
Titling

Binding

Case
Split board
Laced in
Limp vellum

Repair

Rehinge
Reattach:
Reconstruct as orig.

Furbish

Erase
Saddle soap
Cloth cleaner
Potassium lactate
N. oil & lanolin
Touch up color

Other inst.

Inventory
TREATMENT REPORT (OVER)
FRAGMENTS IN FRAGMENT FILE

Figure 2-2. Conservation work order and documentation form. Reprinted with the permission of the Newberry Library Conservation Laboratory.

Treatment Report		

Photographs

	BEFORE - B&W
	RECORD TREATMENT
	AFTER - B&W
	BEFORE - COLOR
	TEACHING SLIDES
	OTHER:

Cost Calculations

Time Record				Materials			Mark-up	Total
DATE	INIT.	HRS.	MINS.	QUAN	DESCRIPTION	COST		
					Total			

Outside Work

			SUPPLIER	DESCRIPTION				
					Total			
			Total hours	Labor				
					Grand Total			

Disposition

To Bindery for:
☐ BINDING   BY _____
☐ BOXING
☐ ENCAPSULATION   DATE _____

Delivered to _____

BY _____ DATE _____

Temporarily out to _____
BY _____   DATE _____

Returned to Lab

BY _____   DATE _____

Billed BY _____ DATE _____

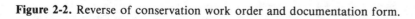

Figure 2-2. Reverse of conservation work order and documentation form.

Accession number_____

CONSERVATION WORK ORDER

Collection: Use:

Item(s):   Intrinsic value:

Media:

Format: Special instructions:

Folder/box number:

Location   Save fragments:

(Above information to be provided by archivist.   Name:_____   Date:____)

Condition statement:

Materials:

Previous treatment:

Treatment	Materials	Time	Cost

Box
  phased box
  solander box
Refolder
Portfolio

Document Repair
  humidify
  surface clean
  remove tape
  wash
  deacidify (pH:)
    aqueous: nonaqueous:
  mend
  encapsulate

Book Repair
  repair torn/loose pages
  reback
  rebind
  leather treatment

Framed Materials
  disassemble/remove from mount
  re-mat and frame
  save original frame

Fumigate

Microfilm

_____

Work accepted by: Date of examination:

Additional information: Photographic record:

Treatment carried out by: Date completed:

Figure 2-3. Sample documentation form. Such forms should be devised to meet the unique collection and treatment needs of individual repositories.

authenticity and continued validity. From the treatment standpoint, it is important to record all procedures and materials used to ensure the possibility of future reversibility, should this become necessary. The limited conservation funds of most archival repositories coupled with the high costs of most treatments lend further rationale to the necessity of documentation to avoid duplication of effort in years to come.

The format chosen for documentation purposes may be either a narrative description or a checklist; a photographic record—before, during, and after treatment—is a useful supplement and may also serve exhibition or similar public relations purposes in educating staff, researchers, and the public regarding archival conservation. Whatever the format, the treatment description should be specific in indicating precise procedures and materials used, including any trade names if appropriate. Other data to be recorded include a bibliographic description of the item or collection treated, statement of original condition, date and place of treatment, name of conservator or firm, and possible other work yet to be undertaken (see Figures 2-2, 2-3). All treatment should be fully documented, whether done on a contractual basis by an outside conservation laboratory or in-house. If necessary, multiple records may be kept for accounting, work scheduling, or other purposes. A copy of the treatment record, however, should become part of the permanent file kept on each collection, along with such other vital records as the deed of gift, accession record, and inventory or finding aid.

3   Nature of Archival Materials

The material nature of the archival record is diverse and potentially limitless, depending upon what is seen as having archival significance. Rapid changes in the technology of recording information will have great impact on the archives of the future. Traditional record materials eventually may be largely replaced by electronic images. In the meantime, however, archivists must be concerned with (1) the support base of collection items, i.e., paper, film, glass, or animal skin, and (2) the medium, or manner in which the information was recorded. In every instance, the archivist must be able to recognize the material nature of the records in order to make informed decisions regarding use, handling, storage, and treatment. Beyond recognition of the various materials that are likely to turn up in a collection, the archivist also must understand how component materials work together. Many archival records are complex rather than simple assemblages. They may be composed of many materials, and also may have interrelated mechanical properties. A book, for example, is constructed of paper, inks, boards, adhesives, thread, and covering material. Ideally, these components function compatibly and in unison to preserve and allow access to information. If any element breaks down, however, the archivist should be able to evaluate the problem and select the appropriate solution.

Since archival records can be complex physical objects having very specific handling and treatment needs, a primary responsibility of the archivist is to become acquainted with the increasingly wide range of record materials, both historical and contemporary. After proper identification, the next steps are deliberately planned storage and care. It is important to know which processes and images are fragile or ephemeral. Also essential is an understanding of how the structural elements of an object—book, scrapbook, film—relate to accessing and preserving its informational content. The archivist must be able intellectually to break down a record into its component parts and to consider its format and information as well as its physical condition, in order to develop systems to manage and preserve the fragile whole.

Paper

Paper is the most common material found in archival collections. Its invention is attributed to Ts'ai Lun in China in approximately 105 AD. Papermaking was primarily a hand process until the development of the Fourdrinier papermaking machine, which was put into operation in 1804. Paper may be defined very simply as fibers that have been reduced to pulp, suspended in water and then matted into sheets. Although a wide range of fibrous material may be used to make paper, it is made primarily from plant fibers, such as cotton, wood, flax, straw, and mulberry, which are rich in cellulose. Cellulose, the most important ingredient in paper, is composed of hydrogen, carbon, and oxygen. It is a stable polysaccharide that serves as the structural element for plants, forming the walls of plant cells. Besides cellulose, plant fibers contain sugars, starches, carbohydrates, and lignin (naturally occuring organic acid).

During the hand papermaking process, suitable fibers are soaked in water and then macerated or beaten so that the fibers flatten out, causing the separation of small hairlike fibers called fabrilles. Originally, beating was done by hand, and it still is to a great degree in the Orient. However, the stamping mill, invented in the 12th century, speeded up the process and still produced relatively long fibers through the use of wooden beaters (or stampers) in a wooden tub. Once the fibers are macerated to a pulp, they are added to a vat of water to

Figure 3-2. Vat paper-making in the United States, 1881. Reprinted courtesy of The John M. Wing Foundation on the History of Printing of the Newberry Library, Chicago, from: J.E.A. Smith, *A History of Paper. Its Genesis and Its Revelations,* Holyoke, MA: Clark W. Bryan and Co., 1882.

Figure 3-1. Vatman dips the paper mold into vat of slurry. Note wooden stampers used to beat pulp in the left background. Reprinted courtesy of The John M. Wing Foundation on the History of Printing of the Newberry Library, Chicago, from: Hartmanno Schoppero, *De Omnibus,* 1554.

Figure 3-3. Forming a sheet of handmade paper, 1983. On this mold, the deckle is round and will form a round sheet of paper. Photograph courtesy of Twinrocker Handmade Paper, Brookston, Indiana.

form a slurry. The water swells the fibers, distributes them evenly in the suspension, and promotes fiber to fiber bonding. A paper mold is dipped into the vat and manipulated until an even layer of slurry rests on the porous screen of the mold (see Figures 3-1, 3-2, 3-3). The slurry is retained by the surround, or top half of the mold, called the deckle. (See Figure 3-4.) Excess water passes through the screen, which traps the fibers, and the remaining mat of fibers is laid (or couched) onto a piece of felt. The paper sheet is formed by mechanical entanglement of the fibers' fabrilles, chemical bonding of adjacent cellulose molecules (i.e., hydrogen bonding), surface tension between fibers, and adhesive action of nonfiber additives.

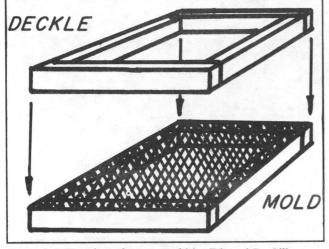

Figure 3-4. Drawing of paper mold by Edward R. Gilbert.

Once a stack of sheets has been made and placed between pieces of felt, additional water is removed by pressing and air drying. Sizing is added to allow the paper to accept writing and printing inks. Without sizing, paper behaves like a blotter and inks feather and spread. Unsized sheets are known as waterleaf. Traditional sizing agents were gelatin and animal glue, which were applied by dipping after the sheets were formed and dry; contemporary handmade papers are often sized with gelatin.

Handmade paper generally has no discernible grain direction because the fibers are aligned randomly as the papermaker manipulates the mold in the vat. This means that handmade paper will not tear more readily in one direction (across either its width or length). Since paper made by hand is formed individually sheet by sheet, no two pieces are exactly alike, nor is a single sheet of uniform thickness throughout. Unless handmade paper has been cut or trimmed (which is seen as sacrilege by some), it has a distinctive deckle (or feathered) edge around all four sides, formed as slurry seeps between the deckle and frame of the mold. Paper-

maker's tears are another distinctive characteristic of handmade paper. These result if a drop of slurry falls onto the sheet after it has been formed on the mold; it is a small roundish impression that is somewhat thinner than the surrounding area because the drop of slurry forces the fibers to disperse slightly. Watermarks are often found in handmade papers. These designs and symbols are wired to the grid of the mold. During sheet formation, fewer fibers settle over the design, resulting in greater translucency in this localized area. The watermark can be seen in the finished sheet through transmitted light. A watermark known as the countermark, introduced in the 17th century, often contained the name or initials of the papermaker as well as the date and place of manufacture. Watermarks are important bibliographic tools in identifying and dating paper and bookbindings.

The process of making paper by machine is essentially the same as the simple hand process outlined above; the scale is obviously much larger and the steps are mechanized. Also, the paper is formed in a continuous roll rather than in individual sheets. The fiber mat is formed on a high-speed screen and carried through succeeding steps to drying, calendaring (i.e., running the paper through cast iron rolls to give it a smooth surface), sizing, and glazing (see Figures 3-5, 3-6). If desired, a dandy roll is employed when the fibers are still wet to create a design (such as laid and chain lines to simulate handmade paper) or watermarks. Machine-made paper has two deckle edges, although it can be manufactured with four simulated deckle edges. Imitation deckle edges also may be created on dry paper by various methods of tearing or cutting. Machine-made papers also have a definite grain direction; the fibers align themselves in the direction of the moving screen. Paper will fold and tear more readily with the grain than against it. Also, when machine-made paper is dampened or pasted, the fibers swell or stretch across their width to a greater degree than with their length. This characteristic has implications for printers, bookbinders, and paper conservators who must know the working properties of material when exposed to moisture or wet treatment.

Unfortunately, the quality of paper has steadily declined since the late 18th century. Prior to that time, papermaking was primarily a hand process using cotton and linen rags as the source of cellulose. As noted above, the fibers were beaten in a stamping mill, which resulted in long, strong fabrilles, and no additives were used that had a deteriorative effect on the paper. Paper from this period is generally still quite strong and flexible.

As the demand for paper increased, however, forcing greater mechanization, processes and materials were introduced which resulted in much poorer quality paper.

Figure 3-5. Fourdrinier papermaking machine, ca. 1900, capable of producing continuous rolls of paper. From: *The Story of Paper-Making,* Chicago: J.W. Butler Paper Co., 1901.

Figure 3-6. Paper running through a vat of gelatin sizing, ca. 1900. From: *The Story of Paper-Making,* Chicago: J.W. Butler Paper Co., 1901.

The introduction by 1620 of alum (potassium aluminum sulphate, an acid salt that degrades to form sulphuric acid) as an agent to harden the gelatin sizing greatly diminished the useful life of paper. The Hollander beater was invented in the Netherlands in 1680 to mechanically macerate the fibers using metal blades against a metal bed plate. The Hollander beater, which replaced the stamping mill, speeded up the pulping process but also resulted in short rather than the more desirable long fibers. The action of the metal blades against the metal plate also resulted in small metallic particles breaking off, which then were included in the pulp. Metallic traces in paper provide ideal starting points for deteriorative chemical reactions, including foxing. The water used in the papermaking process can be another source of trace metals. In 1774 chlorine was introduced to bleach colored rags to a tone found acceptable for paper. If not completely removed, chlorine bleach leaves an acid residue. Beginning in 1850, alum was used in combination with rosin to precipitate this sizing material on the fibers. Rosin replaced gelatin as a more economical sizing agent because it could be added directly in the vat rather than applied after sheet formation. Alum also aided in the dispersal of plant fibers in the slurry.

In the late 18th century increased literacy and the attendant bureaucracy outstripped the availability of rags for paper, and other sources of plant fibers were sought that would be both plentiful and cheap. Experiments were made with a wide range of (by today's standards) curious and wonderful fibers, from potatoes to wasps' nests; but by the middle of the 19th century wood pulp was being used extensively to create inexpensive paper. Wood is the primary source of cellulose fiber for paper being produced today. Wood consists of approximately 45 percent cellulose, 20–25 percent hemicellulose, 25–30 percent lignin, and less than 5 percent of other substances. Groundwood pulp, which is ground or macerated mechanically as its name implies, does not produce strong paper. The fibers are short and a large amount of lignin (which is unstable, light-sensitive, and deteriorates to form acid compounds) is retained. After removing the bark, logs are ground to a pulp on a revolving stone; the resulting pulp thus contains all of the components of wood, including lignin, except for water-soluble materials, which wash away during the grinding process. While groundwood paper is always unstable, it is possible to obtain relatively strong, high-quality paper from wood pulp that has been chemically treated to remove the lignin. Chemical wood pulp is created by cooking chips of wood under pressure at high temperature in a solution of sodium sulfide or sodium sulfite; the cellulose fibers are left in an aqueous suspension and then washed to remove lignin and other undesirable materials.

Acidity in Paper

Conservators generally consider the period from 1850 to the present to be the era of "bad paper." The quality of paper progressively declined, primarily as a result of increased use of alum-rosin sizing and groundwood pulp, both of which introduced a high degree of acidity into paper. Other sources of acid include residual bleaching chemicals, inks, sulphur dioxide and other acid-forming pollutants, and migration. Acid migration (or transfer) refers to the ability of acid to move from an acidic material to items of less or no acidity. This takes place either through direct contact with adjacent acidic materials (secondary materials such as file folders and mat boards, as well as such enclosures as newspaper clippings), or through exposure to acidic vapors in a closed document box or file drawer. It has been determined that acidity is one of the primary causes of paper deterioration. Acidity causes paper to lose its strength by hydrolysis of its cellulose molecules; the polymer chains gradually break down and the paper becomes weak, brittle, and stained, sometimes to the degree that text or images are obliterated. Most of the paper produced today has a life expectancy of less than 50 years, unlike the handmade paper from 300 years ago, much of which is still in very useable condition today. Acidity and alkalinity are measured on the pH scale (see Figure 3-7). This is an arbitrary numerical scale ranging from 0 to 14, 7.0 being the point of neutrality. All numbers above this point represent increasing alkalinity, and all numbers below 7.0 indicate increasing acidity. Since the scale is logarithmic, each numerical unit represents a 10-fold change in acidity or alkalinity. Thus, a pH of 5 is 10 times more acidic than a pH of 6, and a pH of 4 is 100 times more acidic than a pH of 6. While paper conservators are mostly concerned with acidity in paper brought about by modern manufacturing processes and the environment, the archivist must understand that high alkalinity—pH 10.5 to 14—can be equally destructive. Consider, for example, the destructive effect of a strong alkali such as sodium hydroxide (lye). Further research in this area is required.

pH SCALE

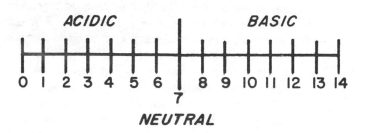

Figure 3-7. pH scale drawn by Edward R. Gilbert.

The concepts of permanence and durability developed as efforts were made to produce papers that were free of acid and that would resist the effects of aging. William J. Barrow was a leader in research and development in this area; the reports of the W. J. Barrow Research Laboratory (cited in the bibliography) document his pioneering efforts. Permanence relates to the ability of paper to remain stable and resist chemical action either from internal impurities or the surrounding environment. Durability relates to the degree to which paper retains its original strength, especially under conditions of heavy, sustained use. A paper may be permanent (i.e., chemically stable) but not durable, and vice versa. Research conducted to date suggests that it is possible to produce permanent/durable papers by controlling the following factors: length of fiber, removal of chemicals used in pulping, the use of tub sizing (preferably gelatin), and removal of all bleaches. It is recommended that groundwood pulp be avoided for archival or heavy-use papers.

Types of Paper

Paper is available in a wide range of size, weight, color, finish, and texture; each variety is designed to meet specific writing, printing, artistic, and storage or packaging needs. Thus, paper of virtually every historical and contemporary type is likely to find its way into an archives. Handmade papers likely will be found in collections that include works of art on paper or fine press books. Handmade Japanese papers with long, strong fibers are commonly used for mending archival documents. By and large, though, the most common type of paper found in archival repositories is modern machine-made paper. The following are the most common types:

Acid-free—Papers with no free acids, having a pH of 7.0 or greater. Care is taken in the manufacturing process to prevent residual or interior acidity. Cotton, chemical wood pulp, or similar fibers may be used. Unless treated with an alkaline substance capable of neutralizing acids, papers that are acid-free at the time of manufacture may become acidic through contact with acidic storage materials or atmospheric pollutants. "Acid-free" has become almost a generic term used by archivists and others to denote a broad range of desirable characteristics of archival storage materials. For example, the term is often used casually to imply that paper and board stock have an alkaline reserve, whether or not this is actually the case. There is a move to standardize and tighten the terminology in many areas of conservation, and precise use of terms is recommended. Use of the term "acid-free" should be dropped in favor of terminology that more accurately conveys the required pH range of the paper or board, i.e., neutral or with an alkaline reserve.

Alkaline reserve—Paper and board stock having an alkaline reserve with a pH of about 8.5–10.0. Treated with an alkaline substance (such as calcium or magnesium carbonate) to counteract or neutralize acid that might later enter the paper from the surrounding air or nearby acidic materials. Papers intended to resist acid for a long period (300–500 years) should have approximately 3 percent precipitated carbonate by weight of paper. Except when otherwise specified, archival storage materials—folders, boxes, wrapping and interleaving papers, etc.—should be fabricated from stock having an alkaline reserve.

Bond—Paper having good writing and erasing qualities, as well as good printing qualities, as most bond papers have printed letterheads. Commonly used for typed manuscripts, correspondence, and forms. Bond paper that has an alkaline reserve is available and may be used for making permanent copies in xerographic (dry-process) photocopy machines.

Cover—Heavy paper stock used as covers for pamphlets or brochures to provide protection for text. Generally durable but not permanent.

Book or text—Range of papers with varying characteristics (appearance, texture, permanence) to meet printing requirements for books, journals, and periodicals. Coated papers (achieved by adding clay fillers or other white mineral pigments) are used for publications requiring fine halftone illustrations.

Decorated—Papers (originally decorated by hand, but now often printed) used for book and pamphlet covers or endsheets. Marbled, paste, and printed papers are often found in ledgers, journals, and day books; quality varies depending upon paper, pigments, and process. Decorated papers can provide useful bibliographic clues and are a subject of study in themselves.

Ledger—Paper originally used for handwritten ledgers and account books, now used for printing. Animal sized, strong, durable, and eraseable, with a uniform surface for writing and ruling lines.

Manifold—Thin translucent paper used for typewritten carbon copies.

Newsprint—Generic term commonly used for the type of paper used in printing newspapers. A soft paper, largely composed of groundwood pulp. Not permanent. Often found in archival collections as second (carbon) sheets, forms, receipts, invoices pamphlets, and newspapers.

Onion skin—Lightweight, durable, nearly transparent paper used for carbon copies of typewritten material. Made from cotton fibers, bleached chemical wood pulp, or combinations.

Parchment bond—Strong, durable paper with a good writing surface. Often used instead of genuine parchment for legal documents and certificates.

Inks

Carbon ink is the earliest of manuscript inks. It is permanent and lightfast and will not damage paper. Most carbon inks are suspensions of lampblack in gum arabic (a water-soluble binding agent obtained from the Acacia tree). Historically, Chinese and India inks were made of carbon soot mixed with a glue size and molded into sticks. A stick would be dissolved in water for use as ink. Carbon inks were used widely until the 19th century and are still used today for calligraphy and art work.

Iron gall ink was made by mixing ferrous sulphate with oak galls and water; the extract was then thickened with gum arabic. Iron gall ink can remain legible for centuries but is susceptible to fading. It dries black on paper but fades to brown over time. The ferrous sulphate oxidizes to form sulphuric acid, which causes the ink to burn into the paper, resulting in a lacy effect (see Figure 3-8). The acid also migrates through to the back side of a sheet or to adjacent paper. As individuals made up their own formulations of iron gall ink, and sometimes introduced additives such as hydrochloric acid, the acid content varied widely. Iron gall ink was impor-

tant to Europeans because it had a good "bite" on vellum and parchment. Thus, iron gall ink continued to be popular after the introduction of paper, despite the fact that it was less suitable on this material. In the U.S., iron gall inks were used almost exclusively during the 17th and 18th centuries.

Printing inks were traditionally made of carbon or soot in boiled linseed oil, which hardened or dried by oxidation. These inks produced a very stable permanent image. Modern printing inks often contain both pigments and dyes, may substitute mineral oils for the more costly linseed oil, and utilize dryers to speed up oxidation, which is necessary for modern high-speed printing processes. They are less permanent than early printing inks, which had no additives.

Inks on typewriter ribbons are pigments or dyes in an oil carrier; they dry by absorption into the paper. Carbon ribbon inks are permanent. Modern manuscript inks are either iron inks or are made from synthetic dyes; the latter are soluble in water are not lightfast. Colored inks have long been used for both writing and drawing; they were originally made from natural pigments and vegetable dyes. Most contemporary colored inks are made from synthetic dyes; while they do not harm paper, they are not permanent. The watercolor inks found in many felt-tip pens are water-soluble and highly susceptible to running or spreading if exposed to water or excessively humid conditions. They are not permanent, and—depending upon the color—are quite light fugitive upon exposure to visible light and ultraviolet radiation. Ballpoint pen inks consist of a mixture of dyes to inhibit the possibility of easy removal, although eraseable ballpoint inks are now available as well. They sit on the surface of paper and are soluble in many solvents.

Animal Skins

Vegetable-tanned leather was the most common covering material for books until the 19th century. The most stable leathers were produced up through the 16th century by a slow tanning process that left protective salts in the skins (see Figure 3-9). These early vegetable-tanned leathers were resistant to decay and acid deterioration. During the late 17th–19th centuries, the demand for leather increased and shortcuts were introduced into the tanning and dyeing processes which eliminated the protective or buffering salts. The resulting leathers quickly deteriorated because of sulphuric acid, which was either present in the skins as a result of the manufacturing process or absorbed from polluted air. The most satisfactory leather for bookbinding today is produced in England. Leather that is stamped P.I.R.A. has met the requirements of the test

Figure 3-8. Textual losses are due to the high acid content of the iron gall ink that was the recording medium of this letter.

developed by the Printing Industries Research Association of Great Britain, which determines the resistance of
vegetable-tanned leather to sulphur dioxide in the air.

Figure 3-9. Flesh and hair must be scraped from skins as part
of the leather tanning process. Reprinted courtesy of The John
M. Wing Foundation on the History of Printing of the
Newberry Library, Chicago, from: Hartmanno Schoppero, *De
Omnibus*, 1554.

Many bound volumes in archival collections are
covered partially or fully in leather, account books,
ledgers, diaries, and presentation volumes in particular.
Leathers that commonly have been used for bookbinding include:

Calf—Used predominantly until the end of the 18th
century. Calf has little noticeable grain and thus is
easily decorated. The surface of calf is delicate and
soft; it readily scratches and mars. Calf is often found
in archival repositories on account books and ledgers
as well as sets of law books.

Goat—Soft, pliable, and strong leather. The grain is
distinctively textured with small ridges and furrows in
an all-over pattern. Goatskin has traditionally been
used for fine bookbinding since the 17th century. It is
also known as levant, niger, morocco, and oasis.

Pigskin—Strong and durable; suitable for large
books. Hair follicles, which are arranged in triangular

groups of three, create a distinctive grain pattern,
which is an identifying characteristic.

Sheepskin—Soft, porous leather, usually grained to
imitate higher quality and more expensive skins. Not
very strong. Natural colored "law sheep" was used to
cover law books.

Suede—Leather (calf, goat, etc.) that has been buffed
on the flesh (inner) side to produce a nap. Often used
for blank books in the 19th century.

The process of chrome tanning was developed in
1858. It is essentially a chemical process by which skins
are treated with basic chromium sulphate. While
durable, chrome-tanned leathers are not very supple
(and thus resist such bookbinding procedures as
turning-in, or wrapping the leather around the edges of
the boards to the inside). They also resist embossing and
gold tooling. Chrome-tanned leathers are used for fine
binding in France, but are not used extensively in the
U.S.

Vellum and parchment were used extensively in the
Middle Ages as writing surfaces for manuscripts; vellum
also has been used since this period as a covering
material in bookbinding. True vellum is the unsplit skin
of a young calf; it is cleaned, preserved by soaking in a
lime solution, scraped to remove the hair, and dried
under tension on a frame (see Figure 3-10). Parchment
(traditionally made from split sheepskin) is also preserved with lime, scraped, and dried under tension. Today, both vellum and parchment are made from the skin
of any small animal, such as calf, sheep, or goat. Both
skins are strong and long lasting; they also are very reactive to changes in the moisture level. They will cockle (or
contract to form wrinkles and puckers) when damp, and
many books covered in vellum have warped boards as a
result of changes in the relative humidity. Vellum and
parchment are not in general use today except
by artists and conservation binders (although parchment is occasionally used for legal documents and certificates). These skins will be found, however, in archival collections that contain early bound manuscripts,
as well as in college and university archives that have
parchment diplomas (the proverbial sheepskin). Both
skins appear smooth and hard; depending on thickness,
they may be translucent or opaque, with a color ranging
from a creamy white to ecru. Vellum can be stained any
color, but usually is not; many vellum skins have faint
vein and hair markings. It is difficult for nonspecialists
to differentiate between parchment and vellum. What is
most important in an archival context is to recognize
that a material is *either* parchment *or* vellum, as their
handling and treatment needs are the same.

Tawed skins may appear in some repositories, especially on 17th- or 18th-century books. Tawed skin is not

Figure 3-10. During the processing of parchment and vellum, the skins are stretched on wooden frames. Reprinted courtesy of The John M. Wing Foundation on the History of Printing of the Newberry Library, Chicago, from: Hartmanno Schoppero, *De Omnibus,* 1554.

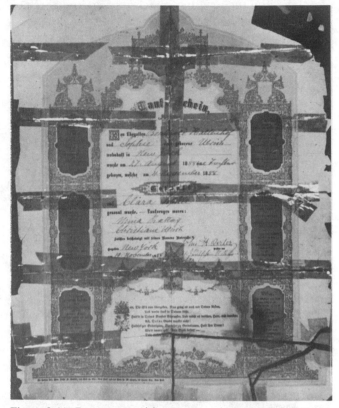

Figure 3-11. Pressure-sensitive tape mends on this brittle document were clearly ill-advised. The plastic carrier is lifting in some areas, leaving permanent stains, and edge losses will continue to occur unless overall support is provided. Reproduced courtesy of the Newberry Library Conservation Laboratory Slide Collection.

tanned (and thus, like vellum and parchment, is not leather), but is preserved in solutions of alum and salt. It is tough and flexible and very white in appearance. Tawed skins (generally pigskin or goatskin) are used today primarily for experimental conservation bindings.

Cloth

Cloth will be found in archives primarily as a book covering. Bookcloth was manufactured in England beginning in the late 1820s; early bookcloth was starch-filled muslin that was colored and sized. Starch-filled cloths, which are still used today, are not durable and are very susceptible to insects, mold, and water. Although starch-filled cloths often provide good color matches for repairing old cloth-covered books, they are not terribly strong and are also vulnerable to water spotting and soiling. Pyroxylin-treated (either impregnated or coated) bookcloth was invented in 1910 in the United States. Though it is durable, washable, and resistant to moisture and insects, pyroxylin-treated bookcloth is not as permanent as starch-filled cloth. A new type of coating based on acrylics is coming into use and may prove more permanent than—and thus replace—pyroxylin. Bookcloth is sometimes embossed to imitate leather, and care must be taken to properly identify the

covering material so that appropriate cleaning and treatment procedures are applied. A wide variety of other fabrics, from velvet to corduroy, have also been used as book coverings.

Other fabrics that may be found in an archival collection include linen (which was often used as a backing for maps and architectural drawings) and silk (used as a lining to support fragile paper documents).

Adhesives

Adhesives are a concern in archival settings for several reasons. First, they are often misapplied and cause damage to a wide variety of materials that come into a repository. Well-meaning people mend treasured letters and photographs with pressure-sensitive tape, for example, and scrapbooks often seem to be virtual catalogs of every known adhesive. Adhesives may break down over time, losing their tackiness; they also may permanently stain documents and initiate harmful chemical reactions that hasten the deterioration of paper (see Figure 3-11). Archivists must contend with these problems and also ensure that only safe adhesives are used with archival materials for mending and mounting. Adhesives are conveniently classified by their setting characteristics:

Heat setting—Waxes and resins, including commercial repair papers applied with a hot iron.

Heat setting and loss of solvent—Animal glues (hide, bone, fish, gelatin). Adhesive must be heated or warmed in a solvent, usually water. Bonding occurs when adhesive cools and water dries.

Loss of solvent—Vegetable pastes, polyvinyl acetate emulsions, and rubber cement.

Chemical reaction—Epoxys and polyesters; urea formaldehyde.

Pressure-sensitive—Cellophane tape, masking tape, archival mending tapes.

Adhesives that are likely to come into, or be used in, an archives include the following:

Animal glues—Adhesives produced from animal hides, bones, etc.; gelatin (used for sizing paper) is a pure form of animal glue. Soluble in water. Traditionally used in bookbinding, though now replaced by polyvinyl acetates. Dries to a hard brittle consistency; often yellowish in appearance.

Methyl cellulose—Synthetic adhesive. Sets slowly; flexible; reversible with water. Very wet; does not

have good bonding strength. Sometimes used for sizing, or added to polyvinyl acetate to improve working properties. Long shelf life; not susceptible to mold growth. Sometimes used for simple paper repairs.

Pastes—Mixture of vegetable (generally wheat or rice) starch and water. Sets slowly; moderately flexible if applied in a thin coat; reversible with water. As pastes are susceptible to mold growth, fungicides are often added. Strong tacky adhesive used in bookbinding and paper repair as well as hinging and lining.

Polyvinyl acetate (PVA)—Synthetic flexible adhesive used in bookbinding. Fast-drying white liquid; not easily reversible. PVA emulsions can be diluted with water or methyl cellulose to slow the drying time. PVA is not susceptible to mold or fungal attack; maximum shelf life of two years. Not an appropriate adhesive for paper repairs.

Pressure-sensitive—An adhesive that will adhere to a surface by means of slight pressure. The carrier can be plastic or paper. Difficult to remove (solvents must be used, see Figure 3-12); leaves permanent stains. Should never be used with archival materials.

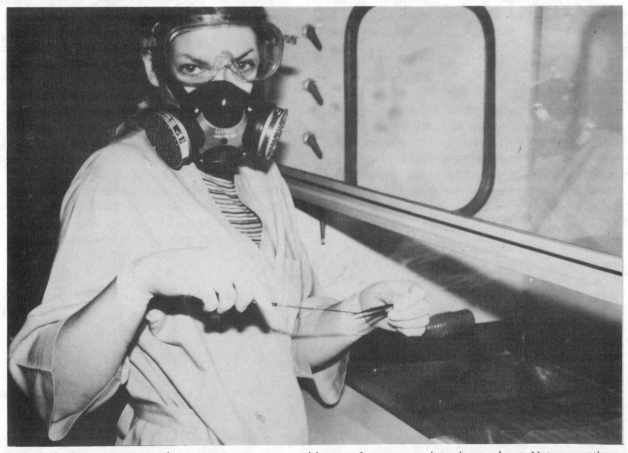

Figure 3-12. Conservator preparing to remove pressure-sensitive tape from manuscript using a solvent. Note precautions: goggles, respirator, rubber gloves, and fume hood.

Rubber cement–Natural rubber dissolved in naphtha or carbon tetrachloride. Loses adhesion over time and leaves permanent stain. Very unstable. Should never be used with archival materials, especially photographs.

Photographic Materials

Photographic images are formed by the action of light on chemical compounds. Very simply, a photograph (print or negative) may be defined as a support upon which an emulsion (image-bearing) layer is coated. The most common photographic emulsion consists of a suspension of light-sensitive silver salts, known as silver halides, in gelatin, although there are other image-forming substances, including other metals (such as platinum) as well as pigments and dyes. There are a number of possible support or base materials, including metal, glass, paper, and film (nitrate, acetate, and polyester). An adhesive sublayer holds the emulsion to the support. Photographs are highly complex structures, and problems with or failure of any of the component parts can mean the destruction of the image. For example, not only may the image-bearing layer be susceptible to such damage as scratches or staining from mold, but the support may fail (i.e., glass may break or plastic may shrink or self-destruct).

Most archival repositories include a diverse sampling of photographic materials representing the entire range of the technological development of photography, from the daguerreotype (invented in 1839) through to present color processes. Archivists must learn to recognize the various types of images in order to provide proper care. Preservation of photographs involves responding to the physical needs of the format and structural materials, as well as the requirements of auxiliary or secondary materials such as mounts, cases, and albums, which are seen as integral to the photographic record. Copying inherently unstable images (including nitrate-base and diacetate film) plays an important part in developing a preservation program for photographic materials.

This very brief overview provides an introduction to materials that an archivist is likely to encounter in working with textual and pictorial records. The readings in the bibliography will provide further guidance. However, reading books and articles must be combined with practical experience with the records themselves. It takes time to train one's eye to discern subtle physical differences between materials. Careful examination and handling of many, many items will help. Advice also should be sought from knowledgeable colleagues (con-servators, bookbinders, archivists, and librarians). To a degree, self-education in this area must correct the deficiencies of most formal archival and library training programs. What is required is understanding archival materials in new ways that combine intellectual interest in their content with a curiosity regarding their physical nature. A number of records appraisal decisions legitimately, and of necessity, relate to considering archival materials from purely physical perspectives; an integrated recognition of historical value and physical need is required. Further, the development of record materials and the crafts associated with them have a fascinating history all their own. Archivists who are capable of understanding and appreciating the records on this level as well will be better overall custodians of collections.

4   Causes of Deterioration

Archival collections contain a wide range of organic materials—paper, cloth, animal skins, adhesives, etc.—that deteriorate over time. These organic substances are composed of complex polymer molecules that undergo a natural aging process as the molecular chains break down, or depolymerize. Natural aging is a slow and inevitable process. While measures can be taken to slow natural aging by providing a sympathetic environment, it is impossible to halt it altogether. The rate of deterioration is dependent upon the inherent chemical stability of the material, in combination with external influences such as the environment, storage conditions, and handling procedures. Some organic materials will age more quickly than others stored in exactly the same environment as a result of their chemical makeup, which may be inherently unstable.

While archivists can do little to alter the innate characteristics of record materials gathered into collections, much can be done to control external factors that accelerate the aging process. Environmental factors that can hasten the deterioration of paper and other materials include temperature, humidity, light, pollution, and biological agents. Independently, each of these factors, if uncontrolled, can cause specific types of damage to record materials, but they also have distinct relationships to one another. For example, the rate of many chemical reactions is dependent on both temperature and water. Thus, the combination of high temperature and high humidity accelerates the action of alum-rosin sizing to generate sulphuric acid in paper. Other actions that speed up the deterioration of archival materials include abuse and mismanagement, as well as disasters, which can cause untold damage or utterly destroy collections in a brief span of time.

Temperature and Relative Humidity

Temperature and relative humidity both have great impact on the rate of deterioration of paper and other record materials, although relative humidity is the more critical factor. High temperature speeds up chemical reactions. For every 18° F increase in temperature, chemical activity of most substances approximately doubles. It has been estimated that the useful life of paper is approximately cut in half with every 10° F increase in temperature. Conversely, with every 10° F decrease, the expected life of paper is effectively doubled.[5]

Relative humidity is defined as the amount of water vapor in a volume of air expressed as a percentage of the maximum amount that the air could hold at the same temperature. The warmer the air, the more water vapor it is capable of holding. Thus, the relative humidity generally decreases as the temperature increases, assuming no moisture were added. The amount of moisture in the air is important for a number of reasons. As stated above, many of the harmful chemical reactions that speed up the deterioration of paper, such as acid hydrolysis, are both temperature- and water-dependent. Humidity causes problems if it is either too high or too low. High humidity speeds up deteriorative chemical reactions. Under conditions of high humidity combined with high temperature, the growth of mold and mildew is encouraged and the likelihood of insect infestation is increased. Under conditions of extremely high humidity, water-soluble inks can offset and coated papers can stick together. Low relative humidity causes materials to become dry and brittle. Paper that is dried out can break and crumble as it is handled and flexed, and covering materials on books (such as vellum) can shrink, causing boards to warp.

As the temperature changes, the relative humidity fluctuates. This fluctuation, or cycling, can be quite drastic, with as much as a 20–30 percent change in relative humidity in a 12–48-hour period.[6] Paper, vellum, and parchment are all hygroscopic materials, which means that their moisture content fluctuates in relation to the amount of water in the surrounding air. Hygroscopic materials are capable of absorbing or emitting moisture, depending on the ambient conditions. Thus, wide swings in temperature (and therefore relative humidity) can be very damaging, as such materials expand and contract in response to changes in the moisture level. While the movement of paper fibers is not visible to the naked eye, the resulting internal stress and dimensional instability is very damaging to paper records over time. Structural composition is important in this context. Bound items—composed of a variety of materials that may react differently (and perhaps in opposition to one another) in response to fluctuation in the relative humidity—will suffer more damage than will unbound single sheets. Warped book covers provide visible evidence of such damage. (See Figure 4-1.)

Figure 4-1. The vellum-covered boards on this book have warped badly. The text block is becoming distorted and the joints are beginning to crack.

Light

Light, or radiational energy, also affects the longevity of collection materials. Light speeds up the oxidation of paper and thus its chemical breakdown. Light has a bleaching action; it can cause paper to whiten and can cause colored papers and inks to fade. Exposure to light can radically alter some photographs and other light-sensitive images such as blueprints. Upon exposure to

---

[5]Paper does not follow the general rule set forth by Arrhenius that substances approximately double their rate of chemical reactivity for every 10° C (18° F) rise in temperature, but instead doubles for approximately every 10° F rise in temperature. Thus, storing paper at 86° F will reduce its life not by half, but to a fourth or less than if it is stored at 68° F. See: *Test Data of Naturally Aged Papers*, W.J. Barrow Research Laboratory, Permanence/Durability of the Book—II (Richmond, Va., 1964), p.20; Robert I. Feller, "Thermochemically Activated Oxidation: Mother Nature's Book Burning," *PLA Bulletin*, 28:234, 238 (November, 1973); D.D. Roberson, "Permanence/Durability and Preservation Research at the Barrow Laboratory," *Preservation of Paper and Textiles of Historic and Artistic Value II*, John C. Williams, ed. (Washington, D.C.: American Chemical Society, 1981), p. 48.

[6]R.D. Buck. "A Specification for Museum Air-Conditioning." Part I. *Museum News*, Technical Supplement No. 6, 43:54, 56 (December, 1964).

light, lignin reacts with other compounds in paper, causing it to darken. Yellowed newspaper clippings and brownish groundwood carbon copies provide graphic evidence of this effect.

All light is potentially damaging, but ultraviolet radiation, which we cannot see, is most active and thus capable of causing serious damage. The shorter the wavelength, the more active or energetic the radiation. Radiation between 300–400 nanometers (one nanometer = one billionth of a meter) has the greatest potential to cause photochemical deterioration (see Figure 4-2).

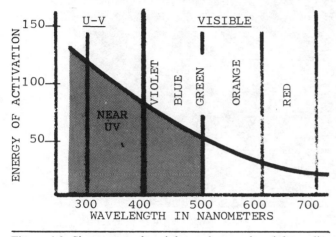

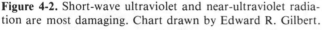

Figure 4-2. Short-wave ultraviolet and near-ultraviolet radiation are most damaging. Chart drawn by Edward R. Gilbert.

Primary sources of ultraviolet radiation are sunlight and fluorescent light; sunlight may contain as much as 25 percent, while fluorescent light may emit 3–7 percent ultraviolet radiation. Visible light, especially in the blue and violet-blue end of the spectrum, also can damage organic materials. Light damage is cumulative; the amount of damage is dependent upon wavelength (i.e., ultraviolet, blue, violet-blue, etc.) and the length and intensity of exposure. Thus, brief exposure under relatively high intensity can be just as damaging as extended exposure to low intensity. Chemical actions initiated by exposure to light continue even after the light source is removed and materials are put into dark storage.

Atmospheric Pollutants

Pollutants in the air also can adversely affect archival materials. Gaseous pollutants include sulphur dioxide, nitrogen dioxide, and hydrogen sulfide, which are products of combustion and other chemical actions; they are thus most prevalent in industrial and urban areas where there are factories and high concentrations of automobiles. Sulphur dioxide and nitrogen dioxide combine with water in the air to form sulphuric and nitric acids, which have a deteriorative effect on paper.

Ozone, another gaseous pollutant, causes oxidation, which embrittles paper. Ozone is a product of the combination of sunlight and nitrogen dioxide from automobile exhaust, and is thus generally more of a problem in urban areas. Ozone also may be produced by electrostatic filtering systems used in some air conditioners, as well as electrostatic photocopy machines.

Dirt, dust, and other solid particles can damage materials through abrasive action. Not only are the surfaces of paper and other record materials (especially photographs) damaged, but, over time, the particles become imbedded in the paper fibers, causing them to break down. Dirt and dust, when viewed under a microscope, appear very menacing, with sharp cutting edges. In the presence of moisture, dirt and pollen can cause permanent stains. Oily soot is especially disfiguring and difficult to remove. Dirt and other solid particles also absorb acidic gaseous pollutants, which they then deposit on collection materials.

While pollution is generally seen as a problem of the cities and industrial parks, changing weather patterns and air inversions mean that pollution is a potential threat to collections in all areas: urban, suburban, and rural.

Biological Agents

Biological agents that can damage archival materials include mold or fungi, insects, and rodents. Mold spores are always present in the air. They will grow whenever environmental conditions are favorable. Warm conditions (temperature generally above 75° F), moisture (relative humidity above 65 percent), darkness, and little air circulation encourage the growth of mold. These factors can vary, however, depending upon the type of mold and whether or not the materials have been previously infested. Pockets of stagnant air also increase the likelihood of mold growth in localized areas. Mold will weaken and permanently stain paper, causing both physical deterioration and cosmetic damage. If left unchecked, mold can obliterate images and text or completely encompass material (see Figures 4-3, 4-4). Mold feeds on the nutrients present in photographic materials and paper, including cellulose, sizing, and gelatin emulsions. When mold reacts with the trace metals (primarily iron salts) present in most paper, the result, known as foxing, is small brownish or rusty patches that are often found on book papers, prints, and drawings. Foxing is fungal growth that occurs under conditions of less moisture than is required for other types of mold activity; its precise relationship to iron is not fully understood.

Insects, rodents, and other pests feed on cellulose as well as other organic substances found in collections,

Figure 4-3. These records suffered water damage and subsequent mold growth. Fumigation is necessary.

Figure 4-4. Advanced mold damage; these records are beyond recovery. Reproduced courtesy of the Newberry Library Conservation Laboratory Slide Collection.

such as paste, glue, gelatin sizing, leather, and book-cloth. Insects that are attracted to archival and library materials include cockroaches, silverfish, termites, and carpet and other beetles (sometimes known as book-worms). Insects generally prefer dark, warm, and damp environments and usually will be active at night when people are not present. The damage they cause is irreversible. They can eat away image-bearing materials (such as gelatin emulsions on photographs); structural damage can also result if a maze of holes or perforations is left in sheets of paper or through entire bindings. Rodents, such as rats, mice, and squirrels, can nibble away at collection items (see Figure 4-5), or eat them in their entirety; rodents like to use shredded paper as a nesting material. Their droppings are also corrosive and can leave permanent stains.

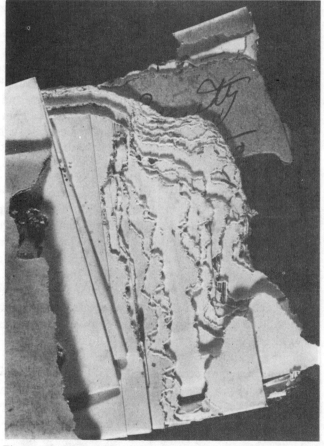

Figure 4-5. Documents exhibiting damage caused by rodents. Reproduced courtesy of the Newberry Library Conservation Laboratory Slide Collection.

Abuse and Mismanagement

Unfortunately, people pose the most constant threats to archival collections. Abuse, whether imposed by archival staff or researchers, intentional or not, results in the same damage and loss of material. Actions that may be considered abusive include careless or rough handling of brittle paper and fragile bindings, destructive photocopying practices, disfiguring manuscripts with notations or marks, and spilling coffee or ashes on material. The list of abusive action is endless. While much damage results from carelessness, abuse also includes such blatant actions as mutilation, vandalism, and theft.

Mismanagement falls more specifically within the realm of the archivist and institutional policies and programs that endanger archival materials through casual inattention, sloppy procedures, or outright sustained efforts to ignore the conservation needs of collections. Mismanagement relates to housekeeping practices as well as processing, storage, and handling procedures that adversely affect the wellbeing of materials. Inappropriate conservation treatments carried out by unqualified personnel are also examples of mismanagement. Broader examples include institutions having neither security programs nor disaster preparedness plans. The lack of a conservation program that is a fully integrated aspect of archival administration contributes as much to the quiet disintegration of materials as the zealous application of inappropriate remedies.

Disasters

Whether brought about by human error or natural events, disasters pose the ultimate threat to collections. The results are immediate, calamitous, and dramatic, unlike the slow and insidious process of deterioration that takes place in boxes and filing cabinets. Disasters, which can result from fire, flooding, storms, earthquakes, or broken steam pipes, can damage or destroy a few items or entire collections. Vigilance and preparedness and recovery plans are the best guards against loss from disasters.[7]

The best response to all of the factors threatening archival collections is informed action to protect and safeguard materials from the hazards of a hostile environment. A controlled environment and proper storage procedures are important components in an archival preservation program. These subjects are addressed in the following chapters.

---

[7]Excellent literature is available on developing disaster preparedness plans. Standard works include pamphlets by Peter Waters and Hilda Bohem, which are cited in the bibliography. For further guidance, see "Disaster Prevention and Recovery Plan," Nebraska State Historical Society, Judith Fortson-Jones, May, 1980 (contact: Conservation Specialist, 1500 R Street, Lincoln, NE 68508).

5   Creating a Suitable Environment

The ideal physical environment for archival materials includes controlled temperature and relative humidity, clean air with good circulation, controlled light sources, and freedom from mold, insect, or rodent infestation. Good housekeeping practices, security provisions, and measures to protect collections against fire and water damage complete the range of environmental concerns. The first steps in providing a suitable environment are to monitor and evaluate existing conditions. Once this data is assembled, necessary improvements can be implemented.

The top conservation priority of every archival repository should be the provision of temperature- and humidity-controlled quarters for the storage and use of archival materials. In a sense, this is a mass conservation treatment because it benefits all items in a repository. *Air conditioning, though it is expensive to install and maintain, is considered to be the most cost-effective means of caring for collections.* Money expended to provide a suitable physical environment is well spent in terms of extending the useful life of collections and avoiding later expenditures for costly restoration.

The wide divergence of climatic conditions across the United States and Canada precludes recommendations regarding any one heating, cooling, and ventilating system that will meet the needs of all repositories. Specific systems must be designed to meet particular conditions of climate, pollution levels, and building construction and design. It is recommended that an engineering firm with a specialty in this area be consulted to develop an appropriate system. The role of the archivist in this context is to know prevailing conditions within the archives, to be aware of the recommendations regarding optimum conditions for the storage and use of archival materials, and to work with the engineers to solve the technical problems within budgetary constraints. Whether purchasing new or renovating existing equipment, a good heating, cooling, and ventilating system should be capable of meeting the following goals. The system should be able to maintain constant conditions of temperature and relative humidity within the prescribed ranges. Gaseous and solid pollutants should be filtered out of incoming air, and ventilation should be sufficient to avoid the creation of pockets of stagnant air.

Temperature and Relative Humidity

Several factors must be kept in mind when establishing specifications for the temperature and relative humidity under which archival materials will be stored and used. First is the fact that there is no easy solution to this problem. Archival collections contain an incredibly wide range of record materials, all of which respond somewhat differently to a given environment. Ideally, separate controlled storage areas would be designed for paper (bound and in sheets), leather, vellum and parchment, and photographic materials. Such practice is not feasible in many repositories, however, and many archival records are assemblages of various materials. Thus, compromises must be made, balancing such practical considerations as building design and construction, energy costs, budgetary restraints, and human comfort, against the nature and use of the collections.

It has sometimes been stated that the temperature that is good for people also is good for paper and books. This is not precisely the case. Theoretically, the colder the temperature at which paper is kept, the longer it will last; freezing thus raises possibilities for actual permanence. Cold temperatures can be expensive to maintain, however, and another consideration works against such practice as well. Working collections need to be accessed on a regular basis. Materials kept in cold storage must be brought to room temperature in stages; if they were brought immediately from cold storage into a room temperature of 65° F, condensation would form on the items. This would be most noticeable if materials were stored at very low temperatures, but also would occur in a temperature change from 55° to 65° F, though the condensation might be imperceptible to the naked eye.

Use of collections must be considered in another context as well. If materials receive heavy use, they need to be flexible and thus require high humidity. On the other hand, high humidity speeds up the rate of deteriorative chemical reactions and encourages mold growth. Materials that are seldom used could withstand low humidity, since a degree of embrittlement presumably would be acceptable in such instances. The variables that must be weighed in designing an environmental system are thus complex and sometimes conflicting.

Taking into account the sometimes opposing requirements of use and preservation, human comfort, and operational reality, the following ranges of temperature and relative humidity are recommended as a reasonable compromise for the storage and use of archival materials:

Temperature: 67° F ± 2° F
Relative Humidity: 47 percent ± 2 percent

These ranges, which are acceptable for a wide variety of materials found in a repository, take a number of factors into account. The allowable fluctuations are not significant in terms of imposing undue stress on materials, and it is unlikely, at any rate, that most systems can maintain conditions within closer ranges. A constant relative humidity of 47 percent ± 2 percent is low enough to avoid problems with mold growth and high enough to avoid problems with materials drying out and becoming brittle. A temperature of 67° F ± 2° F will not unduly accelerate harmful chemical reactions, is satisfactory for human comfort, and is reasonably economical to maintain.

The maintenance of both temperature and relative humidity must be constant within the recommended ranges every day, year round, and heating and cooling systems should not be shut down after office hours or over weekends or holidays. The fluctuation or cycling that occurs as systems are shut down on a daily or weekly basis can cause very serious internal stress and damage in record materials. Slightly greater fluctuations are generally considered tolerable during periods of seasonal transition, as long as daily cycling is not dramatic. No system at all may be preferable, however, to one that subjects material to wide swings in temperature and relative humidity.

American National Standards Institute (ANSI) specifications outline recommendations for the storage of a number of photographic materials (plates, prints, and films; see Appendix D for citations). A compromise for the range of photographic materials (excluding nitrate-base film) likely to be found in a repository suggests a maximum temperature of 68° F (somewhat lower is preferable), and a constant relative humidity of 35 percent. Thus, if at all possible, photographic materials should be given separate storage away from other archival records. ANSI specifications also provide guidelines for the storage of archival microfilm (i.e., master negatives). Requirements for archival microfilm include a constant temperature, not to exceed 68° F, and a relative humidity maintained between 30–40 percent. Such conditions may be easiest to maintain in a vault or similar enclosed area within the archives.

The archivist has a number of responsibilities in the area of controlling temperature and relative humidity. An overall review of the building is advisable, considering construction and energy needs. Windows and doors should be checked for proper sealing, and the need for insulation, vapor barriers, or double or triple glazing on windows should be evaluated. Existing heating and cooling equipment, and its capabilities to meet the specifications, must be evaluated as well. Any malfunctions in the system should be noted, and equipment con- trols should be adjusted and calibrated as necessary. The location of air conditioning equipment must be considered to determine whether it poses a potential threat to collections. For example, such equipment on the roof of the archives building or located near the stacks or vault could result in water damage to collection materials if there were a system failure.

Equally important, the archivist must determine the prevailing conditions in the repository. This necessitates monitoring and recording daily changes in the temperature and relative humidity. Ideally, such a record will provide data on localized areas throughout the archives facility over a period of time; special attention should be paid to holidays as well as periods of seasonal transition. Once this information is assembled (and assuming conditions are not in conformity with recommended levels), the archivist must gain the support of the administration for improving environmental conditions. This is critical, especially in repositories that are maintained on institution-wide heating and cooling systems (which also may be controlled by computer). The archives may comprise but one small area within a complex of rooms or buildings, and persuasive arguments will have to be made to justify the specialized environmental needs of the collection. Special dispensation may be required to bring the archives into conformity with recommended practice, *and* to keep systems operational around the clock. Once specifications for the archives have been agreed upon, effort will be required to implement and maintain them.

Unfortunately, air conditioning systems do not work by magic. Once set, they will not maintain required levels indefinitely. Most systems will require constant adjustment and coddling; and while perfection is not often achieved, a close approximation should be possible. Since most archivists are not familiar with the mysteries of air conditioning equipment or instrumentation, they will need to establish ongoing working relationships with engineers and maintenance crews to achieve the desired results. It is thus very important to have a record of temperature and relative humidity conditions in the archives. Over time, this record documents evidence of system shut-downs or special problems encountered during periods of seasonal transition, which will be very valuable in working with administrators as well as engineers. The archivist should be wary of engineers with pat answers. It generally takes about one year to work out all of the problems in a system and have it respond correctly to seasonal weather changes that affect indoor conditions. Maintenance and engineering staff are more likely to respond to the needs of the archives if they are informed regarding the specialized needs of the collections and made to feel that they are partners in preserving valuable material.

If system-wide air conditioning is not feasible, portable air conditioners, humidifiers, and dehumidifiers may be employed. They have obvious limitations in output and cannot effectively maintain desired conditions in large areas, but, with care and regular monitoring, they can often achieve good results. Electrical wiring should be checked to ensure that there is no system overload, and any source of water and potential leaking should be checked daily. If possible, portable dehumidifiers should be outfitted to drain automatically. Humidifiers should be watched closely for mold growth, and a regular cleaning program should be instituted to avoid this problem.

Air Quality

Air circulation and filtration are other important elements that must be addressed in providing a suitable environment for archival materials. A good ventilation system will provide for circulation of air in and around stack areas. Pockets of stagnant air can create mini-environments (i.e., localized variations in temperature and relative humidity), which, under the right conditions, can encourage mold growth. Pollution levels within the archives also must be determined, and appropriate filters that will eliminate specific pollutants should be installed. As such monitoring can be difficult and costly, it is recommended that archival repositories take advantage of information that can be acquired from state environmental protection agencies regarding the levels of various pollutants in their region. While such information cannot be exactly equated with pollution levels within a building, it will give a good indication of which pollutants pose problems in the region and their relative levels. Specific monitoring and detection equipment is described in the following section.

Filtration devices should be incorporated into heating and cooling systems to remove harmful gases, dirt, and other solid particles from incoming air. Adsorption systems remove gaseous pollutants, while mechanical filtration systems remove solid particles; archives need to be outfitted with both. Gaseous pollutants are removed from the air with filters of activated charcoal or ceramic pellets, both of which adsorb harmful gases. Mechanical filtration with fiberglass filters will remove solid particles. It would be prohibitively expensive (and perhaps impossible) to achieve 100 percent efficiency with mechanical filtration devices; 95 percent is considered acceptable. To be effective, all filters must be monitored for their efficiency and changed on a regular basis.

Electrostatic filters are capable of removing solid particles from incoming air but are not acceptable for archives or libraries because they produce ozone. Scrubbing systems, in which incoming air is passed through alkaline water washes, can be built into central air conditioning systems to remove sulphur dioxide and similar gases. Such systems are expensive, however, and need constant maintenance; they may have to be used in combination with adsorption systems to be fully effective. Window air conditioning units equipped with filters will remove some particulate matter, but no gaseous pollutants, from incoming air.

Monitoring and Detection Equipment

Archives staff or conservation personnel should be responsible for monitoring environmental conditions within the archives. A sophisticated environmental system is only as good as the monitoring system that backs it up; the two are equally important and must go hand-in-hand. The importance of knowing prevailing conditions has been stressed already. Since the archivist has primary responsibility for the care of collections and must work both with administrators and engineers or maintenance personnel to achieve desired conditions, he or she will place a greater priority on the need for monitoring conditions in a consistent manner. Further, it is often advisable to have a system of checks and balances; the person responsible for maintaining conditions (the engineer) should not also be charged with the monitoring function. Such a situation exemplifies the benign distrust that an archivist must exhibit on behalf of the collection. In addition, actual room conditions can vary with thermostat settings or readings, and an independent check is thus further warranted.

It is desirable to take daily readings of temperature and relative humidity in the archives. Depending on the size of the facility, it may be necessary to take readings in several locations throughout the building. Ideally, a record of changing conditions would be gained with a hygrothermograph, which creates a graph, recording time and the corresponding temperature and relative humidity. The benefit of such a device is that it will continue to work whether or not staff are present, providing a record of conditions after office hours and over weekends and holidays.

At a minimum, however, every archives should own a thermometer and hygrometer. These are relatively inexpensive devices and are readily available from conservation and scientific supply houses. While they are not extremely precise and do not create an ongoing record of conditions, they will provide readings of temperature and relative humidity within tolerable error. These manual devices require the keeping of a log or chart (see Figure 5-1). While readings can be taken only when staff are present, such an approach provides

TEMPERATURE/RELATIVE HUMIDITY LOG

Date	Day	Time	Temp.	RH	Location	Remarks	Staff
	Monday						
	Tuesday						
	Wednesday						
	Thursday						
	Friday						
	Saturday						
	Sunday						

Average conditions for week:

Measuring devices used:

Figure 5-1. A manual record of temperature and relative humidity must be compiled if non-recording instruments are used to monitor the environment.

at least a starting point in the assembling of data on the environmental conditions within the archives. Also, the instruments are within the financial means of every institution. Dial hygrometers, which are small enough to be used within enclosed areas and which may be placed unobtrusively in exhibit cases, tend to lose their accuracy over time and should be tested periodically against a sling psychrometer. Portable electronic hygrometers and thermometers are now available that will provide very accurate readings with ease.

The sling psychrometer is a manual instrument outfitted with two thermometers (see Figure 5-2). The dry bulb provides a reading of temperature. The wet bulb, which is covered with cotton wicking and wetted with distilled water, indicates temperature change (caused by evaporation) as the psychrometer is rotated at a constant rate for approximately two minutes. The relative humidity is then calculated from the two temperatures using a slide rule or chart, which accompanies the instrument. If the two thermometers are well matched, the

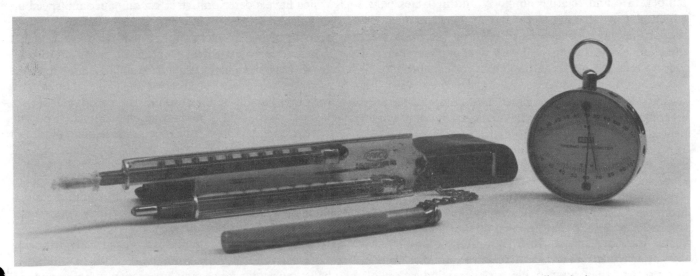

Figure 5-2. Sling psychrometer (left) and thermo-hygrometer (right). These are inexpensive non-recording devices.

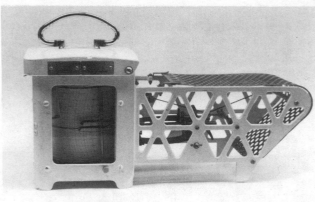

Figure 5-3. An hygrothermograph provides on-going documentation of changes in the temperature and relative humidity.

sling psychrometer is very accurate; it is used to calibrate other monitoring devices (such as dial hygrometers and hygrothermographs). Sling psychrometers obviously cannot be used in enclosed areas or narrow aisles between stacks; since they are nonrecording, they also require the creation of a manual chart of changing conditions of temperature and relative humidity. Aspirating psychrometers work on the same principle as sling psychrometers but draw air in over the two thermometers with a battery or electrically operated fan. They can thus be placed in small areas as no manual rotating is required.

Hygrothermographs are precise instruments that record the fluctuation of temperature and humidity (see Figure 5-3). They are outfitted with sensing devices (such as horsehair filaments) and a spring-wound or electrically driven drum covered with calibrated graph paper. The sensing element responds to changes in the temperature and relative humidity and activates pens, which plot the changes on the paper. The drums can be set for one-day or one-week revolutions, at which time the chart has to be replaced with new paper. While expensive initially, hygrothermographs are capable of providing continuous precise readings. They must be recalibrated occasionally against an accurate psychrometer. Depending upon the size of the archives, it would be useful to have several hygrothermographs to locate in key positions, such as a vault or microforms storage area. With care, they may be rotated on a weekly basis to various locations within the archives.

Humidity indicators are strips of paper treated with a moisture-sensitive chemical, which changes color in response to changes in the relative humidity. Exposed strips are matched against a calibrated color chart to give approximate readings of relative humidity. While not precise, they do provide a general indication of changed conditions. They can be useful in exhibit cases.

As stated earlier, it is potentially difficult to monitor pollution levels within archival repositories. The instruments that detect the presence of various gaseous pollutants are expensive and require specific technical expertise to operate. It may be necessary to employ the advice and services of the state environmental protection agency, the chemistry department at a local college or university, or an engineering firm to determine the level of pollution within the building. Local readings by the U.S. Environmental Protection Agency (EPA) of exterior pollution levels provide fairly accurate comparisons with conditions inside buildings. It may be possible to develop a cooperative arrangement with a nearby chemistry department that has access to portable gas detectors capable of detecting levels of such gases as sulphur dioxide and nitrogen dioxide. The presence of ozone cannot be detected as easily; it is best in this instance to rely upon EPA readings and assume that exterior and interior levels will be fairly close.

Simple indicators are available that detect the presence of specific gases such as sulphur dioxide and hydrogen sulfide. Test papers are impregnated with a chemical that reacts with a color change in the presence of the particular gas; the strip is then matched against a calibrated color chart to indicate the degree of concentration. These are not extremely precise, but at least they will indicate the presence of harmful gases. It is recommended that the services of a consulting engineer be engaged to determine precise levels of harmful pollutants within a repository and to develop appropriate filtration systems.

Light

Archival materials must be protected against ultraviolet (UV) radiation and active visible light, both of which have a deteriorative effect on paper and speed up chemical reactions. While ultraviolet radiation (which is emitted primarily from sunlight and fluorescent light) poses the greatest threat to archival materials, the effects of visible light should not be underestimated. Light sources throughout the archives must be evaluated, and measures should be taken to protect materials from exposure. Means of illuminating the archives and the presence of windows must be considered. (Windows also pose a potential security breach and must be considered in this context as well.) The degree of exposure must be evaluated. If all items are boxed or wrapped, damage from exposure to light will not pose a serious threat, though the vast majority of archives do have unprotected items sitting on open shelves. In processing or reading rooms, a wide range of materials may be briefly exposed while they are being used; while in exhibition halls, particular items may be exposed to light, often to very strong light, for several months.

Ideally, stack areas should have no windows at all, even if items are boxed. If windows are present, they should be painted over or, preferably, boarded up. Windows in processing areas or reading rooms may be handled differently, in part for aesthetic reasons and human comfort and in part because materials are exposed for relatively brief periods of time. Windows in these areas should be outfitted with UV-filtering shields, which are available in rigid sheet form (such as Plexiglas® UF3) or in thin rolls that can be applied directly to the insides of windows. As an intermediate step—or a further precaution—window shades, blinds, or opaque curtains may be used to limit the amount of sunlight entering the area. Architectural features, such as eaves or overhangs, also may be a help in this regard. Another means of reducing the level of ultraviolet radiation in archival quarters is to paint walls and ceilings with paint containing UV-absorbing zinc white or titanium dioxide. Light (from any source) reflected from surfaces painted with these pigments contains little ultraviolet radiation.

Fluorescent light tubes should be covered with UV-filtering sleeves; these are flexible plastic covers that contain a UV-absorbing material and that slip directly around the fluorescent tubes. Despite manufacturers' claims, UV-filtering screens do not last indefinitely. They must be changed on a periodic basis; every 7 to 10 years is recommended. Fluorescent tubes that have been coated directly with a UV-absorbing material also may be purchased, though they are a more costly alternative. Maintenance crews, if not supervised, may unintentionally discard UV-filtering sleeves or replace coated tubes with regular fluorescent lights. In some large institutions, outside firms are hired to change fluorescent lights on a regular basis. As such service contracts are fulfilled throughout institutional offices and buildings, special archival concerns may be forgotten if the archivist is not vigilant. While UV filters and coated fluorescent tubes must be replaced periodically, it is not cost-effective to discard them prematurely.

Incandescent lights pose no significant threats to archival materials from ultraviolet radiation, and thus are the preferable light source in archives. Despite the fact that incandescent lights are somewhat more costly to operate than fluorescent lights (and many institutions have switched to the latter for this reason), good arguments may be made on behalf of incandescent lighting. First, there is generally no reason to have lights constantly on in stack areas. If incandescent lights were turned on only when material had to be retrieved or refiled, there would be an energy savings in addition to reducing the threat to the materials from light damage. Further cost savings would result because no filtering devices would be required. Over time, this could effect a substantial savings, since filtering sleeves must be replaced periodically. The primary concern with incandescent light is the possibility of heat buildup; this problem, however, is associated with incandescent bulbs in enclosed areas, such as exhibit cases, and would not be a problem in stacks or processing rooms.

New lighting found in many reading and exhibit areas, particularly those with high ceilings, may include high-intensity quartz lighting. These lights should be checked for their UV, blue, and violet-blue contents, and retrofitted with appropriate filters if needed.

As a general practice, light levels in archives could be lowered substantially both by keeping lights off when they are not necessary and by reducing the wattage. When fluorescent lights are used they are generally installed to the point of excess; lighting systems should be adjusted to allow turning off every other range. Timed shut-off switches also should be considered for storage and stack areas.

Actual light levels within the archives (and especially in exhibition areas) should be monitored. Meters that measure both visible and ultraviolet light are available, although the latter are costly. Some photographic light meters may be used to measure foot candles. Assistance in monitoring levels of ultraviolet radiation may be sought from local art museums, universities, or lighting engineers.

Housekeeping

Housekeeping practices in the archives have great impact on the preservation of collections. An atmosphere of orderliness and cleanliness is a positive impetus to maintain good conditions, and creates a positive impression with visitors and donors. Clean surroundings also discourage insects and rodents from settling into the archives. Further, housekeeping activities provide an opportunity to observe conditions throughout the repository and note problems (such as harmful shelving practices) that otherwise might go unnoticed.

Food and drink should be strictly prohibited from the archives storage, processing, and reading areas. Kitchen facilities and staff lunch rooms should be kept scrupulously clean and should be sufficiently removed from areas where archival materials are stored and used. Accidental spills can damage or stain archival records and, equally important, crumbs and garbage will attract insects and rodents. Insects can be a particular problem in tropical climates, but they are a potential threat in any archival repository no matter its locality. At the first sign of insect or rodent infestation, action must be taken. The services of a qualified licensed exterminator should be engaged; and it also may be useful to consult with an entymologist from a local university or natural history museum if insects cannot be identified. Any chemicals that are used in archival settings must be non-toxic to humans and nondamaging to record materials. Chemicals used to control pests should never be placed in direct contact with archival materials, nor placed in archives storage boxes.

Stacks and storage areas must be kept clean of debris and any material that is extraneous to collections. An ongoing program of dusting shelves and boxes will help to control the amount of airborne dirt that can settle into boxes and folders. Shelves, storage containers, and the exteriors of bound volumes may be cleaned with treated dust cloths (One-Wipe® cloths are recommended), or Endust® may be sprayed onto a piece of soft fabric such as cheesecloth. These products are recommended for such uses in archival and library settings; they readily pick up and trap the dirt rather than spreading it around from one surface to the next. Another aid in cleaning shelves, boxes, and bound volumes is a portable tank-type vacuum cleaner, which will remove heavy accumulations of dirt. The suction should be low, and cheesecloth or a piece of nylon screening should be placed over the nozzle to prevent fragments of bindings or paper records from being sucked into the machine. After initial vacuuming, it may be necessary to complete the job with treated dust cloths; very fragile items should only be dusted by hand.

If shelves are exceptionally dirty—or if they have housed mold-infested materials—wet cleaning is desirable. One cup of Lysol® Disinfectant per gallon of water is a satisfactory cleaning solution. The active ingredient in Lysol® is the fungicide o-phenyl phenol. Rubber gloves should be worn, and the shelves should be allowed to dry completely before reshelving collection items.

Any cleaning that is done by maintenance or janitorial staff should be done during regular working hours when the archivist is present to supervise. This is a precaution from several perspectives. Many archives processing areas appear cluttered to the unpracticed eye, and well-meaning janitors may inadvertently discard materials that were intended to be saved. Any water coming into the archives must be carefully controlled. If floors are to be washed or waxed, care must be taken that records storage cartons are not permanently affixed to the floor as the wax dries. (Despite the fact that archivists know that it is not good practice to store boxes on the floor, the practice persists in bulging repositories.) Further, it should be ascertained that any cleaning supplies or solvents used in the archives pose no threat to collections because of dangerous fumes; sensitive photographic emulsions are especially susceptible to damage or alteration from solvent fumes. Prod-

ucts containing oil, chlorine, alum, peroxides, and ammonia should be avoided; paint and turpentine fumes are also destructive. All cleaning supplies should be stored well away from the archives. A final housekeeping concern relates to the security breach that is posed if maintenance staff have access by key to the archives after hours.

Security

Security is an issue that encompasses all aspects of archival work, and should be considered as it relates to processing collections, supervising readers, and providing theft deterrents. In the present context, however, security is an issue that must be addressed in providing a safe environment for archival materials.

The archives building and its perimeter must be evaluated to determine possible routes of unauthorized access or egress. Within a building, the layout of the archives quarters must be evaluated, paying particular attention to windows, doors, and skylights. Emergency exits with crash bars should be outfitted with alarms. Heavy-duty locks should be installed on doors and windows, and the need for window grills or bars determined. Intrusion alarms at doors and windows should be installed and connected to monitoring panels at the security office, local police station, or commercial security firm. The need for motion detectors with remote alarms should be evaluated as well.

If the archives storage, processing, and reading rooms are not all contiguous, patterns of access and use must be scrutinized. Off-site storage facilities must be considered in these contexts as well. Stack areas should be closed to all but archives personnel, with limited access allowed in other parts of the archives quarters. Researchers should always be monitored in the reading room, for example, and any visitors brought into the processing areas should be supervised. The archives should be keyed on its own system separate from the rest of the institution, and key distribution should be limited and strictly controlled. There is no reason for everyone on staff to have access by key or combination to stack or high security areas such as vaults; access to these areas should be on a need-to-use basis. Distribution of keys to non-archives staff should be avoided at all costs. Maintenance or security staff should not have unsupervised access to the archives.[8]

---

[8]For further information on archival security, see: Timothy Walch, *Archives and Manuscripts: Security.* Basic Manual Series. Chicago: Society of American Archivists, 1977.

Fire and Water Protection

A final broad environmental issue—securing the archival quarters against fire and water damage—is integral to conservation and security concerns, and to disaster preparedness as well. Every archives must be outfitted with automatic fire detection and suppression equipment. Smoke and heat sensors with warning alarms in the repository as well as alarms connected to the security office and fire station are mandatory. Several factors should be considered when selecting a system to contain or suppress fire, including the proximity of the archives building to the local fire department and the construction and layout of the building. If fire-resistant building materials were not used in construction, or if the layout of rooms or stack areas will encourage the spread of fire, the need for an adequate fire suppression system becomes even more compelling.

Several automatic fire suppression systems that activate via heat sensors are in use in archives and libraries. High-expansion foam systems employ a biodegradable detergent concentrate which, upon being mixed with water, expand approximately 1,000 times to form bubbles. Upon contact with heated surfaces or fire, these bubbles release water, which then forms steam. The foam has a cooling and quenching effect. The conversion of water to steam absorbs heat energy and results in a lowered oxygen level, which cannot support combustion. Total flooding of a sealed area is required for this system to be effective. The amount of water damage to materials is potentially minimal because of the low water content of the foam.

Other automatic suppression systems that require total flooding of a sealed area employ gas. Carbon dioxide, which reduces the oxygen level to the degree that combustion stops, is one such system. The oxygen, however, is reduced to such a degree that human life would be threatened; for this reason carbon dioxide is not generally used. The Halon (halogenated hydrocarbon) system, which is less toxic and more effective than carbon dioxide, also interferes with the combustion cycle to suppress the fire. The Halon system does not damage books and papers and leaves little residue after use. It is an effective fire suppressant within limits but generally provides protection for only a matter of minutes, and it is not effective against smoldering fires. There are several additional drawbacks. Halon is expensive to install and requires a tightly sealed area if it is to be effective; it is thus often used for confined spaces that are readily sealed, such as vaults or rare book rooms. High concentrations or prolonged exposure to Halon may pose a health hazard.

Automatic sprinkler systems are more economical than the Halon system, especially for large areas, and have been greatly improved in recent years. Early concerns over the possibility of accidental discharge have seldom been supported in actual fact. Dry or wet pipe systems are available that provide protection for a period of from one-half to four hours. With dry pipe systems, supply pipes are filled with pressurized air; pressure is released when heat-sensitive sprinkler heads open, and water is directed only to those heads. Dry pipe systems can take a bit of time to activate, and, as there is the possibility of dry pipes becoming obstructed with rust or corrosion, they should be flushed periodically. Dry pipes are often used where there is the possibility of pipes freezing. Given the slower reaction time with dry pipes, wet pipe systems may be preferable. With either system, it is important that sprinkler heads operate independently of one another. They should activate with devices that detect a rapid increase in temperature, and thus release water only over the affected area. Sprinkler systems provide quick response and will protect archival records from being irretrievably lost to fire. Concern over possible water damage should be balanced against improved techniques of restoring water-damaged materials. Given the relative expense, sprinkler systems are the most viable fire suppression option available for archival repositories. In some situations, fire insurance premiums can be reduced as a result of installing a sprinkler system; this savings can offset installation costs within a decade.

To be effective, all fire detection and suppression systems must be checked on a regular basis to make sure they are operational and functioning properly; otherwise, a false—and potentially tragic—sense of security could persist. All archives staff should be informed of the fire detection and suppression systems protecting the repository. They should know what kind of system is in use and its operational characteristics. The location of manual fire alarms should be known as well. The archives should be equipped with several portable fire extinguishers (ABC or Halon variety). These should be checked on a regular basis and all staff members should be trained in their use.

A water detection system should be installed if the archives is outfitted with a sprinkler system. Water detectors are also desirable if the archives is susceptible to natural flooding, surrounded by water pipes, or located near restrooms. The water detectors react in the presence of water, not under conditions of high humidity. They have an audible alarm and also may be outfitted with remote indicators. In conjunction with smoke and heat detectors, they provide complete protection for the archives against fire and water damage.

6   Storage of Archival Materials

Storage Equipment

The layout of the archives storage area must provide an efficient use of space and meet the physical needs of the collection. Shelves should not be placed directly against outside or basement walls because of the possibility of excessive moisture buildup or actual leaks. Also, shelves should be positioned parallel with the direction of air flow in the room to allow good circulation in and around stacks. If book trucks or ladders are to be used, aisles will have to be large enough to accommodate them. Oversized materials require more aisle space for access and shelving than do smaller record formats. Factors to consider in determining the height of shelving units are ceiling height, proximity to light fixtures or pipes, and potential awkwardness or difficulty of lifting heavy boxes. In a warehouse setting, high ranges of industrial shelving may be used, although safety factors for staff and material must be considered. Heavy-duty ladders that have platforms rather than narrow steps or rungs should be employed wherever transfer cases or document boxes must be lifted to high levels.

Storage systems should provide overall support and protect materials from physical or mechanical damage. Storage areas and equipment must be designed to meet the preservation needs of special record formats, such as oversized material, photographs, bound volumes, and sound recordings. Decisions about these systems should be based on the format and condition of the material, and not on traditional practices that mandate keeping disparate formats in a collection together despite their physical needs. Good intellectual controls, i.e., an inventory and location file, should overcome any resistance to separating a collection into parts to provide for its greater protection.

Good shelving equipment must be heavy-duty, constructed of non-damaging materials, and designed to impose no stress on collections. It is recommended that all storage equipment, including conventional library shelving, industrial shelving units, map cases, and filing cabinets, be constructed of steel with a baked enamel finish. The finish should be smooth, not bumpy or abrasive, and there should be no sharp edges or corners that could function as cutting edges and thus damage material.

Ranges of library and industrial shelving are commonly used in archival settings for storing document boxes, transfer cases, bound volumes, and oversized records. These units should have shelves that adjust vertically to accommodate materials and boxes of varying sizes. To increase their sturdiness, free-standing units should be bolted together as well as to the floor, and they should be equipped with back and side braces to further avoid the possibility of collapse. Shelves should sit on a base four to six inches off the floor to provide an extra measure of protection for archival materials in the event that flooding results in water collecting on the floor.

Wooden shelves are not desirable for the storage of archival materials because of the possibility of pitch, resin, peroxide, and acidic products leaching out and damaging records. Oak, which traditionally has been used for book cases and shelves, has a particularly high formic acid content. Unfortunately, many archives and special collections departments store their treasured volumes and records on beautiful wooden shelves in reception or reading areas. While the decor is pleasing, it poses potential problems for the materials. If wooden shelves are already in use and the likelihood of change is not great, precautionary measures should be taken. Raw wooden shelves should *never* be used. Wood must be properly sealed with two or three coats of polyurethane varnish to prevent lignin and other damaging materials from leaching out. After varnishing, shelves should be "cured," or allowed to dry for several weeks, before material is reshelved. An alternative to varnishing shelves is to line them with heavy (5-mil) polyester to provide a protective barrier between the shelves and the records stored on them. Appropriately sized strips of polyester can be cut most economically from a roll; and the strips may be held in position on the shelves with double-coated tape (the same as that used for encapsulation).

Map or blueprint cases also should be constructed of steel with a baked enamel finish. Drawers should be no more than two inches deep, although shallower drawers (3/4 inch) are preferable. Deep drawers encourage overstuffing and inflict greater mechanical stress on items during retrieval and refiling. Drawers should be outfitted with fabric dust covers or rear hoods to protect the contents from slipping over the backs or being caught up and damaged as drawers are maneuvered. High-quality, heavy-duty map cases are expensive but prove their worth over time. They should have locks, and drawers should roll easily on ballbearings rather than sliding in grooves, which often results in their becoming misaligned or stuck. Map cases also should be equipped with stop devices to prevent drawers from sliding completely out of the unit when they are opened.

The location of shelving for oversized materials is important, whether map cases or industrial shelving are used. Access to and from filing equipment should be direct and free from obstructions. Filing will be less hazardous if there is room for drawers to be pulled out completely to the stop position. Also, there should be a large flat surface near the oversized shelving unit where folders and items can be placed to expedite filing and sorting.

Filing cabinets serve a number of purposes for archival storage. These, too, should be made of steel with a baked enamel finish. Wooden filing cabinets, wooden map drawers, and containers that have raw wooden interiors should be avoided. Closed wooden containers offer greater hazards than book shelves due to the build-up of decomposition by-products in an enclosed space, whereas open shelves allow these by-products to be diluted in the surrounding air. Filing cabinets should be evaluated to determine if they have any moveable parts that could damage archival materials. For example, back supports or spring-type devices designed to hold contents upright may exert too much pressure on fragile material, or may allow papers to get caught up in the system and thus suffer damage. Potentially harmful features should be removed.

If the archives is the repository for archaic filing equipment as well as historical records, the suitability of the equipment for housing valuable collections must be evaluated. The type of material, finish, and mechanical features must be considered. For example, the action of a drawer rotating open in a circular motion rather than rolling on a flat plane could damage fragile material as it moves about. Spring clamps may exert too much localized pressure on brittle items. Filing equipment that is not suitable for storing archival materials, if it cannot be discarded, should be recycled to other uses, such as storing office supplies.

Storage Materials

All paper and board stock used in conjunction with archival materials, such as boxes, file folders, envelopes, and mat board, should be acid-free and buffered to have an alkaline reserve with a minimum pH of 8.5. In addition, archival storage materials should contain no lignin, groundwood, or alum-rosin sizing. Some photographic materials are excluded from this recommendation, as noted on page 44. Storage materials that have an alkaline reserve are available in a wide variety of standard sizes and formats to meet virtually every collection need. In addition, suppliers are willing—for a fee—to fabricate folders and boxes to specialized sizes. Also available are paper and board stock that allow the skillful archivist to construct custom-made storage units. Acidic filing materials, of which there are endless examples ranging from manila folders to glassine negative sleeves, do not provide long-term protection for archival materials. They are inherently unstable and will break down over time; it is not at all uncommon to see top edges missing from old manila file folders. More importantly, acid will migrate from these enclosures to archival records stored in them. For example, corrugated cardboard boxes emit substantial quantities of peroxides and lignin by-products, which are especially harmful within closed containers.

Some archivists and administrators argue that it is a waste of money to use folders and boxes that have an alkaline reserve on materials that have not been deacidified. There are other ways of looking at this issue, however. The information that is currently available on the damage caused to records from acid—whatever its source—is conclusive. It renders decisions to keep valuable records in acidic containers unconscionable and unenlightened. Further, it is incorrect to assume that all archival papers are inherently acidic; some are quite sound and do not require deacidification. It is a basic conservation principle that any materials brought into contact with a collection must be non-damaging; suspect or nontested materials should be kept away from valuable records. Thus, even a beginning archives can institute sound conservation practice by using only safe storage materials. There is a further, perhaps psychological, advantage to replacing acidic file folders and boxes with containers that have an alkaline reserve: records that show evidence of care and attention will elicit careful handling, while records that look timeworn and sit in ragged dirty folders and boxes give the impression that they have little value to the repository or anyone else. (See Figure 6-1.)

A wide variety of plastic materials are being used to store and protect archival records. The recommended plastics have several positive attributes. They are inert, or chemically stable, and will undergo no changes that will have an adverse effect on material stored in them. Further, they allow clear visual access to records, are strong, and protect fragile materials from mechanical damage that could result from handling. Perhaps the most common plastic found in archival repositories is polyester, often referred to as Mylar®, its DuPont tradename. Polyester is used to encapsulate brittle paper, to construct protective folders, and also has many uses in mounting exhibits. Plastic envelopes and sleeves are being used increasingly for housing photographic prints and negatives. They allow immediate visual access and also protect sensitive photographic emulsions from fingerprints.

Plastics that are safe to use with photographs and other archival materials include, in addition to polyester, polyethylene, polypropylene, and triacetate. The sheets of black paper that are often found within inert plastic sleeves when purchased should be discarded; these sheets are acidic and will damage materials stored

Figure 6-1. This collection would benefit physically by removal from the acidic and dirty envelopes in which it is stored. Improved storage conditions would also present a better image to researchers and potential donors.

in contact with them. As a precautionary measure, the pH level of any paper inserts in commercial plastic sleeves should be tested before use. Polyvinylchloride, which is used in a number of commercially available photographic albums, sleeves, and slide enclosures, has no place in an archival repository. It is not inert but readily degrades upon exposure to heat and light, emitting plasticizer by-products and harmful gases that are very damaging to records.

When purchasing any storage materials for archival records, it is important to specify the exact requirements of the materials in precise language. American National Standards Institute (ANSI) or government specifications should be cited as appropriate. The term "archival quality" may be used, though it is imprecise. When ordering paper and board stock, pH range should be specified; groundwood papers and those with alum-rosin sizing should be specifically excluded. Orders for plastic materials should explicitly exclude plasticizers, surface coatings, and UV absorbents or inhibitors. It is safest to purchase storage materials directly from reputable archival and conservation suppliers. It is in their best interest to work with both archivists and manufacturers to keep quality high and within recommended specifications. As a precaution, however, it is always wise to double check an order. For example, once a shipment of boxes and paper is received, it is a simple matter to conduct several spot tests to check the pH level (see Appendix B5 for instructions) to make sure it is within the proper range. Orders for all archival storage materials should specify that no substitutions are acceptable. Questions should be raised if problems develop with a product, or if there is any suspicion that specifications have not been precisely honored. Ques-

tions may be addressed to both the supplier and the manufacturer; reputable suppliers will correct any problems with new shipments.

It is essential to know exactly what a product consists of before purchasing it. This is a special problem with plastics. It is often impossible to determine the composition of a product from packaging materials or advertising claims. In such instances, clarification (via the product data sheet) should be requested from the manufacturer. Local art, photographic, and stationery supply stores should not be viewed as appropriate sources for archival storage materials. While the paper *may* have an alkaline reserve and the photographic sleeve *may* be polyester, it is unlikely that salespeople will know the precise composition of their product lines. Similar cautions should be taken when purchasing other archival and conservation supplies. The terms "archival" and "archival quality" are commonly used to denote characteristics of permanence and are often included in advertising literature to invoke the impression that products have keeping qualities and non-damaging characteristics. They may indeed, but it is always advisable to evaluate the source and know whether or not products and materials have been independently tested for their safe use with archival records.

Storage and Handling of Specific Record Formats

Archival records exist in a wide range of formats. While they can be preserved compatibly under the environmental conditions described in the preceding chapter, some records have specialized filing and storage requirements because of their physical format or condition. Appropriate storage practices for a number of archival record formats are described below.

Unbound Records

This category encompasses a wide range of materials: correspondence, legal documents, financial records, leaflets, minutes, and broadsides. The list is potentially limitless, and, in terms of their storage requirements, may include pamphlets, publications, and small booklets (such as constitutions and membership directories) as well. Virtually any paper record that meets the size limitation should be stored in file folders and boxes that have an alkaline reserve. Based on collection format and need, many repositories find it advantageous to adopt either legal- or letter-sized supplies and to use them consistently. Such uniformity expedites shelving and filing systems. Envelopes and pamphlet boxes are also useful for filing pamphlet collections and small-format items. Many repositories have traditionally used document boxes that are designed to sit upright on shelves, with file folders perpendicular to the shelves within boxes. This approach is satisfactory when records are in good condition, but it may also result in fragile and brittle papers standing on edge, forced to bear their own weight. This may be more stress than some papers can bear. Thus, uniform flat storage for archival records is recommended to alleviate this problem. Flat storage provides overall support for records and avoids problems of curling often associated with upright storage. The adoption of flat storage would necessitate a reorientation of upright boxes, the repositioning of box labels, and possibly the adjustment of shelves. Flat or clam-shell document boxes thus would be more suitable for this purpose than upright boxes, though the latter could certainly be adapted. While the shifting of an entire collection to flat storage might seem overwhelming, it should be considered. New shelving practices could be instituted slowly over time, with fragile or brittle items given priority for immediate shifting. At any rate, repositories should be aware of revised thinking in this area and take it into account, especially when renovating or planning new quarters. At a minimum, flat storage should be adopted where the physical condition of collections requires it.

Unbound Oversized Materials

Unbound oversized items often found in archival repositories include posters, blueprints, architectural drawings, photographs, and maps. They should be placed in file folders that have an alkaline reserve and stored flat in map cases. All folders should be cut to the same size as the drawers to ensure that they do not get misplaced or pushed to the backs and crumpled. The size, weight of contents, and maneuverability of the folders must permit safe handling. In some instances, two people will be required to safely retrieve and file oversized folders (see Figure 6-2). The number of items per folder will depend on condition and value of material. At times, one item per folder will be warranted; however, since oversized materials are inherently awkward to handle and very susceptible to damage because of their size, the maximum number of items in a folder should be ten to twelve. Large pieces of paper cut to the same size as the folders may be used as interleaving sheets, both to protect fragile materials and to help bear the weight of items as they are being taken in and out of folders. Wide, heavy-weight, paper that has an alkaline reserve can be purchased by the roll and cut to size for this purpose. If extra support is required to keep

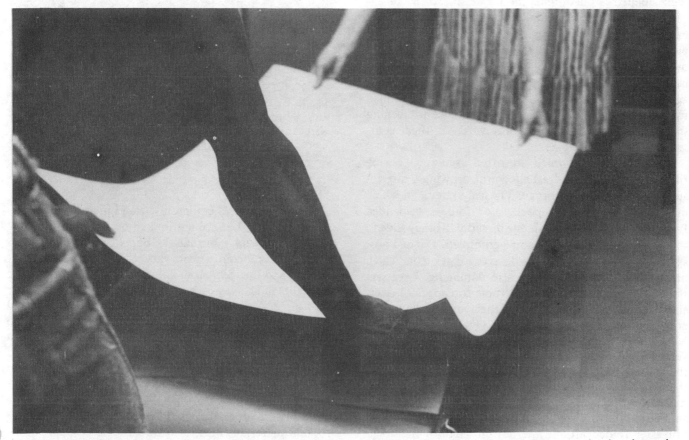

Figure 6-2. Oversized records are often endangered because of the sheer awkwardness of their format. Preservation is enhanced when two people handle them.

fragile items or materials with flaking images rigid and intact as they are being handled, a piece of alkaline mat board may be placed within a folder to keep items from flexing or bending. Especially large items may be folded once (with, rather than against, the grain of the paper) and stored in folders as well. If there is more than one fold, however, the points at which the folds intersect become very weak and will break down in time. If map cases are not available, oversized folders may be wrapped and placed flat on industrial shelving units. Depending on the sizes of the items to be stored, large, flat document cases are another alternative; these also may be placed on industrial shelves.

If items are too large for flat storage, an acceptable alternative is to roll materials around the outside of neutral pH tubes. Wide-diameter cardboard tubes may be used as well if they are first covered with either paper that has an alkaline reserve or polyester. The tubes provide rigid support for oversized items; under no circumstance should material be slipped inside a tube. Sheets of neutral pH tissue paper should be positioned on the items as they are rolled to serve an interleaving function. The rolled items should be wrapped in strong paper to protect the contents from light and dirt, and then labelled. Rolled items should be stored flat on industrial shelving or on top of a map cabinet, and not upright in bins or standing on the floor. Maintenance of proper environmental controls makes it possible to store oversized materials in a rolled state without having them become dried out and inflexible, and thus suffer damage as they are opened for use. Items that have been rolled for a long period and exhibit any resistance to opening should be humidified before any work on them is attempted (see Figure 6-3).

Vertical systems, which are often used for working files of blueprints and architectural drawings, are not suitable for archival storage. Vertical systems in which materials are stored in pockets or folders suspended from sliding rails often damage materials as they slide to the bottom of units and become crumpled. Pin and post systems, which employ self-adhesive hinges from which materials are suspended, are also damaging. Excessive strain is placed along the vulnerable top edges of oversized items, which must bear their own weight; the adhesive also may be damaging. Oversized items that have been encapsulated, however, may safely be stored vertically. A border of polyester is left to extend beyond the top edge of the capsule, and the unit is suspended from this edge using clips or pegs. Thus no strain is placed on the document. Static electricity keeps it from falling to the bottom of the capsule, and a strip of polyester folded around the bottom edge of the document keeps it from coming into contact with the double-coated tape. Oversized materials also may be encap-

sulated and then rolled. If either approach employing polyester is used, materials will still require protection from light.

Figure 6-3. These records were rolled without any interior support, and have thus suffered a great deal of damage as they were crushed, flattened, and bent. Humidification may be required before they can safely be opened for examination and treatment.

Bound Volumes

Bound materials commonly found in archival repositories include, but are not limited to, letterpress books, diaries, ledgers, journals, albums, and scrapbooks. Their storage requirements vary with size and condition. Small- and medium-sized volumes may be stored either upright on shelves or within folders and boxes if they are integrated with archival records. Volumes stored within folders and document boxes should be filed in such a way as to avoid physical distortion; spine down within folders is best for most volumes. Similarly sized volumes should be shelved together to ensure uniform support and thereby discourage warping of the boards or other physical distortions, which could result if large folios were interfiled with small volumes. Shelving bound materials with no regard to size considerations will result either in small books being damaged as they are jammed at the backs of shelves, or large volumes suffering structural damage if they are shelved next to small volumes that cannot provide proper support. Volumes on shelves should be kept vertical and not allowed to lean or slant, which could result in warped structures. Bookends should not have sharp cutting edges and should be thick enough that volumes are not inadvertently jammed onto them and thus damaged. Volumes that have loose or missing boards (i.e., covers) or that are otherwise not intact may be handled in one of several ways. At a minimum, all broken or weak bindings should be tied, using unbleached cotton or linen tape. The flat tape should wrap around the four edges of the book without exerting excessive pressure;

function properly, they must be constructed to the precise dimensions of the volume and thus require skill to make. While expensive, solander boxes are warranted for highly valuable bound records (see Figure 6-5). Slipcases do not provide safe storage from a conservation standpoint. Volumes are abraded every time they are slipped in and out of the cases, and spines are left exposed and thus suffer from light damage (see Figure 6-6).

Figure 6-5. A drop-spine box provides physical support, protects valuable bindings from light and dirt, and allows easy, non-damaging access to the volume. Such boxes also afford great protection to their contents in the event of a disaster.

Figure 6-4. The linen tape will keep the boards on this weak volume intact until boxing or repair is possible.

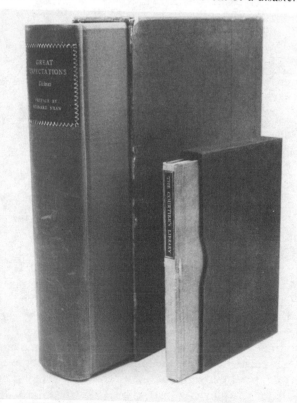

the knot or bow should be positioned across the fore-edge of the book so as not to create an indentation on the cover or interfere with shelving practices (see Figure 6-4). Greater protection may be provided by wrapping weak volumes in strong wrapping paper or polyester book jackets, or by placing them in phased boxes. Phased boxes were developed at the Library of Congress to provide intermediate protection to materials waiting further treatment; they are easy to construct (see Appendix B11) or may be purchased in several standard sizes from archival suppliers. Solander, or drop-spine, boxes afford the greatest protection to bound volumes both during handling and in the event of a disaster. To

Figure 6-6. Volumes stored in slipcases suffer abrasion and faded spines. In addition, spines are often scratched in careless attempts to remove volumes from their slipcases.

In general, the bindings on large or oversized volumes are not strong enough to support their text blocks. They therefore require additional support and should be stored flat on shelves rather than upright. Ideally, shelves should be adjusted so that volumes are shelved in stacks no more than two or three high; the temptation to pull the bottom volume out from under a stack should be avoided. If flat storage for oversized volumes is impossible, they may be stored spine down on shelves. This will result in some abrasion of the spines but, given the structural weakness of large volumes, is less likely to result in books separating from their covers. An adequate sorting surface should be located near oversized shelving upon which volumes may be safely placed during retrieval and refiling. Scrapbooks and albums, which are sometimes oversized, also should be stored flat. They often contain loosely tipped-in items and enclosures that could fall out if the volumes were stored upright. As a further precaution, scrapbooks and albums should be wrapped or placed in large, flat document cases.

Photographic Materials

Every image (print and negative) should be stored in its own envelope or sleeve. These should be made either of paper or an inert plastic, such as polyester, polyethylene, polypropylene, or triacetate. There are advantages and disadvantages to either approach. Since paper is opaque, photographs will be protected from light, but they must be pulled in and out of paper sleeves for each viewing, thus possibly abrading the images. Paper envelopes with center seams should be avoided; envelopes with seams along one side are acceptable, but photographs should be inserted with the emulsion side away from the seam. Flap-type seamless paper envelopes are now available and are preferable to seamed enclosures.

Plastic envelopes and sleeves provide immediate visual access to the images without hands-on contact. They are more expensive than paper, however, and further disadvantages include the possibility of moisture buildup within the sleeves, which can result in ferreotyping (i.e., the transfer of the gelatin image to the smooth plastic surface). Plastic sleeves also can build up static electricity, which can attract dirt and dust.

At this time, enclosures made either of an inert plastic or paper that has an alkaline reserve are recommended for the safe storage of photographic materials; the selection of one over the other will depend upon the resources of the repository and access requirements. There is evidence, however, that alkaline conditions accelerate the yellowing of albumen prints. (Albumen prints were produced in the U.S. from roughly 1850 to 1895. The paper was extremely thin and the prints were generally affixed to standard-sized mounts, such as carte-de-visite, cabinet, and stereo cards. They generally appear brownish in color, sometimes with a yellowish cast, and somewhat glossy.) For this reason, recommended storage enclosures for albumen prints are either neutral paper envelopes without carbonate buffering, or inert plastic sleeves.[9] As some photographic conservators are considering extending this storage recommendation to photographic materials other than albumen prints, archivists are advised to keep current with the photographic literature.

Once enclosed in individual envelopes or sleeves, photographs should be placed flat on shelves in boxes that have an alkaline reserve. If vertical storage is used in filing cabinets, hanging folders are recommended to inhibit items from slumping in drawers and becoming crumpled or curled. Photographic prints on paper are predisposed to curl because the emulsion layer sits on one side of the paper; this imbalance or unequal pull on the paper creates a tendency for the print to curl in toward the emulsion. Improper filing practices will exacerbate this tendency, resulting in damage to the emulsion layer.

Oversized photographs either should be stored flat, or, if absolutely necessary (as with panoramas), rolled as described in the preceding section. Although photographs generally should be removed from frames for storage, oversized photographs that are received in frames may pose less of a storage problem if they are retained in this format. If such practice is followed, however, framed items must be disassembled to remove harmful backings and mounts, and then reassembled with safe materials before placing the items in long-term storage. (See Figure 6-7.) Photographs that are affixed to brittle cardboard mounts are endangered if the mounting boards are chipping or breaking off dangerously close to the images. Such photographs should be given additional support by slipping a piece of slightly larger neutral pH board behind them in their enclosures, and then storing them flat. Cased photographs, such as daguerreotypes and tintypes (see Figure 6-8), may be protected by wrapping them in tissue paper and placing them flat in boxes; microfilm boxes are ideal for the smaller cased photographs. Glass negatives and lantern slides also need to be individually sleeved. If they do not have their own specially grooved storage containers, they should be stored on end in heavy-duty, boxes that have an alkaline reserve; rigid supports (neutral pH board) should be placed between every ten to fifteen glass plates to keep them upright. Glass negatives and lantern slides should never be stack-

[9]James M. Reilly. "Albumen Prints: A Summary of New Research About Their Preservation." *Picturescope* 30:36 (Spring, 1982).

Figure 6-7. Acid will migrate from poor quality mounting and backing materials directly to the framed photograph. Staining, caused by the raw wooden backing, will eventually disfigure the front of the photographic print. Reproduced courtesy of the Newberry Library Conservation Laboratory Slide Collection.

Figure 6-8. Cases that house daguerreotypes, ambrotypes, and tintypes are often fragile and may have broken hinges. Cased photographs should be wrapped individually and stored flat. Gloves should be worn when handling them, and no repair attempts should be made.

ed; given their weight and fragility, the bottom images especially will be susceptible to breakage.

Microfilm

Use copies of microfilm may be stored within the temperature and humidity ranges specified for other archival materials. Master negatives, however, must be given separate storage in a strictly controlled environment free of gaseous pollutants. The temperature should not exceed 68° F, and the relative humidity should be maintained between 30 and 40 percent. To be considered archival, microfilm must meet precise standards of film quality, processing, and storage as outlined in the American National Standards Institute specifications (ANSI PH1.28-1976 and ANSI PH1.41-1976, or latest revisions thereof; see Appendix D for full citations).

Microfilm should be stored on noncorrosive metal or inert plastic reels, and placed in containers or boxes constructed of nonferrous metal, inert plastic, or board that has an alkaline reserve. Vertical storage in steel cabinets with a baked-enamel finish is recommended. Microfilm should not be wound too tightly on reels, and strips of alkaline paper with string ties should replace rubber bands as a means of keeping film from unrolling. Microfilm should be inspected (randomly, if the holdings are extensive) every two years. If there are signs of blemishes or deterioration, replacement copies should be made.

Sound Recordings

A primary concern in the preservation of sound recordings is keeping the dust level in the repository to a minimum. Dirt and dust can not only damage playback equipment, but, more importantly, it can distort the sound if it gets into disc grooves or miniscule pits in magnetic tape. As a further precaution against dust, sound recordings should be stored in cabinets with tight-fitting doors.

Disc recordings should be shelved fully vertical at all times. Because the disc shape is vulnerable to warping, discs should not be allowed to lean or slant, as this could result in distortion of their shape as well as sound. Rigid dividers separating shelves into compartments accommodating approximately twenty discs each should be used to maintain proper vertical storage. Because of their weight, shelves must be heavy-duty, and discs should never be stacked. Nor should they be allowed to extend out over the edges of shelves, because of possible breakage. Cellophane shrink-wrap, found on modern discs, responds to changes in environmental conditions and thus could cause discs to warp. It should be removed. Original paper or glassine inner linings on shellac and vinyl discs should be replaced with inert

polyethylene or paper liners that have an alkaline reserve, which are available from archival suppliers. Acetate and nitrate discs should be stored in paper envelopes. Original packaging and jackets should be protected from light damage as many of these items are seen to have artistic and historic significance.

Repositories that maintain collections of older discs may have difficulty with playback if compatible equipment of the appropriate type and vintage is not available. Because of differences in stylus, construction, or record grooves, modern stereo equipment is often unable to accurately reproduce sounds from older recordings. A solution that alleviates the need to maintain a museum of phonograph equipment is to transfer the disc to a master reel-to-reel tape. The services of a professional sound laboratory that has access to the appropriate equipment should be sought. Such a reproduction would serve as a use copy to protect the original from excessive handling, and also would preserve an accurate representation of the recording as it was meant to be heard.

Magnetic (reel-to-reel and cassette) tapes should be stored away from stray magnetic fields—created by electrical motors or other sources of magnetic energy—as well as transformers or high voltage lines because of the possibility of sound alternation or accidental erasure. Some repositories prefer to store magnetic tapes on wooden rather than metal shelves, but in practical experience neither surface seems to affect sound quality. Problems with dust may be reduced by storing reel-to-reel and cassette tapes in small polyethylene bags within their original packaging. Vertical orientation on shelves is recommended.

Cassette tapes are not considered acceptable for long-term archival storage; if possible, they should be dubbed to 1.5 mil polyester reel-to-reel tape. If cassette recordings must be retained, C60 and C90 lengths are preferred to the longer lengths, which are more susceptible to breakage and significant print-through. Cassette cases with screw fittings only should be used as they can be opened safely in the event the tape tangles.

Magnetic tapes deteriorate from use because during playback they ride directly against the reading heads; after repeated use the sound can be noticeably degraded. Thus, it is advisable to make use copies of magnetic tapes and to retire the originals to storage. Research use of cassette and reel-to-reel tapes should be monitored, and use of the fast-forward speed on the playback equipment should be prohibited as it can distort the tape tension. The rewind speed also can cause tape tension to fluctuate. Thus, tapes should be stored in the played (or "tails out") position to ensure a steady tension throughout.

Videotapes

Videotapes are also susceptible to alteration through exposure to stray magnetic fields and thus have the same storage requirements as magnetic reel-to-reel and cassette tapes. At the present time, videotapes are largely a commercial phenomena that are undergoing rapid technological changes with relatively little concern for stability. While videotapes are being used increasingly to meet the short-term needs of the media and as a training vehicle for educational institutions and industry, contemporary videotapes do not meet archival standards for permanence. Since videotapes are increasingly finding their way into archival collections, however, preservation efforts must focus on handling and maintenance of this potentially unstable medium.

During playback, videotapes—like cassette and reel-to-reel tapes—ride against decoding heads and are thus somewhat degraded after each use. Use copies of valuable videotapes should be made, as well as duplicate first-generation copies from which additional use copies may be made as needed. An original tape should then only be used if another master reference copy is required. Playback machines must be cleaned regularly, and all research use monitored. Tapes should not be tightly wound, and fast-forward and fast-reverse, which can cause tapes to stretch somewhat, should be avoided. Videotapes should be stored in the played position and rewound only at the time of the next use. 🌳

---

7 Integrating Conservation and Archival Administration

Conservation must be seen as integral to every activity in an archival repository. Each time a collection item is used and handled, whether by archival staff in processing, patrons in conducting research, or preparators mounting an exhibition, there is a potential for damage or loss. Every function must be carried out from a conservation perspective. This conservation concern, or consciousness, can be developed, in part, by careful forethought—that is, thinking through all archival activities from a conservation standpoint and considering at each phase: What are the steps we will go through to accomplish this task? What are the potential dangers to the material? What staff members will be involved and what difficulties should they anticipate? Contingency plans should be developed for potential problems, and a clear chain of command should be identified to expedite decision making and cope with emergencies. As a result of this approach, often termed conservation management, collections will be less endangered and better cared for, and the repository will develop a reputation for being careful and conscientious

with collections. The conservation aura created in a repository will be evident to virtually everyone having contact with the institution: staff, researchers, donors, professional colleagues, and the general public. Such a reputation can be only an asset in dealing with potential donors, in seeking financial support, or in negotiating cooperative programs with other institutions.

Conservation is basic to the very mission of an archival institution. It is inherent in the goal to collect historical material for research, exhibition, and similar cultural and educational purposes, and should be seen as closely aligned with, and integral to, such other concerns as security, collections maintenance and development, housekeeping, and reference services. Conservation responsibility crosses job lines and should be identified as part of every position description. Ideally, conservation will be mandated from the highest administrative level and work outward to encompass all staff activity. If such an ideal situation does not exist, however, development of a conservation approach to archival management can begin through the efforts of a single staff member having the interest and some training. An appropriate first step is the scrutiny of all archival functions from a conservation perspective to determine whether changes in policy or procedures are required that will enhance the useful life of collections. Persistence and politic agitation for change will be required to effect change and spread the conservation message.

At every stage of archival activity, the archivist must take responsibility for the care and protection of the collections. This advocacy role is a primary professional duty, which may at times be undertaken in seeming isolation. For example, other institutional priorities, or the weight of tradition, may mandate actions that pose threats to archival material, such as the continual exhibition of institutional treasures or the constant fetching and handling of unique items on behalf of board members or special guests. At an appropriate point, the archivist should begin to raise conservation and security issues that can be readily recognized as sensible and obvious. Implementing change in long-held institutional practices may be difficult, and persistence and patience will be necessary. Collection materials clearly need an advocate, and no one is better suited to the job than the archivist or curator. The archivist should serve as the intermediary between the safety and physical requirements of the material and all demands placed on it.

Depending upon the size of the archives staff, specific archival and conservation duties may be spread among a number of individuals or carried out by only one or two people. Staff size, however, should have no bearing on a conservation program that emphasizes proper storage and handling procedures for all material and takes a conservation approach to all archival functions. Much of conservation management is good common sense. What is required is seriously thinking about conservation and imposing sound preservation practices on all aspects of archival administration. The following sections consider archival functions from a conservation point of view. Although terminology and means of implementation may vary from one repository to another, all are recognizable archival functions. The conservation approaches suggested may be adapted to meet specific institutional policies and needs.

Field Survey

During the initial survey of records before they are brought into the repository, it is important to identify potential preservation problems. The physical conditions under which collections have been stored over a period of time will provide many clues to the resulting physical problems of the collections that will need to be addressed. For example, if the records have been stored for years in an attic that, depending upon the season, is alternately extremely hot or extremely cold, the papers may be dried out and brittle. If the collection has been stored in a damp or leaking basement, the records may be moldy or mildewed as well as somewhat pulpy, and thus very fragile. The storage area and storage containers also must be observed for evidence of insect or rodent infestation. It is important to conduct an initial conservation survey at the same time that other records appraisal functions are taking place. The eye to careful detail should extend beyond the intellectual content of the papers and their historical value to encompass the physical conditions to which the materials have been subjected, thus allowing sound observations and conclusions to be drawn regarding their present physical state.

The format of potential accessions also should be considered during the field survey. Unusual or especially fragile formats, such as oil paintings, three-dimensional objects, or glass plate negatives, may pose special transport and storage problems. Collections presenting severe physical problems that will require substantial treatment should be evaluated against the institution's ability to adequately preserve these materials. A potentially difficult and emotional situation may exist if the archivist is called in following a disaster to salvage and acquire damaged documents. One may find extremely valuable items which, though they would greatly enhance existing holdings, are damaged beyond recovery. An example would be water-damaged records that exhibit extensive mold growth at an advanced stage. Some quick decisions would have to be made, depending upon the degree of damage and the time that had elapsed since the disaster occurred. In some cases, it

might be virtually impossible to appraise the value of the collection because of the extent of damage. Unless a repository has extensive conservation resources and is fairly certain of the value of the material, the decision must be against such salvage attempts. Conservation resources tend to be very scarce and should be expended only when the value of the material is known. A negative decision in such a case is in effect a positive decision on behalf of existing collections, both in terms of reserving scarce staff and conservation resources for material of known value *and* of unwillingness to risk contaminating existing holdings by acquiring infested records, thereby greatly enlarging the problem.

The inventory created as part of the field survey generally includes information on the scope and content of the collection and its estimated size. Other information should be recorded to expedite the packing and moving of the material and reduce the likelihood of damage or loss: highly valuable or fragile items that may require special handling or security precautions should be noted, and it is particularly important to note any evidence of mold or insect infestation (see Figure 7-1). The overall range of collection formats represented should be considered so that necessary packing supplies and moving equipment will be available when needed. The goal is to record special problems and needs so that each succeeding step can be undertaken safely and efficiently. A thorough field survey of the collection should ensure that there are no surprises or unanticipated problems for the packing crew, which should be well equipped to deal with all items, be they oversized rolled documents or loose daguerreotypes.

Transfer of Material

Once the decision to acquire a collection has been made, provisions for its safe packing and transport to the archives must be implemented. Questions to consider at this stage of activity include: What personnel will pack and load the material? Are they archives staff or physical plant crew, and, if the latter, does the archives have authority over them to specify handling procedures? Have personnel who will actually do the packing been trained in proper boxing and handling techniques, with an emphasis on fragile items? It is important that an archivist supervise these functions on site. Ideally, the person who conducted the initial field survey should oversee the packing and transport functions, because that individual has firsthand knowledge of the range and condition of the physical objects to be handled.

It should be known to all involved exactly who is in charge and who has decision-making authority. The easiest situation will be one in which only archives staff

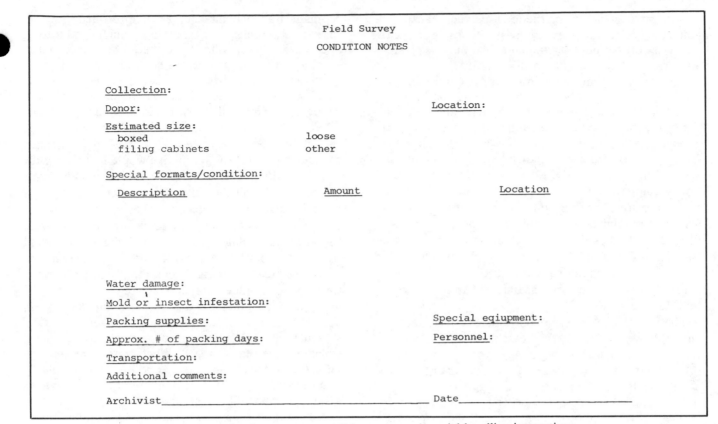

```
                            Field Survey
                          CONDITION NOTES


     Collection:

     Donor:                              Location:

     Estimated size:
        boxed                  loose
        filing cabinets        other

     Special formats/condition:
       Description            Amount              Location




     Water damage:
     Mold or insect infestation:

     Packing supplies:                   Special eqiupment:

     Approx. # of packing days:          Personnel:

     Transportation:

     Additional comments:

     Archivist_____  Date_____
```

Figure 7-1. Sample field survey form that incorporates condition notes and special handling instructions.

participate in the move. They have been trained to be sensitive to the importance and often fragile condition of the material, and can be most easily oriented to proper packing and moving procedures. The problems will be compounded a bit in large institutions if physical-plant personnel are involved in the move. They may be less likely to acknowledge the archivist's authority over the situation and may be eager to get the job over with quickly and thus proceed with other duties. Further, they may be more familiar with handling heavy machinery or lab equipment than boxes of brittle paper, and may tend to impose heavy-duty handling on fragile material. The best course in such a situation is, over a period of time, to orient the crew to the value and importance of archival material and its special physical needs. It is quite likely that they will come to understand the necessity of the archives' regulations and become real friends of the collection. If it is necessary to contract with movers outside of the institution, similar problems of orientation may exist. In addition to determining their familiarity with handling archival material, it will be necessary to gauge their reliability. It may be useful to consult other local libraries, historical societies, or museums regarding carriers they have found satisfactory; fine-art movers may be the best choice.

Another factor that must be considered when dealing with physical-plant crews, as well as outside moving companies, are union and work regulations regarding breaks, quitting times, weight limits on lifting or moving material, and similar matters. It is important to conform the packing and transfer of archival material with such regulations, and to assure the security of the material at all times. It is thus necessary to estimate the number of working days required to pack the collection. Once the actual move is underway, it should be known if the truck is returning directly to the archives or making other stops around the area. Is the work day likely to end before all moving and unloading is completed, with the result that archival material is left all night on a truck or loading dock? The security of the collection will be in jeopardy in such a situation. There have been unfortunate instances of material being left on loading docks and discarded as rubbish by overzealous maintenance crews. Combined with concern for security while the material is in transit is consideration of possible damage by inclement weather. Depending upon the season, what is the likelihood of snow, rain, or high winds on moving day? Flexibility to adjust schedules to adapt to changes in the weather will add a further measure of protection to the collection.

Issues of safety and security are compounded when

making arrangements for the long-distance transfer of collections. Generally, the archivist will not be on site to supervise proper packing and labelling, but it is possible to provide the donor with detailed instructions. Repositories and museums in the off-site location may be able to provide advice or recommend local professional packers and craters. Crating material can be very expensive but may be warranted in some instances, especially with highly valuable, unique, or fragile items. Crates are constructed specifically around the dimensions of the material, and through a series of protective layers guard the object against movement, breakage, and moisture. The best method of transportation is generally the quickest, to avoid excessive physical handling and the possibility of the material being left at transfer points until a truck is completely filled. Air transport, if available, should be used. All items being shipped should be insured against possible damage or loss.[10]

The actual packing of material should integrate archival concerns for order with conservation concerns for safe transport. Varying record formats will require different methods of packing. Records transfer cases should be used to transport groups of material in traditional archival formats (single sheets in file folders, bound volumes, photographs) as well as other small items that the transfer cartons will accommodate (such as motion-picture film, cassette and reel tapes, memorabilia, and three-dimensional objects). The transfer cases must be strong, dry, and assembled properly so that the bottoms will not give way under the weight of their contents; boxes should not be filled to capacity with extremely heavy items. Series of file folders should be packed so that they will be maintained in an upright position with no leeway for moving about or items becoming separated; both overstuffing and underfilling transfer cases will cause damage, especially to brittle records. Filing cabinets that are to be moved to the repository need special attention. Contents of drawers must be evaluated to ensure that fragile items will not move about in transit. It may be necessary to secure a series of folders by adding a bit of support at the back of the drawer if it is not completely filled and folders are likely to move during loading and shipping. An empty document case will serve this purpose satisfactorily. All file drawers must be secured so that they will not open during the move, damaging their contents or perhaps disrupting the order of the material. Strong cord tied around the cabinet will serve this purpose best; reinforced strapping tape may work but also may damage the finish on the cabinet when the tape is removed.

---

[10]For an excellent discussion of this subject, see: Caroline K. Keck. *Safeguarding Your Collection in Travel.* Nashville: American Association for State and Local History, 1970.

Small, fragile items that are unprotected, such as cased photographs, diaries, albums, campaign buttons, and lantern slides, will require special handling. Sturdy envelopes in varying sizes can be used to enclose many small items, which then can be safely placed in transfer cases. Unprotected rolled items, which may be both brittle and oversized, may be slipped into oversized tubes for protection if the diameter of the tubes is large enough that they pose no resistance to or pressure on the rolled documents. An alternative would be to wrap the rolls in sturdy kraft paper. No attempt should be made to open tightly rolled or folded documents on site. Glass plate negatives pose problems if they are not housed in protective boxes having grooved separations. To avoid breakage, glass plates should be individually sleeved in strong paper envelopes; they can then be placed on edge in strong boxes with rigid separators (such as heavyweight mat or binder's board) between every ten to fifteen plates to provide extra support and keep them upright. Glass plates that are already broken or cracked should be placed between two piees of strong board, which are then taped together before slipping the unit into an envelope. If unprotected, loose pieces are placed in an envelope, they will suffer more damage, perhaps making it impossible to later piece the negative together and copy the image. Glass plate negatives and lantern slides are very heavy; care must be taken that boxes are not filled with them to the breaking point. Three-dimensional objects should be wrapped in tissue paper or plastic sheeting for protection against scratching or abrasion before being placed in a transfer case. Several such items in a single box should be separated by stuffing to inhibit movement. Items with a painted or glazed surface that is flaking or chipping should be wrapped with extreme caution in tissue paper and kept from jostling or making contact with other items. Framed items under glass must be protected to avoid breakage of the cover glass and thus possible damage to the item. Cover glass should be taped (an X, corner to corner, will suffice to keep the glass intact) in the event it should break. Before wrapping, frames with fragile corners or elaborate plaster decoration should be protected against breakage by padding with pieces of soft cloth, such as flannel or felt. Picture wires and protruding screw eyes, both of which can be damaging, should be removed. The surfaces of paintings—oil and watercolor—must be protected against dirt and abrasion with sheets of tissue paper or glassine. After measures have been taken to protect the image, cover glass, and fragile portions of the frame, the entire unit should be wrapped in protective material, such as bubble-pack. Unframed paintings and other works of art will require rigid support before wrapping to avoid damage to the canvas or other image-bearing surface. Any flaking medium, such as charcoal or pastels, should be wrapped in paper rather than plastic, which, through static electricity, could cause the image to lift or move.

If a potential accession contains substantial numbers of works of art, such as watercolors, charcoal and pastel drawings, or oil paintings, it is wise to seek expert advice, from a museum conservator if possible. The archivist may not be knowledgeable regarding the various mediums and may need assistance both in identification and devising proper packing procedures. Also, physical condition should be evaluated to determine if transporting the items will be hazardous and whether special precautions or stabilization are necessary. Advice also might be required in evaluating the art works, both in terms of artistic merit and monetary value, to help determine appropriate disposition.

It is advisable to have a range of packing materials on hand to meet the needs of all collection formats. Supplies should include the following: strong transfer cases, tissue paper, kraft paper, plastic sheeting, shock absorbing material (such as bubble-pack or styrofoam pellets), heavy cord or twine, binder's board (.080 inch thick) or mat board in various precut sizes to serve as rigid supports, envelopes and folders to protect fragile items, and oversized tubes. It is an unnecessary expense to use conservation-quality packing and wrapping materials. *It is important to remember, however, that packing supplies are intended to provide interim support and protection over a relatively short period of time.* They must be replaced with the approved long-term storage materials after processing. If more than one or two months are likely to elapse between receipt of material and accessioning, packing materials that are placed in direct contact with collection items (envelopes, folders, etc.) should be fabricated of paper stock that has an alkaline reserve. Acidic wrapping materials are not acceptable for long-term storage.

Much archival field work takes place in curious, out-of-the-way settings. Packing a collection often must be done under conditions that are less than ideal. Safety precautions must be taken for personnel, and efforts must be made to keep collection items as clean as possible. A supply of cotton gloves, which can be discarded as they become soiled, will be a help in this regard. As soap and water may not be handy, commercially available treated washcloths may also prove helpful in keeping hands clean.

On-site cleaning or conservation treatment of items is generally best avoided. Activity should focus on providing stable and safe transport; broken or cracked items may require rigid support by a piece of stiff binder's board, but repair attempts should not be made. Conditions during packing and moving can be chaotic enough without trying to improvise a lab in a setting that is likely dirty and poorly lit. It is advisable to consult with a qualified conservator before attempting to move highly valuable items that may be further damaged in transit because of their poor condition. In such cases, limited remedial action may have to be undertaken on site by qualified personnel to allow for safe transport.

All containers, boxes, and file cabinets should be marked clearly with the name of the collection and the repository; also, all items should be sequentially numbered before anything is moved from the site. A written inventory of numbered containers should be kept, with brief references as to contents. Labels also should include any specific handling instructions; glass and other fragile material should be so labelled. Proper labelling and the container inventory serve as security measures, which represent another point of contact between archival administration and conservation management.

Receiving Room Procedures

The next series of functions relates to activities undertaken as the material is received into the archives. Whether the receiving room is an elaborate space adjacent to a loading dock or is as simple as a backdoor passageway, the procedures are the same.

The first step is to check the inventory to make sure that all material can be accounted for and that it has arrived intact. It is important to have a secure place available for incoming collections to be housed while they are awaiting integration into the archival workflow.

During the field survey, any evidence of mold or insect infestation should have been noted. All incoming materials in which there is the slightest evidence of infestation must be fumigated. These items must be kept segregated in a secure area while they are awaiting treatment to avoid contaminating the entire holdings. Fumigation procedures are outlined in Chapter 10.

Accessioning

Functions generally associated with accessioning involve preliminary recordkeeping on newly acquired collections. Accession, or identification, numbers are assigned at this time, donor and location files are created, and initial systems of bibliographic control are instituted. Potentially damaging packing materials should be discarded at this time. Records also may be transferred into alkaline-buffered document cases as part of the accessioning procedure. For archival purposes, however, it is recommended that either original file folders be retained until arrangement and description activities are begun, or that original folder titles and file designations be transferred—at least temporarily—to the new folders. Appropriate policies also should be developed regarding the disposition of duplicate materials or categories of items or objects that are seen as extraneous to the archival holdings. If such materials can be removed from the collection (discarded, returned to donor, or sent to another library or curatorial department) during accessioning, valuable storage space can be saved and staff time will not be wasted later on processing or treating out-of-scope items.

In many institutions, the creation of the preliminary inventory (often synonymous with an accession record) represents the first detailed review and evaluation of the contents of a collection. The level of descriptive review will vary among institutions and with type and value of

collection; however, the creation of the accession record provides an ideal time to consider the physical state and conservation needs of collections in addition to intellectual concerns of identification, subject content, and manner of arrangement. Staff members compiling the accession lists should be trained to identify materials (papers, inks, animals skins, types of photographs) as well as common physical problems, and to record this information for future reference and use in establishing treatment priorities. Such recordkeeping can become part of an overall conservation needs survey, and such a survey is less overwhelming if at least portions of it can be incorporated into other archival functions. Further, by recording information on the conservation needs of

---

CONSERVATION WORKSHEET

Collection_____ Accession no._____

Donor_____ Location_____

Item(s)/series*	Folder	Box	Work required**	Date completed	Staff

Special requirements:

Additional comments:

Open for research: Date:

Accessioned by_____ Date_____

*Describe records requiring treatment as   **refolder
 well as special formats: rebox
   newspaper clippings   humidify
   scrapbooks/albums   remove fasteners
   bound volumes   interleave
   framed items   remove from frame
   photographs   photocopy
     -prints   clean
     -negatives   mend
       -glass   encapsulate
       -nitrate
   oversized materials

Figure 7-2. Sample conservation worksheet to be compiled as collections are accessioned.

collections as they are acquired (i.e., during the accessioning process), the conservation survey may be kept current. A checklist may be devised that can be filled out as the accession record is compiled. In this way, conservation problems are segregated intellectually, if not physically, making it easy to locate batches of related work when there is time to tend to it. The conservation checklist also can be used as a work sheet; as tasks are completed they can be initialed and dated by the staff member who did the work (see Figure 7-2).

Accessioning that is conducted down to the folder or item level will afford much information about the contents of a collection and its physical condition. Sound archival practice mandates such an approach in all but large and highly repetitive series. Conservation data that might be recorded during the accessioning process includes information on the location of highly unique formats and objects that would classify as art, as well as brittle or damaged material that is in immediate need of physical support or reinforcement. Treatments (such as silking, cellulose acetate lamination, or polyester encapsulation) that have already been carried out should be noted, as well as any evidence of treatment breakdown. The location of such items as newspaper clippings or similar highly acidic materials that can cause damage to adjacent items should be recorded. The location of photographs requiring special handling or enclosures should be listed, as well as the presence of glass plate negatives and similar fragile or fugitive images, such as cellulose nitrate film or color prints. Physical problems that should be noted include evidence of tears, surface dirt and stains, tightly folded or rolled documents, framed items requiring disassembly, and bound volumes with boards detached.

A new level of evaluation and decision making is thus imposed upon the accessioning process. Staff must be trained to recognize various types of material and to make informed decisions regarding their physical condition and need for treatment. Security concerns may also come into play at this stage. Material that is valuable in monetary terms, has artistic merit, or has the potential to evoke strong emotional or acquisitive reactions should be separated from the collection to avoid the possibility of theft or defacement. Good copies may be kept in the collection for research use, and the original items may be filed in a separate secure location. In addition to identifying material that requires extra security precautions, material that is in very fragile condition and subject to damage or loss if exposed to any kind of handling should be closed to research use until the necessary treatment can be undertaken. In such cases, good reproductions can serve as working copies to meet the research needs of patrons and the requirements of staff as further processing of the collection continues.

Preservation copying must be done with extreme care to avoid further damage to the material.

For reasons of both security and conservation, it is recommended that research access to collections be prohibited until the accession process is completed. It is unwise to make material available for research use until decisions have been made regarding its physical stability. Further, it is impossible to be sure that nothing is lost or missing following research use if no intellectual controls exist. Contents of a collection must be precisely known if they are to be protected.

Arrangement and Description

At this stage of processing, collections are analyzed at the item, folder, or series level for subject content and organization. Decisions are made regarding arrangement of the collection and information is recorded that will be used to create collection descriptions, inventories, and guides. Adherence to sound archival practice in these matters is essential. Appropriate systems of archival arrangement, precise descriptions, and sure knowledge of the location of collection items at all times are basic elements uniting two interlocking components of archival administration: conservation and security. These are constant themes that should undergird all archival activity.

A number of specific conservation concerns may be addressed as arrangement and description functions are carried out. The checklist created during the accessioning process will highlight specific problems needing attention. These are best addressed by the archivist as part of the overall decision-making process regarding retention of specific groups of material and collection organization. Within the context of these decisions, the material can be evaluated and conservation treatment priorities assigned based on the condition of the materials and their relative values. Decisions about archival arrangement and conservation treatment should be integrated at this point to ensure uniform approaches to collections management and efficient use of time spent on collections review.

While a collection is being organized, destructive fasteners, accretions, and other items viewed as foreign should be removed from the records. Foreign objects include paper clips, staples, rubber bands, string or colored tape, ribbons, brads, locks of hair, or pressed flowers (see Figure 7-3). These items can convey much useful information about the collection. The manner in which a creator arranges records into particular groups will often give the archivist invaluable clues as to the importance and interrelationships of records. For example, fasteners used to unite groups of material can tell the archivist a great deal about how the creator of the

Figure 7-3. Collection of paper fasteners and devices assembled in the Manuscript Division, Preparation Section, Library of Congress. Photograph courtesy of the Library of Congress.

records viewed and ordered the world. It is thus important to leave these clues in place for the archivist to use in evaluating the collection and gaining intellectual control over it. Once the order and relationships among materials have been established, however, any object that can cause mechanical or chemical damage should be removed. Metal fasteners can rust, leaving permanent stains; they also can function as cutting edges against which paper will break as it is flexed over a period of time. Pressed flowers and similar organic materials can cause permanent staining through acid migration. Items that are damaging to surrounding material because of their acid content but are seen as integral to the collection may be either filed separately or kept within their file sequence but physically isolated to protect adjacent material. It may be appropriate to develop a separate filing and cross-reference system for bulky and potentially damaging items—pressed flowers, campaign buttons, locks of hair—that are deemed worthy of retention (see Figure 7-4). Highly acidic materials, such as newspaper clippings, should, at a minimum, be interleaved between two sheets of thin polyester (2-mil) or bond paper that has an alkaline reserve to inhibit acid migration. A small group of acidic materials also could be placed at the back of a folder behind protective sheets of polyester or alkaline-paper. If there are large numbers of acidic items requiring interleaving, it may be useful to consider a quicker and less bulky solution, such as dividing the

material into two folders (i.e., Folder 20 A—Correspondence; Folder 20 B—Clippings). Enclosures in bound records also must be removed if they are likely to cause chemical damage to adjacent pages through acid migration, or if their bulk will cause physical distortion of the binding.

Most often, archival materials are retained in original file folders until arrangement and description processes are underway, as the folders help to keep the records in their original order and also usually contain information that aids in identifying and dating the material. As final decisions are made regarding arrangement, however, original filing enclosures, which generally are of poor quality paper stock and highly acidic, should be discarded and replaced with file folders that have an alkaline reserve. Material requiring special protection, such as photographs, should be individually sleeved at this time also. Several common-sense factors should be considered as file folders and document boxes are filled. Folders and boxes should not be overstuffed, as this can result in much damage as brittle material is forced in and out of containers. The number of sheets that can safely be placed in a folder will depend upon the condition of the material and its value. There may be in-

Figure 7-4. Delegate badges and buttons retained in folders with textual records will cause physical stress and distortion in the latter.

stances when one item per folder is warranted, both for physical protection and reasons of security. If material is very brittle and has not been encapsulated, it is advisable to place a small number of sheets in a single folder to avoid excessive abrasion and possible breaking. In such cases, a simple precaution would be to interleave brittle documents between sheets of alkaline paper, allowing the interleaving sheets to bear the burden of handling as pages are turned. Folders should be scored to accommodate the thickness of material placed in them; when paper is in good condition—strong, flexible, and not discolored—fifty to seventy-five sheets may be safely placed in a folder.

Document boxes should be filled so that folders do not have excessive pressure placed on them; both overstuffing and underfilling are to be avoided. The attempt to place too many folders into a box will result in a great deal of damage to their brittle contents as folders are pushed and crammed into place. The impulse is to work a tight-fitting folder into its box using both hands, and brittle paper will just break into pieces under such stress. On the other hand, if a box that is to be shelved upright is only partially filled, the contents will take on a permanent curve or curl (see Figures 7-5, 7-6). This may be avoided by adding non-damaging material at the backs of the boxes to take up excess space. For example, museum board that has been laminated to the proper thickness may be placed behind the last folder to keep the contents upright. The problem of curling records

Figure 7-6. Such a configuration is especially damaging to photographs and brittle documents.

will be avoided altogether, however, if boxes are stored flat on shelves.

A supply of both 2½-inch and 5-inch document cases as well as flat storage boxes should be kept on hand to help reduce the problem of properly filling boxes. Very small collections, consisting of one or two folders, are probably best stored in a filing cabinet with appropriate dividers between collections.

A number of other basic conservation procedures may be incorporated into arrangement and description functions. Such techniques as humidification, surface cleaning, mending, and polyester encapsulation may be easily learned by the archivist through basic training and practice, and carried out as other archival functions are implemented. Technicians or other personnel also can be trained to do such tasks, which can be quite time-consuming depending upon the size and condition of the collection.

In archival settings, such treatments as surface cleaning and mending are carried out to stabilize the material, protect it from further damage, and ready it for safe use by researchers. Except in rare instances of highly valuable items that are important as artifacts or artistic works, archival conservation treatments are not carried out to improve the cosmetic appearance of material. Rather, surface cleaning is undertaken to remove gritty dirt or soot, which can obscure or abrade images or text and can cause further damage by becoming imbedded in the paper fibers. Mending is done to repair past damage and stop the tears from becoming worse. Humidification of tightly rolled or folded materials, such as documents, blueprints, drawings, and photographs, allows them to be safely opened and evaluated for archival significance and further treatment requirements. The goal is the continued availability of the records; improvements in physical appearance, while pleasing, are of secondary importance.

The recommended steps that will help to integrate conservation measures into archival processing call for the compilation of an initial conservation worksheet during accessioning procedures. This provides an interim record on the physical condition of the collection,

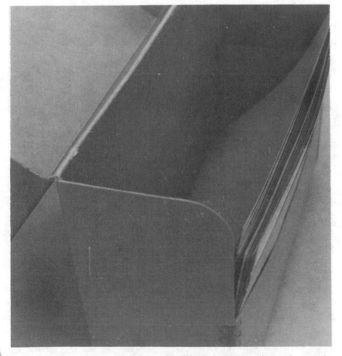

Figure 7-5. Contents of underfilled boxes oriented to sit upright on shelves will take on a definite curve or bow in a short period of time, as seen in Figure 7-6.

which will aid in making determinations regarding research access and also will assist the archivist during processing. Next, during arrangement and description activities (which may take place long after the collection is received and accessioned), appraisal decisions are made regarding retention of material and its relative importance. Treatment priorities also should be established at this time. Ideally, all work on a collection—intellectual as well as physical stabilization and protection—should proceed simultaneously at this stage. This is not always realistic, however, and a flexible system should be developed that allows time and resources to be allocated to immediately address at least the most pressing problems. Records requiring humidification or that are too fragile to be handled by researchers should be given top priority for treatment. As much work as possible should be done on a collection at the time of processing, not only because it is difficult to find time to get back to complete the "detail" work once processing of a new collection has commenced, but because when treatment is integrated with processing, the finished collection will truly be ready for research use. Such tasks as cleaning and encapsulation are most compelling when the collection surrounds the processor on desks and sorting tables; once hidden away on shelves, neatly filed in folders and boxes, it is too easy to ignore the problems. A systematic approach that encompasses decisions and actions regarding organization and physical treatment should be devised. If several people can be involved simultaneously to complete various phases of the work—archivist, technicians, student assistants, and volunteers—all the better, although in many institutions the archivist will function alone in every capacity.

The conservation checklist developed for use in accessioning can be expanded to double as a processing worksheet; thus, all routine processing and conservation tasks can be listed along with special problems. Such a list can provide the framework for archival processing to conservation standards. Also, since there will be occasions when it will be impossible to complete all of the work on a given project at one time, the checklist will help to gauge progress and provide a permanent record of treatment completed as well as that still pending. Such a method helps to assure a uniform approach to processing collections.

Instructions for basic conservation procedures that may be incorporated into archival processing are located in Appendix B.

Research Use of Collections

Although record materials are subject to damage throughout their life cycle, proper archival controls will provide a high degree of protection after they are housed in a repository. Once properly arranged, described, physically reinforced or protected, and stored, collections are ready to withstand the rigors of research use. It is in this area of activity that collection materials are most susceptible to damage or loss, and special precautions are mandatory to safeguard them. While the majority of researchers using archival collections are conscientious, honest, and sensitive to the value and condition of the materials they wish to use, there are exceptions. For this reason, it is necessary to establish rules regarding access to and use of collections, to promulgate reading room rules, and to enforce their uniform compliance. The atmosphere created by the staff will have a direct impact on researchers and other visitors; the manner in which staff conduct themselves when handling archival material will provide the best model for orienting researchers to proper procedures.

Reading room regulations should be developed to meet the particular needs of an institution and its collections, and should be adhered to strictly. These rules and procedures should be written down and thoroughly understood by all archival staff. In addition, they should have the concurrence and support of top administration. This is especially important if irate researchers object to rules and complain to the president, dean, or chief administrator. The institution should present a common front in protecting its material, and staff members should not be chastised or overruled when implementing approved policy. To be effective, reading room rules and procedures must be carried out uniformly; one exception, made one time, negates a rule and may open the door not only to further infringement but to charges by researchers of favoritism or preferential treatment if they are denied privileges that are granted to others. Rules regarding access to materials should apply not only to researchers and outside visitors, but to institutional staff as well. This can pose sensitive political problems if one is faced with an emeritus director or a scholar who is seen as influential and who has been given special privileges in the past. The goal is to provide uniform protection to the collections, considering both conservation and security concerns; this goal can be achieved fully only by monitoring all use of the holdings. The manner of dealing with a group of "special" users, and eventually eliminating this category, will vary depending upon the numbers of such individuals, the severity of the problem and any known or suspected examples of mishandling or "borrowing" of material, and the support of the administration. At a minimum, such situations should be perceived as problems and closely monitored while devising acceptable solutions. A few researchers may become disgruntled as access and use policies are tightened; some may take it as a personal affront, feeling that their personal integrity has been challenged. Every effort should be made to ease this transition period by informing researchers very clearly about the need for policy changes (discussing national trends involving the theft of materials, preparing exhibits on mutilation, etc.) and by requesting their support as active partners in preserving the material.

All researchers entering the archives reading room should sign a daily register. A secure place should be designated for hats, coats, briefcases, large purses, and backpacks, none of which should be allowed at reading tables. As a security precaution, the archivist or reading room supervisor should request positive identification of the researcher as a formal part of the reference interview. At this time, potential users also should be informed of all regulations regarding access to and use of materials. These rules should be posted in a prominent place in the reading room (cards on reading tables are hard to ignore), and also should be printed on a form the researcher is required to read and sign to indicate compliance. These preliminary procedures should take place before the patron is given access to any material.

Rules governing the use of archival and manuscript material relate to physical handling, copying regulations, and legal issues pertaining to publication and copyright, as well as general behavior in the reading room. Drinking, smoking, and eating by both researchers and staff should be strictly forbidden in the reading room. Pencils only should be allowed for taking notes; fountain, ballpoint, and felt-tip pens can cause permanent damage even if done unintentionally. It may be useful for the archives to provide researchers with pencils; some institutions do not allow any personal note-taking materials and provide both pencils and paper, which researchers must use. Rules should specify the proper way to handle archival material, and should state that the researcher is to maintain material in the same order as found. If the researcher notices any potential problems, either in arrangement, identification, or physical condition, these should be brought to the attention of the archivist.

There should be a policy on access to fragile material that is awaiting conservation treatment and to material that has not yet been accessioned and is thus not protected by intellectual controls. If access to such materials is to be allowed, the conditions under which it is to be made available must be precisely spelled out. In situations where access will clearly jeopardize the material, the archivist must be assured of administrative support in denying use.

A policy should be established regarding use of original items when preservation copies are available. Access to the original should be allowed only in special circumstances when physical examination of the item

will provide answers to questions that will be left unanswered by the reproduction. Verification of the authenticity of a document is obviously an acceptable use, as is examining the paper (watermarks, chain lines, etc.) to help date the item. Casual researchers will not have such needs. Researchers who insist that they cannot gain a true understanding of the content unless they are allowed to use and handle the material in original format should not be indulged.

Researchers should be carefully and obviously monitored as they use material. Archives stack areas should be closed to all researchers, and archival material should be noncirculating, even to institutional staff. A staff member should be in, or have visual control of, the reading room at all times. As a further security precaution, video cameras with remote viewing capabilities may be installed in the reading room to give more actual protection—or at least to enhance the impression of tight security. A paging system that will not diminish the security of the reading room should be devised. This may be difficult if staff numbers are limited and if there are several remote archives storage areas. In such situations, researchers should be required to request the total amount of material they anticipate using in a given day; this can then be retrieved at one time, kept near the reading room, and made available for use in small batches.

The amount of material actually given to a researcher at one time should be carefully controlled. Researchers naturally prefer to have everything at their fingertips; to them, a book cart filled with boxes of material would be preferable to boxes handed out singly. This approach, however, eliminates effectual control over the security of the material. With a large number of boxes, it is possible for a researcher essentially to build up a fortress, obscuring the view of the reading room monitor. Ideally, the monitor should be placed in a position that allows unobstructed visual control of all that is going on in the reading room. The actual number of boxes, folders, or items delivered to a researcher will vary with the value and condition of the material and the nature of the research. It is useful to have a standard policy (such as no more than two boxes at one time), with provision for reducing the amount of material as necessary. With highly valuable material, it is not unreasonable to make only one item or one folder available at a time. With certain valuable series, it may be worthwhile to make an item count of the content of each folder; this number should be placed prominently on the outside of the folder to emphasize the fact that the actual contents are known. If such precautions are to be employed, an item count must be made before and after research use so that researchers are not unfairly accused of retaining material. In all cases, researchers should be required to turn in all archival materials before leaving the reading room. It is then possible to account for all material; such a procedure also helps to impress upon researchers the fact that they are responsible for the material they have used. For a number of reasons, compiling use statistics among them, it is advisable to keep sheets or forms that record patron requests. The archives then has a permanent record of all persons using specific portions of collections. If materials turn up missing, it is possible to determine last use and at least the basis for a list of people who warrant special scrutiny the next time they enter the archives. The fact that a certain patron had used a collection, however, would not be sufficient ground for making accusations regarding theft, or for denying future access. Institutions can also use patron forms to help prove custody or ownership of collections, as they document the fact that material was in the repository as of a given date.

For reasons of security, some repositories mark all manuscript and archival material with an ownership stamp. This practice can be a useful theft deterrent as well as an aid in proving ownership when attempting to recover lost or stolen material. While it is unlikely that a determined or sophisticated thief will be deterred by markings (many of which can be obscured, bleached, or cut out), such devices will inhibit casual, or spur-of-the-moment, thievery. If the decision is made to mark collection material, a non-destructive method should be selected. An early approach to marking ownership, especially for library books, was to use a seal that embossed or perforated the name of the institution directly in the paper. This approach causes permanent damage to the paper fibers and should be avoided. Traditional rubber stamp inks are highly acidic and should be avoided as well. Invisible inks not only may be acidic, they do not provide the psychological inhibition to theft that is a primary reason for marking material. The Library of Congress has developed a permanent, non-acidic ink specifically for the purpose of marking manuscripts. It is available in black or blue and is designed for use with a balsa wood stamp pad. It will be provided without charge to any library or repository requesting it. A nicely designed stamp need not be seen as visually offensive or disfiguring, and the ink from the Library of Congress will not damage the paper. Institutions interested in implementing a marking program should write the Library of Congress Preservation Office for their free leaflet on the subject as well as a bottle of marking ink, which will last several years.

Researchers should be given specific instructions regarding proper ways of handling archival materials. This is especially true with brittle items; it is not inappropriate, for example, to tell researchers how to turn pages or to ask a researcher not to lean upon or take notes on top of material. (See Figure 7-7.) Material in

Figure 7-7. If brittle scrapbook pages are not turned carefully, mounted materials will suffer loss and damage. The album pictured would benefit from interleaving sheets that would help to support the weakened pages as they are turned. Interleaving sheets should not be used, however, if their bulk will damage or distort the binding structure.

special formats may also require special handling instructions. If photographs are not stored in clear plastic sleeves, researchers should be given clean white cotton gloves to wear while handling them. (See Figure 7-8.) Gloves should also be used when handling albums or scrapbooks containing photographs, as well as unprotected drawings, artwork, and posters.

If researchers are using sound recordings and are allowed to operate phonograph machines or cassette or tape recorders, they should be carefully informed how to handle the recording and operate the machine. Written instructions should be posted on the equipment as well. Use copies should be made of all sound recordings; these copies may be made on an on-demand basis to meet research needs if it is not feasible to copy the entire collection. It may be necessary to charge a fee to cover copying costs. Under no circumstances should researchers be allowed to handle original recordings, given the ease of damage or breakage. If it is virtually impossible for the institution to provide use copies of sound recordings, a policy should be instituted whereby staff must handle the items and run the playback equipment for re-

Figure 7-8. Gloves should be worn when handling unprotected photo albums. This album would benefit from the creation of a good microfilm copy which could be used in place of the original, which is quickly breaking into pieces.

searchers. Researchers also should be instructed how to operate microfilm and microfiche readers; reference copies of all films should be made from the master negatives.

A policy on photocopying must be established. Photocopying is a great asset for researchers, as it speeds note-taking and the time that must be spent in a repository. Institutions also may see photocopying as a deterrent to theft. There are, however, a number of conservation concerns relating to photocopying that must be addressed, balancing the needs of the researchers against the physical needs of the collections. Some collection items should never be photocopied because of their poor physical condition. These include extremely brittle sheets that cannot withstand physical handling, tightly bound volumes of brittle paper, material in rare books or fine bindings, oversized items that must be excessively manipulated to get a complete image, and scrapbook pages with material tipped-on so that sheets flap about and are susceptible to bending or cracking off (see Figure 7-9). Repeated copying of the same docu-

Figure 7-9. Such a scrapbook should not be subjected to photocopying, which would greatly endanger the booklets that are precariously tipped-on and already damaged. Microfilming is a feasible though time-consuming alternative.

ment should be avoided, given the potential for damage resulting from the cumulative effects of light (and sometimes heat) associated with copy machines. Duplicates of heavily copied items should be made, which can then be used to fill copy requests. Photographs are often copied to create access files or assist long-distance researchers in selecting images. This is acceptable practice as long as individual decisions are made regarding the ability of the item to withstand copying (based on such factors as the item's condition and its vulnerability to light). Repeated copying of a single photograph should be avoided by the use of duplicate prints.

Photocopying should be seen as a privilege that is allowed if it will not endanger the material. Researchers should request copies on a form devised for this purpose. This request process implies decision-making rather than pro forma action. Notices should be posted to the effect that photocopying will be done at the discretion of the archivist, and that the decision to copy or not will be based both on legal requirements (such as copyright and donor restrictions) as well as physical condition.

Researchers should not be allowed to make their own copies. Generally, their goal will be to get the sharpest image possible, regardless of the physical strain placed on the item. Thus, photocopy machines should not be located in reading rooms, and only staff who are properly trained should make copies. Institutions that rely upon self-service copy machines as a means of avoiding their obligations to uphold the copyright law will have to reevaluate their policies toward copying material that may be protected by statute. For institutions sustaining heavy research use, the photocopy workload may at times be quite heavy. Researchers must be re-educated so that they do not expect immediate copies or compliance with their every request. While an archives will want to maintain a good service stance and the support of the research community, the emphasis on service must be meshed with the institutional priority of maintaining collections for future use. In some cases, this will require refusing applications to photocopy material.

While the ideal photocopy machine for use with archival material in a range of formats has not yet been developed, there are several factors to consider when selecting a machine. The size and position of the copying surface is most important and must be evaluated in terms of the type of material that generally will be copied. Most repositories will need to copy single sheets of paper as well as material in bound volumes; oversized materials cannot be accommodated by most photocopy machines, which allow for a maximum exposure of 8½ inches by 14 inches. A sloped copying surface that allows bound volumes to be opened to a maximum of 90°–110° (rather than a full 180° if books are placed face down on a flat glass platen) will allow good copies to be made without damaging the binding. The copying surface should be stationery so that material is not subject to movement and possible damage. Also, moveable plates preclude the copying of bound volumes. The automatic feed device, a feature on many copy machines, should never be used with archival material. Most photocopy machines are temperamental at best, and paper can easily get caught and crinkled in automatic feeders.

Microfilming may be seen as an alternative means of copying items that will not withstand the physical strain of being placed on a photocopy machine or that present problems because of poor image quality. Volumes with tight bindings can be filmed using book cradles to avoid the damage that would result if such bindings were forced flat on copying surfaces. Through image reduction, oversized materials, such as newspapers, can readily be copied via microfilm. Microfilm also may be used successfully to copy images that are barely legible. Letterpress books, for example, which are composed of tissue-like paper and contain faint images (which may have bled through to the opposite side of the sheet), often can be copied more satisfactorily by microfilming than by photocopying.[11]

Whatever copy process is used, a system for tagging items to be copied should be devised that does not require the researcher to remove items from a folder. Any item removed from its file location is at risk of being lost, and the staff time required to refile material is greatly increased if researchers remove items for copying. A copy request form may be developed that will describe the item to be copied, indicate location, and list special copying instructions. A form printed on long strips of paper that will extend beyond the length of letter- or legal-size folders can serve the dual purpose of a tag and a request form (see Figure 7-10).

[11]For a discussion of various copying options and technical specifications, see: Carolyn Hoover Sung, *Archives and Manuscripts: Reprography*. Basic Manual Series. Chicago: Society of American Archivists, 1982.

```
+----------------------------------------------------+
|            Photocopy Request Form                  |
|                                                    |
|  One form must be filled out for each request      |
|  and placed as a marker with the item to be        |
|  copied.  Do not remove archival materials         |
|  from folders.  Photocopy requests will be         |
|  granted in accordance with the copyright          |
|  law (Title 17 U.S. Code) when physical            |
|  condition permits.                                |
|                                                    |
|  Name_____   |
|                                                    |
|  Date_____   |
|                                                    |
|  Collection_____   |
|                                                    |
|  Folder_____Box_____   |
|  Title or description of item to be                |
|    copied_____   |
|                                                    |
|  _____   |
|  Number of pages_____   |
|  Special copying instructions_____   |
|                                                    |
|  _____   |
|  Approved by_____   |
|  Date copying completed_____   |
+----------------------------------------------------+
```

Figure 7-10. Sample photocopy request form.

Exhibition Practices

Exhibits of archival and manuscript material serve many outreach and educational purposes. Since exhibits are so public, they also invite scrutiny of institutional practices, which become manifest in an exhibition: historical accuracy in identification and descriptive practices, quality of exhibit design, and methods of display and mounting. The general public as well as potential donors and professional colleagues (all of whom are becoming more knowledgeable consumers of exhibits), will evaluate the overall quality and professionalism of an institution through its exhibition practices. Thus, sound conservation exhibit procedures are necessary not only to protect the material displayed, but to protect and enhance the reputation of the institution as well.

Depending upon staff size and how integral exhibits are seen to be to the mission of the institution, varying emphasis will be placed on exhibition programs and staff allocated to carrying them out. No matter how large or small the program, nor whether an entire crew of designers and preparators is involved in major installations, the goals and conservation concerns are the same. The archivist or curator must serve as the conduit between the public outreach needs of an exhibition and the physical requirements of the collections. In some instances, the responsibility of acting as the advocate or caretaker of the collections will necessitate refusing to have an item displayed on the basis of its value or uniqueness, its sensitive physical condition, or because of unacceptable security provisions. Further, the advocacy role played on behalf of collections may sometimes bring the archivist into conflict with other institutional staff, administrators, or other institutional goals. An ongoing process of education is required; in this regard it may be useful to prepare an exhibit manual or list of guidelines as helpful ammunition. Not all battles will be won, and some compromises will have to be made. At a minimum, however, anything that goes on exhibition over the objection of the archival or conservation staff should be well documented and carefully monitored while on display for any evidence of damage or increased (speeded up) deterioration. It should go without saying that the archivist must abide by the same restrictions placed on exhibition personnel.

A number of questions must be considered as part of the planning process for any exhibit. The initial series of questions relate to the selection of material for exhibition, and the decision to use original items or copies. The latter, if well done, are often quite acceptable, and may be the only viable option in travelling exhibits or other situations where exhibit security and physical controls are not assured (for example, in nonsupervised institutional space, student unions, banks, and shopping centers). The actual physical condition of an item also should be considered. Is it strong enough to withstand exhibition? Does it require repair or restoration before it can be displayed? Is the image (certain photographs, inks, and colorants) fugitive and likely to be affected to an unacceptable degree by any exposure to light? The location and security of the exhibit area also must be scrutinized. Is the area isolated with no traffic by staff? Are there security guards present, or should there be? Exhibit cases should be locked and located in a secure area.

Other questions relate to environmental concerns. What are the sources of light in the exhibit area, and can the light level be controlled? A maximum light level of five footcandles is recommended for museum exhibits and the display of valuable archival and library materials. Five footcandles is approximately equal to the output of one 150-watt incandescent bulb at a distance of three to four feet (a light meter may be used to measure the light level). Five footcandles is obviously quite dim, and it will be impossible to maintain this level for exhibits located in archives reading rooms or reception areas. While lights should be dimmed whenever possible (both to conserve energy and protect collection items), additional precautions must be taken to protect materials on display from exposure to ultraviolet radiation. Of special concern are sunlight coming in through windows, overhead fluorescent tubes, and light sources within exhibit cases, which pose even more problems due to the possibility of excessive heat buildup. Track lighting with beams aimed directly on an object is also a problem. Curtains or shades should be drawn over windows, and window glass covered with an ultraviolet filtering screen. Ultraviolet filters should be placed over fluorescent tubes and quartz lamps, and track lighting aimed away from displayed items. To avoid possible heat buildup, light fixtures within cases should be turned off. Plexiglas ® UF-3 is an ultraviolet absorbing material that may be used as glazing in frames or placed directly over items in cases; in both instances a mat should be used to separate the document from the plexiglass filter.

An exhibit case is a minienvironment and efforts must be made to maintain temperature and relative humidity within the ranges prescribed for the storage of archival materials. An exhibit case should not be airtight; lack of circulating air could contribute to the buildup of excessive heat and moisture. One or two small air vents may be drilled around the base of a case to alleviate this problem. A dial hygrometer may be placed inconspicuously in the corner of a case and read daily to determine relative humidity; humidity indicator cards, which react to changes in the moisture level, also may be used. Generally, the most effective and inexpensive means of controlling temperature and relative humidity within exhibit cases is to maintain proper levels in the room where the cases are located.

It is recommended that original materials be exhibited for a maximum of three months. This may not be feasible in all instances given the expense of mounting exhibits. It should be realized, however, that exhibition and exposure to light are endangering the materials to at least some degree. Items on exhibit are less secure than when in archival storage, and exposure to light will initiate chemical actions that will continue even after materials are put back into dark storage in folders, boxes, and cabinets. As in other matters, compromises have to be made; what must be considered or negotiated is the degree to which security measures and physical protection should be compromised to meet exhibition needs. It is important that the decisions reached be tempered with the knowledge that some degree of loss, however gradual, is going to occur. The maximum acceptable degree of loss over time should be consciously considered, though it is unlikely that easy or uniform answers will be forthcoming. Such informed decisions, however, are the basis for meaningful compromise.

Permanent exhibition of any item should be avoided. It may be possible to develop a rotation system for quasi-permanent installations, identifying a series of similar items that can be placed in an exhibit on a periodic basis to illustrate a given issue or concept. The tendency to place institutional treasures on permanent display should be discouraged, perhaps citing the extensive precautions undertaken by the National Archives to protect the permanent exhibition of the U.S. Constitution and Declaration of Independence.[12] Although few items will warrant such treatment, parallels may be drawn to items that have great institutional significance.

Exhibit preparation and method of matting and mounting raise important conservation considerations. Here, again, the archivist or curatorial staff must demand strict adherence to conservation procedures. Items may require cleaning, mending, or physical support prior to exhibition. All materials used in matting should be archivally stable and safe. Mat board that has an alkaline reserve and contains no groundwood should be used for constructing mats. This board may be purchased from archival suppliers in sheet form; precut mats in standard sizes are also available. Care should be taken that no adhesive or pressure-sensitive tape is placed directly on archival materials. Polyester photo corner mounts are ideal for exhibits, as items can be safely removed and the mats reused. Polyester envelopes and

[12]National Bureau of Standards. *Preservation of the Declaration of Independence and the Constitution of the United States.* NBS Circular 505. Washington, D.C.: U.S. Department of Commerce, July 2, 1951.

sheets have many uses in constructing an exhibit. No adhesives are required and items can be hung on boards simply by pushing pins through the polyester. Archives are often required to mount quick rotating exhibits in reading room settings. In such situations, polish and design are often of less concern than conveying information about archival holdings. Polyester sleeves or slings are a great asset in these instances, and should replace the practice of displaying unprotected items by the artful positioning of push-pins to hold material in place. Spur-of-the-moment exhibits are perhaps the most common of archival exhibits. These, too, deserve conservation and security consideration; thinking about such measures and instituting even minor changes can be a step forward in implementing or upgrading a conservation program.

Another category of activity that is common in archives and has overtones of an exhibit is the show-and-tell session, when archival materials—again, often special treasures—are brought out to inform and impress visitors and distinguished guests, potential donors, or students. Such practice is probably most common in settings where the archives functions as a teaching laboratory in colleges and universities. Students need to become familiar with the range of archival materials and how they are used in historical research. Such situations need to be controlled, and, ideally, should take place within the archives area to further emphasize the idea that such materials do not circulate or leave the building. It is advisable to have a checklist of all items brought out for such show-and-tell sessions, and to make sure that items are physically protected. Documents should be encapsulated, photographs enclosed in polyester envelopes, and bound volumes sturdy and intact. If such teaching activity takes place on a regular basis, it would be advisable to assemble an "archival sample kit" containing duplicates and discards that can be handled with fewer concerns for security and preservation of the material.

When lending materials to other institutions for exhibition purposes, the same considerations as those outlined above should be considered: physical condition of material, treatment needs, duration of exhibit, type of exhibit cases, security provisions, and environmental controls. In addition, the reputation of the borrowing institution and its staff should be evaluated. If the loan proves to be acceptable, a loan agreement should be drawn up that specifies conditions of the loan, including duration of total loan period and period of actual exhibition, means of transport to and from the borrowing institution, type of physical protection and security, and method of mounting and display. The agreement should also include provisions for insurance, which will necessitate placing a monetary value on the material and providing a complete physical description. A photo-

graphic record is a useful supplement to the narrative description so that condition may be compared before and after lending, should any doubt arise regarding damage. The method of mounting may be expressly specified by the lending institution; a statement requiring written permission before any repair or restoration work is done is an added precaution. It is essential to keep copies of any materials that are loaned, both as a security back-up and for internal use by researchers and staff.[13]

[13]For information on all aspects of developing an exhibits program, see: Gail Farr Casterline, *Archives and Manuscripts: Exhibits*. Basic Manual Series. Chicago: Society of American Archivists, 1980.

8 Implementing a Conservation Program

The first step in implementing a conservation program is to establish priorities and goals. Conservation should be seen as integral to every activity within the archives. If this approach is accepted, the task of instituting a conservation program will be much easier. It is very likely that many procedures and policies basic to the development of a full-scale program are already in place. For example, regular dusting and cleaning and the use of non-acidic storage materials are common in most repositories, even those that would deny having a conservation program. It is important to recognize these and similar actions as preservation functions because they provide good departure points for further program development. All such activities need to be included under the conservation mantle.

In planning and implementing a conservation program, it is advisable that a staff member or a committee be appointed with designated responsibility for the conservation effort. Ideally, this will be an individual or group with some knowledge of conservation and the nature of the collections; at a minimum, however, there should be enthusiasm, interest, and a willingness to learn. It would be helpful if the individual or committee responsible for conservation planning were formally appointed by the chief administrative officer or board, because the planning effort would then generate more cooperation, and the eventual implementation of necessary changes would be easier. Even informal efforts, however, can initiate positive results.

The designated or even self-appointed individual or committee should assemble information, coordinate the planning process, and initiate review of the archives facility and its environment. Perhaps as important as these efforts is the fact that a recognized body will be working on behalf of conservation within the institution. This acknowledgement of conservation need and responsibility is a positive first step in program implementation.

It should go without saying that the archivist and/or archival staff should play a key role in this planning process, from initiating the effort to directing the conservation committee. The number of individuals appropriately involved will depend on the size and type of institution, and on whether or not an archival conservation program is to be coordinated with conservation planning within a larger institutional setting (such as a university library or presidential museum). Even if it is a committee of one, however, the archivist alone can do a great deal within the confines of the archives to improve procedures and implement a viable preservation program.

Initial actions should revolve around setting goals and developing common understandings about the parameters and thrust of a conservation program. In this context it will be necessary to evaluate present conditions in the following areas: environment, building and archival quarters, archival functions and their preservation impact, physical needs of the collections, and staff. (Specific survey approaches are suggested in the next chapter; archival functions were considered in Chapter 7.)

The actual setting of program goals must be closely related to conditions identified in the evaluation process and degree of need. Goals and their attendant costs may then be developed. It is useful to categorize goals in terms of their time requirements (short-term, intermediate, and long-range) as well as financial implications (minimal, moderate, and substantial). In developing a plan of action, it is useful to include both short- and long-term goals, and changes that require little as well as more substantial expenditure of funds. Not only is such an approach realistic, but it also allows program implementation to begin immediately. This is necessary to sustain staff and administrative interest and support. The process of evaluation and reaching consensus on a set of goals is time-consuming and potentially exhausting; if program changes are deferred too long, interest will wane.

Immediate attention should be directed toward instituting necessary changes in the way archival materials are handled, processed, and stored. Improvements in these areas may require staff orientation and training and the acquisition of supplies, but the actual outlay of funds should be minimal. An equal priority is evaluating environmental conditions. Major changes in this area are likely to be costly and require several years. Here, too, however, it is possible to identify such short-term goals as improving housekeeping practices or installing light filters. Depending upon the physical condition of the collections and staff capability, another short-term goal can be the institution of basic conservation procedures (such as mending, cleaning, and encapsulation) as a part of processing. The conclusion that a conservation laboratory is an immediate priority is generally not warranted for most institutions. In this area, as in others, program implementation must be gradual and keyed to actual need as well as the ability to meet high standards. Much good can be accomplished by instituting basic or remedial procedures as a part of archival processing; the development of a full-scale laboratory is better left until intermediate steps have been fulfilled and the repository has a sound program of conservation management. There is no reason, however, not to include the development of a conservation laboratory or workshop as a long-range goal.

Administrators may have to be convinced of the importance of a conservation program and allocating resources to support it. If an initial committee effort to determine conservation need was authorized by administrative order, that is a very positive first step. Further levels of sanction and support will be required, however. Good communication is always important, and good archivists know the value of written documentation! During the data gathering and evaluation process, progress reports should be submitted to keep administrators informed. A final statement of findings and needed changes or improvements also should be prepared. Since proposed goals will have some policy and financial implications, the concurrence of the chief administrative officer or board is mandatory. In this context, it is important that the committee know the mission and overall goals of the institution, and develop conservation priorities within this framework.

Good two-way communication between administrators and conservation advocates may not be enough. If further convincing becomes necessary, several approaches may be attempted. Tours of the archives to show examples of deterioration, especially in highly visible collections, may be helpful. Data should be presented on causes of deterioration and costs of restoration. Examples of conservation programs at other prestigious institutions may provide the capstone to such persuasive approaches.

Once the concept of a conservation program has been accepted, and common goals established, several activities must commence. A conservation policy statement should be written and approved to guide program implementation. Also, conservation must become a line item in the institution. That is, the conservation program must be visible in the budget and on the staff roster.

Conservation Budget

Budgeting for conservation can begin by evaluating current expenditures for conservation-related supplies and services, and uniting them under a conservation heading. Assembly of such expenses as archival storage materials, extermination services, and a subscription to a conservation newsletter provides evidence that a conservation program does in fact exist, even if it is in its infancy. Somewhat more difficult will be acquiring additional funds to meet the goals of an expanded program. The allocation of internal funds for conservation purposes should be feasible; the degree will depend on administrative support and acceptance of the program. Rapid increases in funds should not necessarily be expected, as all new programs must prove their worth. In this context as well, progress reports should document need as well as any improvements brought about as a result of increased or special project funding. Such reports help to assure that funds are being spent wisely, and encourage continued support.

Outside funds also may be sought to support the conservation effort. State, local, and national public funding agencies, as well as private foundations, often grant monies to preserve significant research materials; some institutions have even been able to acquire start-up funds for conservation laboratories. The archives also should look close to home for conservation funding. Donors may be convinced to endow funds to meet the preservation needs of their collections, or to make a gift for the restoration of an item of particularly high value. A friends group also may be encouraged to become interested in the conservation program. Through gifts or special fund-raising efforts, a friends group might support a particular preservation project or outfit a workshop. Gifts should be publicly acknowledged (with the donor's permission) through newsletters, receptions, or the placement of plaques. Fund-raising is consuming of staff time and requires ongoing nurturing and attention. The rewards can be very great, however, and also may help to loosen institutional coffers once the value outside agencies and individuals place on the collections and their preservation is recognized.

The amount of money that should be budgeted for the conservation effort will depend on the needs of the collection and number of staff members with conservation responsibility. Supplies, equipment, and services also must figure into the equation. Unfortunately, little data is available on exactly how much institutions with conservation programs actually spend. A reasonable goal, however, is at least 15 – 20 percent of the total institutional budget.[14] The conservation program must receive such consistent ongoing support if it is to make any progress; current preservation problems are too great to expect miracles from piecemeal or haphazard approaches.

Conservation Personnel

Every archival repository should have a designated preservation officer. This position should evolve out of the initial move to develop a conservation program. Whether the preservation position represents a new staff position or is simply the archivist accepting added responsibilities, it must be made a formal part of the individual's job assignment. Ideally, it should appear in a written position description and also should be evident in the position title. Such titles as Archivist and Preservation Officer or Director and Head of Conservation may seem lengthy and a bit ambitious, but they do get the point across and help to keep conservation visible.

The preservation officer has a number of responsibilities to fulfill or oversee. These include the following:

(1) Institute preventive conservation measures. This is a policy-level responsibility that requires the evaluation of all activities and procedures from a conservation perspective. Ongoing review is necessary to ensure that high standards are maintained.

(2) Coordinate all conservation effort within the archives. Serve as liaison with other divisions or institutional departments.

(3) Monitor environmental conditions; agitate for necessary improvements. Maintain record of daily conditions of temperature and relative humidity.

(4) Conduct conservation survey.

(5) Coordinate all treatment activities, in-house or contractual.

(6) Ensure that accurate records of examinations and conservation treatments are maintained and become part of the permanent file maintained on each collection.

---

[14]Alan Calmes, Preservation Officer at the National Archives and Records Service, Washington, D.C., reports that approximately 25 percent of that portion of the NARS budget allocated to records holding activities is devoted to preservation services. James E. Potter, State Archivist, Nebraska State Historical Society, indicates that the combined budget for conservation and microfilming equals 32 percent of the Archives Division's budget; of that percentage, approximately 15 percent is allocated for conservation. Michael McColgin, Conservator at the Arizona Department of Library, Archives and Public Records, reports that conservation is budgeted for about 40 percent of the Archives' personnel budget.

(7) Develop an inventory of available preservation and restoration services, including manufacturers' and suppliers' catalogs.

(8) Order and monitor quality of archival and conservation supplies.

(9) Develop safe exhibit practices and procedures.

(10) Monitor housekeeping practices.

(11) Coordinate security program.

(12) Build a technical conservation library.

(13) Represent the archives at professional meetings and develop contacts in the conservation community.

(14) Plan and implement a disaster preparedness program. (Working on a disaster plan is a good way to involve the entire staff in conservation activity.)

(15) Train staff in conservation procedures.

The last point deserves special attention. Staff training is an ongoing responsibility. All staff should be oriented to basic conservation philosophy, practice, and techniques as they pertain to archival materials. Proper ways of handling and storing materials should be stressed. Training and orientation must be directed toward staff at all levels—administrative through student and volunteer workers—and mechanisms must be established for continued training and for orienting new staff members. (See Figure 8-1.) A concise conservation manual or policy statement specifically keyed to the procedures of the repository is a helpful training aid and may be given to new staff as they are hired. Lists of specific "dos and don'ts" are also useful. Means should be devised to encourage staff to be active participants in the preservation process. Periodic problem-solving sessions where specific topics—such as problems with over-sized records —are discussed help to get everyone thinking about particular issues from a conservation perspective. A number of excellent audiovisual presentations are available on conservation topics (see Appendix E). These can provide the focus for a number of staff training sessions.

The above list of responsibilities to be carried out by a preservation officer is by no means exhaustive; in some institutions such tasks as overseeing preservation microfilming or supervising a photographic laboratory would also have to be included. It does, however, give a sense of the breadth of responsibility. The duties are extensive enough to warrant a full-time position in a large repository with diverse program elements, although an archivist working alone with little or no assistance can also incorporate these functions into work routines.

It is important for the preservation officer to read widely in the conservation literature to keep abreast of changes in the field. The preservation officer also should attend continuing education seminars and workshops and join conservation organizations as further means of keeping current as well as making useful contacts. Colleagues at other institutions can provide much help and information, and visits to similar institutions with fully developed conservation programs can be very valuable learning experiences.

Figure 8-1. Staff should be given opportunities to attend continuing education workshops on conservation philosophy and procedures. Photograph by Hugh Talman, National Archives and Records Service.

9   Conservation Survey

The development of a sound archival conservation program must be based on a thorough understanding of the physical plant and environment, the range and formats of collection materials, and archival procedures and policies. A number of elements that are seen as routine archival tasks, and therefore far removed from the mystique of conservation, do indeed play a vital role in the overall development of a conservation program and in the ultimate preservation of archival materials. Once data is gathered regarding the scope and character of holdings, storage capabilities, and processing procedures, it is possible to compare present conditions against developing standards of archival conservation. As a result of such self-study and evaluation, a needs assessment statement can be developed which may be used to design a phased preservation program.

Self-Study Questionnaire

The following questions have been designed as a brief guide to consideration of a manuscript or archival repository from a conservation perspective. The questions focus on types of material, policies and procedures, and the physical environment. They will also serve as an aid in turning a critical eye to current archival and conservation practices. While there are no right or wrong answers in such a data-gathering exercise, the questions are certainly leading in that they highlight areas of conservation concern.

1. Types of material held by repository:

    ____handwritten documents and records on paper:
       ____single sheets   ____bound format
    ____typewritten material (correspondence, reports, etc.):
       ____with handwritten notations
    ____all-print material
    ____copy methods represented: ____letterpress ____carbon ____mimeograph ____thermofax ____other
    ____bound volumes:
       ____diaries and journals   ____ledgers and account books   ____scrapbooks
    ____newspapers
    ____photographic prints (black and white) on paper

    ____photographic prints (color) on paper
    ____cased photographs: ____daguerreotypes ____ambrotypes   ____tintypes (ferrotypes)
    ____photographic negatives on film: ____safety film   ____nitrate base
    ____glass plate negatives
    ____motion-picture film: ____safety film ____nitrate base
    ____sound recordings: ____cylinder (Edison) ____disc   ____cassette tapes   ____reel-to-reel tapes
    ____videotapes
    ____computer tapes
    ____records in microformats: ____microfilm ____microfiche
    ____works of art on paper: ____framed under glass
    ____architectural drawings: ____renderings ____tracings
    ____blueprints and similarly processed reproductions
    ____maps and charts
    ____posters and advertising broadsides
    ____three-dimensional objects

2. Dates of holdings:
    ____pre-1850 ____%
    ____1850–1900 ____%
    ____post-1900 ____%

3. Size of holdings:
    ____items ____linear feet

4. Where are the records stored? ____separate stack area ____open shelves ____departmental office ____warehouse ____basement ____attic ____closets/cupboards ____other

5. How are the records stored?: ____boxed on shelves ____boxed on the floor ____filing cabinets ____map cases ____other

6. Are the shelves or storage units: ____wooden ____metal
    Type of finish: ____polyurethane varnish ____baked enamel ____paint ____other

7. What types of storage containers are used?
____alkaline boxes ____transfer cases ____miscellaneous cartons ____alkaline file folders ____manila folders ____tubes ____other

8. Is the storage area/reading room:
____air-conditioned
____temperature- and humidity-controlled: temperature maintained between ____degrees F and ____degrees F, with relative humidity between ____% and ____%.
____outfitted with air filtration device(s)
____surrounded by or near steam or water pipes
____susceptible to leaks or flooding
____outfitted with water detection system
____outfitted with smoke/fire detection system
____outfitted with fire suppression system: ____ sprinkler system ____gas system (Halon type, etc.)
____equipped with fire extinguishers
____subject to insect or rodent infestation
Are the monitoring and detection systems operational? Are these systems inspected periodically? Are staff members trained to use fire extinguishers?

9. Is the storage area/reading room illuminated with:
____incandescent light ____fluorescent light ____direct sunlight ____quartz light
Are protective shades or ultraviolet filtering devices used?

10. Who has access by key to locked storage or vault areas:
____entire archives staff ____designated archives staff ____volunteer or student employees ____other institutional staff ____maintenance staff ____engineers ____security personnel ____other
Is there an intrusion alarm system? Is the system operational?

11. Does the repository have a written disaster plan? Is this institution-wide, or does it apply only to the manuscripts/archives division? What natural disasters are likely in the local geographic area?

12. Are researchers monitored at all times? Are reading room rules posted and enforced? Is there a written policy covering abuse or possible theft of material?

13. Is the archives staff trained in:
____proper ways to handle manuscript and archival material
____basic conservation procedures
____emergency procedures

14. Is there anyone on staff with designated conservation responsibility or conservation expertise?

15. Are funds allocated for conservation purposes? Amount per year: ____; ____% of total budget.

16. Is there an in-house conservation laboratory facility? Are treatments carried out by trained personnel? Which of the following are undertaken:
____surface cleaning ____washing ____removal of pressure-sensitive tape and other intrusions ____deacidification ____mending ____reinforcement ____encapsulation ____lamination ____leather treatment ____treatment of three-dimensional objects ____other

17. How many staff hours per week are spent on conservation activities?

18. Does the repository contract for outside treatment services? How have these services been evaluated?

19. Are preservation/security copies of valuable records and photographic prints and negatives made for research use?

20. Has a preservation microfilming program been instituted?

21. Are original materials (manuscripts, photographs, posters, etc.) placed on exhibition? What conservation and security measures are taken?

22. Has a condition survey of the repository's holdings ever been undertaken?

23. Have conservation treatment priorities been established and, if so, on what basis?

24. Characterize the overall conservation needs of the institution:

Condition Survey

Following a review of repository-wide conditions and policies, attention should be directed to the needs of individual collections or items for protection and support. A condition survey is the best means of gathering data needed to evaluate treatment priorities. A simple conservation checklist may be devised for recording infor-

NEBRASKA STATE HISTORICAL SOCIETY

   Condition Survey Report: Paper   ____ Archives   ____ needs repair
                                         ____ Library   ____ needs cleaning
Date of Examination: _____   ____ Museum   ____ needs leather treatment
Surveyor: _____   ____ needs container
Title: _____   Primary Protection: Paper:
_____   ____ binding   ____ discolored
                                          ____ full   ____ dirt
Number: _____   ____ half   ____ stained
Dimensions: _____   ____ quarter   ____ brittle
No. of Pages/Units: _____   ____ leather   ____ tears
_____   ____ tanned   ____ missing/loose leaves
                                              ____ suede   ____ foxing
Type of Item: ____ other   ____ insertions
   ____ book   ____ cloth   ____ clips, pins, bands, etc.
   ____ manuscript   ____ paper   ____ soluble inks, colors
   ____ pamphlet   ____ rot/abrasion   ____ illustrations
   ____ periodical   ____ soil   ____ sewing deterioration
   ____ broadside   ____ loose/broken spine   ____ tape
   ____ certificate   ____ torn headcap   ____ glue
   ____ architectural   ____ broken/missing board ____ backing
   ____ map   ____ metal binder   ____ mildew
   ____ card   ____ box   ____ insect/rodent damage
   ____ newspaper   ____ torn/broken   ____ other _____
   ____ work of art   ____ tied/wrapped/envelope, etc.
   ____ photograph   ____ other _____ ____ parchment
   ____ other _____

Figure 9-1. Condition survey report form. Reproduced with the permission of the Nebraska State Historical Society.

mation on physical condition either of individual items or entire collections. The survey form should be as detailed as deemed necessary and should be specifically designed to meet the unique characteristics of an institution's holdings (see Figures 9-1, 9-2).

Although the idea of undertaking a condition survey may seem overwhelming, collection size or limited staff should not be seen as deterrents. It may be necessary to utilize a sampling technique if the holdings are very large (an approach as simple as surveying every tenth container or item may suffice), or to consider other means of integrating the data-gathering process into ongoing archival functions. For example, condition forms could be filled out during accessioning or processing activities, or before reshelving collections that have been used for research. Whatever method the condition survey employs (i.e., sampling or an item-by-item evaluation), or whether the information is gained over a period of time as part of other archival duties or acquired more quickly as a special project, the assembled data will provide a good overview of the scope and nature of the physical needs of the collection.

The specific type of information sought in the condition survey will vary depending on the material nature of the records. It is advised, however, to make the survey instrument simple to fill out, with easily ascertainable categories of information. The background and training of potential surveyors should be considered as well. Nontechnical personnel will need to be trained to recognize the physical characteristics of the material they are likely to encounter; they should not be expected to make chemical determinations regarding stability of material. The survey instrument should be as extensive in coverage as is feasible, considering a variety of possible future uses for the information gathered. At a minimum, a condition checklist should include the following categories of information: name and location of item or collection; brief biblographic description; type of material (paper, leather, photographic print, etc.); media (pencil, typewritten, manuscript ink, etc.); format (single sheets, scrapbook, oversized, etc.); observable damage (surface dirt, brittleness, evidence of prior treatment, etc.); type and quality of storage containers; and the date and name of the surveyor. Many of the determinations can be subjective and it will be necessary, as far as possible, to ensure that surveyors are trained to work from common understandings of terms and conditions. In some instances, it may be desirable to make simple readings of surface pH using nonbleeding indicators; this step will, however, add considerably to the time required to complete the survey. Treatment recommendations also can form part of the survey checklist, including such options as: reboxing or refoldering material, relaxing rolled or folded documents, removing harmful enclosures, surface cleaning, mending, physical support through

Sequence Number _____

CHECKLIST FOR FY 1983 NBS PRESERVATION SURVEY
OF NARS PAPER TEXTUAL HOLDINGS
PART I (To be completed by archival staff)

SURVEYOR _____   TODAY'S DATE _____

RG _____   SERIES TITLE _____

SERIES DATE SPAN _____

DATE SPAN OF DOCUMENTS SAMPLED _____   LENGTH OF SERIES (linear) _____

                                          Yes   No
1. Disposable Series . . . . ( )   ( )
2. Intrinsic Value . . . . ( )   ( )
   a. If "Yes," then which specific characteristics or qualities does it contain
      (see SIP 21): 1   2   3   4   5   6   7   8   9
                    ( ) ( ) ( ) ( ) ( ) ( ) ( ) ( ) ( )
   b. If "No" and 14a indicates presence of colored inks, are the colors significant?
                                          Yes,   No,
                                          ( )   ( )
   c. Do the characteristics of intrinsic value apply to the series or the sample unit
      only? ( ) Series   ( ) Unit Only

3. USE: ( ) at least once a month   ( ) at least once a year   ( ) less than once a year
                                          Yes   No
4. In NARS A-1 . . . . ( )   ( )
5. Microfilmed . . . . ( )   ( )
6. Published (other than by microfilm)   ( )   ( )
   Change 9d second part to "Yes" if folders are needed for arrangement control.

PART II (To be completed by preservation staff)

SURVEYOR _____   TODAY'S DATE _____

STACK AREA _____ ROW _____ COMPARTMENT _____ SHELF _____ SEVENTH _____

BOX/VOL. LABEL _____

ID. NO. OF FOLDER SELECTED _____   TOTAL NO. OF FOLDERS _____

ESTIMATING GUIDE

(Few) = 5% or less
(1/4) = about one quarter of the contents
(1/2) = about one half of the contents
(3/4) = about three quarters of the contents
(All) = almost all of the contents 95% or more

7. Sample Unit Size: ( ) 1/3 cu. ft. ( ) 1 cu. ft. ( ) Vols. (No. of Vols.____)
                      ( ) Other
   If vols. or other give height _____ depth _____ thickness _____

8. Loose paper: ( ) Few ( ) 1/4 ( ) 1/2 ( ) 3/4 ( ) All

9. Housing of loose papers
   a. Container: ( ) Archives box ( ) FRC Box ( ) Tray ( ) Roller Drawer
                  ( ) Other (Specify other)_____
   b. Overloaded: ( ) Yes ( ) No
   c. Quality of container: ( ) Good ( ) Fair ( ) Poor
   d. Folders used: ( ) Yes ( ) No   If "No," are they needed: ( ) Yes ( ) No
   e. Condition of folders: ( ) Acid ( ) Non-acidic

10. Bindings of Volumes (Indicate the Volume Number in each category)
    a. Type of binding: _____ Library _____ Unique/Historic _____ Ledger _____ Post
    b. Covering material: _____ Buckram _____ Cloth _____ Paper _____ Leather
    c. Minor red rot _____   g. Spine detached _____
    d. Major red rot _____   h. Minor sewing damage _____
    e. Loose binding _____   i. Major sewing damage _____
    f. Improperly shelved _____

                          Few   1/4   1/2   3/4   All
11. Paper Size
    a. index cards   ( )   ( )   ( )   ( )   ( )
    b. smaller than letter ( )   ( )   ( )   ( )   ( )
    c. letter/legal   ( )   ( )   ( )   ( )   ( )
    d. larger than legal but
       under 4 sq. ft.   ( )   ( )   ( )   ( )   ( )
    e. 4 sq. ft. and larger ( ) ( )   ( )   ( )   ( )

12. Type of Support
    a. newsprint/ground wood ( ) ( )   ( )   ( )   ( )
    b. tissue paper   ( )   ( )   ( )   ( )   ( )
    c. handmade paper   ( )   ( )   ( )   ( )   ( )

Figure 9-2. Survey instrument. Reproduced with the permission of the National Archives and Records Service.

	Few	1/4	1/2	3/4	All
d. book/writing paper	( )	( )	( )	( )	( )
e. parchment	( )	( )	( )	( )	( )
f. other (specify_____)	( )	( )	( )	( )	( )

13. Type of media

	Few	1/4	1/2	3/4	All
a. handwritten	( )	( )	( )	( )	( )
b. typewritten	( )	( )	( )	( )	( )
c. printed text	( )	( )	( )	( )	( )
d. press copies	( )	( )	( )	( )	( )
e. impermanent copies	( )	( )	( )	( )	( )
f. photographs	( )	( )	( )	( )	( )
g. drawings	( )	( )	( )	( )	( )
h. hand-colored printed maps	( )	( )	( )	( )	( )
i. other (specify_____)	( )	( )	( )	( )	( )
j. damaged special media	( )	( )	( )	( )	( )

14. Use problems

	Few	1/4	1/2	3/4	All
a. colored inks	( )	( )	( )	( )	( )
b. faint image	( )	( )	( )	( )	( )
c. brittle	( )	( )	( )	( )	( )
d. folded	( )	( )	( )	( )	( )
e. rolled	( )	( )	( )	( )	( )
f. homogeneous format	( )Yes ( )No				

15. Previous treatment

	Few	1/4	1/2	3/4	All
a. laminated	( )	( )	( )	( )	( )
b. laminated w/o tissue	( )	( )	( )	( )	( )
c. silked	( )	( )	( )	( )	( )
d. other (specify_____)	( )	( )	( )	( )	( )

16. Major damage by:

	Few	1/4	1/2	3/4	All
a. tears/breaks	( )	( )	( )	( )	( )
b. water/mold	( )	( )	( )	( )	( )
c. acidic ink	( )	( )	( )	( )	( )
d. tape	( )	( )	( )	( )	( )
e. glue/paste	( )	( )	( )	( )	( )
f. corrosion stains	( )	( )	( )	( )	( )
g. other (specify_____)	( )	( )	( )	( )	( )

17. Loss of information ( ) ( ) ( ) ( ) ( )

18. Abundant loose dirt/dust on document ( )Yes ( )No

19. % unused (blank pages or part empty) _____%

20. Active mold, insects, or rodents ( )Yes ( )No

Figure 9-2. Survey instrument (reverse).

polyester encapsulation or mounting, removal from frame, treatment of bound volumes, removal of inappropriate prior treatment, and deacidification.

The survey form should be designed to ensure that each collection or item is considered from the same perspective. It should be emphasized that the basis for recording condition data is evaluation of physical evidence; a careful, trained, and consistent eye is required, not laboratory analysis, although this may be necessary before making some treatment decisions. Once all collections have been surveyed, the data gathered may be used to develop priorities for treatment. Physical condition will then be considered in conjunction with such factors as historical value, uniqueness, and incidence of research use. The following categories of information may be used to develop a condition survey tool specifically designed to fit the needs of individual institutions.

Collection: Location:

Date of survey: Conducted by:

Box and folder number:

Type of material: Inclusive dates:

Format:

Media:

Type and quality of storage containers:
  folders/envelopes:
  boxes/cartons:

Condition of collection:
  general appearance:
  tears/abrasions:
  surface dirt and dust:
  water or other stains:
  discoloration:
  embrittlement:
  evidence of mold or mildew:
  insect damage:
  harmful means of attachment (pins, brads, paper clips, etc.):
  enclosures (pressed flowers, clippings, etc.)

Additional observations:

Use of collection:

Priority ranking of collection for treatment:

Recommended treatments:
  refoldering: deacidification:
  reboxing: mending:
  removal of foreign materials: removal from frame:
  surface cleaning: encapsulation:
  preservation copying:

Establishing Treatment Priorities

Data gathered on the physical condition of collection items must be considered in combination with the resources available for conservation treatment and the relative value of the material as the basis for setting treatment priorities. Archival material may be regarded from a number of perspectives, and values attached accordingly. In part, the assignment of values will determine which records must be maintained in their original format (and thus may require physical treatment), and which records may be copied to preserve their informational content. For example, a document may have importance because it is unique (i.e., it contains information found in no other place); this type of document, however, either may be very scarce (giving it added value), or it may be representative of masses of similar documents (such as case records or constituent mail). Informational value must be weighed against artifactual value. Is the physical form a subject for study? Does the item have artistic or aesthetic merit? Is it useful for exhibition purposes? Age may be another criterion on the assumption that early records are scarce and thus take on added value. Some records have legal values that must be considered; other records may be of suspect authenticity, in which case it is necessary to maintain them in original format so that they may be physically examined. Records relating to the founding of an organization or institution—charters or constitutions, for example—are generally seen to have high artifactual value, as are records that relate to the primary collecting focus of an institution. Use is another factor that must be considered. Collections that receive a high level of research use are likely very important to the institution; these also may be in the poorest condition because of the high degree of handling they receive. Such factors must be considered and weighed in determining, in priority order, which collections require immediate physical treatment, which can be copied, and which can safely await future action. Given the inherent nature of archival materials, there is no standard formula that can be applied uniformly to assess the relative values of collection material. The criteria used will vary from institution to institution, each developing its own set of factors to evaluate unique collections.

Evaluating Conservation Treatment Services

Following the condition survey and the ordering of collections according to physical need and value, specific remedial actions and treatments can commence. Treatment options will be determined in part by fiscal resources, staff competency, and the possibility of sending work to outside conservators.

In-House Conservation Laboratories

As part of the overall process of evaluation, it is important to evaluate in-house capabilities for undertaking conservation treatments. The training and skill level of conservation personnel must be scrutinized in the same fashion that contractual services are evaluated. The range of treatments that can be safely undertaken in-house must be based upon the level of staff ability. Unless the in-house capability warrants it, work on valuable items or treatments requiring a high level of craft and technical skill should be left to professional conservators. (See Figure 9-3). It is better to attempt no treatment at all than to carry it out poorly.

Figure 9-3. Conservator removing an acidic cardboard backing using mechanical means—a task that requires patience and exacting skill. Photograph courtesy of the Northeast Document Conservation Center.

It is potentially awkward if the archivist/preservation officer must evaluate the staff capabilities and quality of work produced in an existing in-house laboratory. In such instances, the weight of institutional inertia will be particularly burdensome if conservation personnel are poorly trained or have no formal training at all. Unfortunately, such situations are not all that unusual. The scrutiny must extend beyond personnel to the tech-

niques they carry out. It must be determined if a proper range of treatments is being implemented, and whether individual treatment decisions are being made based on need and condition of the material. If in-house work does not meet high standards, the archivist must be willing to agitate for change, either in treatment systems, personnel, or both. While this may be difficult, the archivist must act in the best interests of the collection. Some possible solutions include:

(1) Halt inappropriate procedures by administrative order and provide rationale for the decision and direction regarding suitable treatments.

(2) Place the workshop under the supervision of trained personnel, either the preservation officer or a qualified conservation technician.

(3) Provide opportunities for staff training to build up skills. Possible avenues include workshops or internships in conservation departments at other institutions.

Evaluating Outside Conservation Services

The need for evaluating conservators who may be selected to work on institutional treasures is very important. The scarcity of qualified paper and book conservators is compounded by their tendency to be clustered in or near large urban centers. There are virtually no conservators in large portions of the country, although, to be sure, there may be individuals who advertise qualifications that are not justified. This renders the selection process even more difficult as contacts may have to be made by mail and telephone. It must be stressed that it is the archivist's responsibility to select a qualified conservator and to ensure that appropriate treatments are carried out. Treatment decisions are made jointly by the archivist, who knows the value and significance of the records, and the conservator, who is aware of the physical nature of the materials and the viable treatment options. When turning work over to a conservation laboratory, the archivist takes on rather than gives up responsibility; he or she must make final decisions regarding treatment recommendations and evaluate the quality of the work.

It is often useful to talk with individuals at other repositories, libraries, and museums when seeking a qualified conservator. They may be able to recommend individuals with whom they have worked and have been satisfied. The American Institute for Conservation and the Guild of Book Workers also maintain lists of their members, and while such lists do not constitute a recommendation or endorsement, they do provide a starting point to determine if there are people working in a given locality. The least satisfactory course is to consult the telephone directory; while a qualified individual may indeed be listed, there will be many others who are not.

Look with a wary eye at picture framers and library binders who claim to do restoration work. Department stores and photo labs are also getting into the business of "restoring" old family photographs and albums; their methods probably are not appropriate for archival materials—nor for treasured family records, for that matter.

If at all possible, it is advisable to visit the conservator's studio or laboratory before actually contracting for work. It is not inappropriate to ask to see samples of work, or to ask for information on the individual's background and training. A great deal may be learned from visiting the actual workplace; the way materials are kept and tools are cared for will indicate a great deal about the overall approach taken to conservation. In establishing an initial relationship, it may be useful to have several sample jobs done on items that are not terribly valuable. These may be evaluated for quality of work and cost. For purposes of comparison, two or three similar jobs might be sent to different conservators.

A customer has the right to expect that a conservator will:

—be sensitive to the importance and value of a document and its historical period

—use sympathetic styles and materials in any restoration treatment

—use only high-quality supplies

—not skimp on time or materials

—exhibit a high degree of craft skill

—complete work within a reasonable, or at least agreed upon, period of time

—provide a written report of all treatment

—provide security for material

—indicate whether any part of the work is to be subcontracted out to other labs

—make reasonably accurate estimates of cost of treatments

Not all of these factors will be immediately evident, but they should be borne in mind as appropriate expectations and evaluated over time.

One of the archivist's primary responsibilities in this area is to develop the ability to evaluate the quality of any treatment undertaken, whether it involves a simple in-house repair or a major restoration job done by an outside conservator. It is necessary to be able to differentiate between work that is done skillfully and work that is only passable. This involves training one's eye to see the whole object as well as details. Much careful looking will aid in developing the requisite knowledge. Concern over aesthetics must be integrated with practical requirements regarding use and function. The archivist must be a knowledgeable consumer of conservation services to adequately protect the collections in his or her charge.

10 Conservation Treatments

Mass conservation procedures are often seen as the coming panacea for archival and library collections. In theory, mass procedures would allow large volume treatment of materials evidencing the same problem; individual handling of items would be minimized, and the cost per item for treatment thus radically reduced. The only area where mass treatment may be feasible in the near future is deacidification and, even here, the projected cost per item may not place such advances within the financial reach of many institutions. Thus, it is imperative to consider the provision of a temperature- and humidity-controlled environment as a mass preservation tool that is realistically within the range of the majority of institutions. Such controls will effectively slow the rate of deterioration of most materials, and should be a top priority.

The concept of "phased preservation" as developed at the Library of Congress is relevant in this context. It involves collections maintenance (that is, reboxing, refoldering, and reshelving materials, and providing protective encasement for individual items) while devising appropriate survey techniques to establish priorities for future treatment. This phased approach encourages repositories to allocate resources for preservation measures that will benefit all holdings by housing them in a protective and nonthreatening environment, while making plans and allocating funds for physical treatment of specific materials as appropriate.

Controlling the environment and providing proper storage fall within the realm of preventive maintenance. Treatment procedures are a step beyond this. In an archival context, physical treatment is intended to return damaged materials to a usable condition with the goal of preservation and stability, not cosmetic improvement. An alternative to physical treatment is substitution, or transferring the informational content of unstable records to a more stable medium, such as microfilm. A conservation survey provides a systematic procedure for determining the nature of the problem and specific preservation needs. Treatment priorities can then be established based on the data gathered and the intrinsic value of the records. It must be determined whether it is necessary to preserve the document in its original format *and* its informational content, or if only the latter is deemed important. This is a basic decision that determines whether preservation of the original material is required or some form of preservation copying will suffice.

Treatment options for stabilizing and supporting archival materials must be weighed against several factors before any action is taken. The archivist must understand the extent and nature of the problem, the range of available solutions, and the feasibility of following any given option, based on the availability of resources and technical expertise. In this context, decisions must be made regarding tasks that can be competently carried out in-house and those that need to be sent to outside specialists.

The problem to be remedied must be clearly understood before any physical treatment is undertaken. Often, symptoms are obvious. For example, a document may be discolored and brittle to the degree that it crumbles at the slightest touch. The problem in this instance is clearly brittle and weakened paper. Other problems, such as tears and stains, can be found through physical examination. Laboratory analysis may be required, however, to determine the specific nature of these problems, and to assist in determining factors such as the age of the item, pigments or inks used to record information, fiber content, precise readings of acidity level, and the present of groundwood.

The solution to the problem of preserving weak and brittle paper would appear to be to select appropriate means of stabilization and support. Deacidification may be required to slow the process of acid deterioration by neutralizing the acids and providing an alkaline reserve to inhibit the return of the paper to an acidic state. The decision whether to deacidify or not should be based upon a number of factors, including the processes available, the quality and condition of the paper, and the type of inks or colorants and their reaction to water or solvents. If the decision is made to deacidify the brittle document, its chemical condition will be stabilized. Its physical condition (i.e., degree of brittleness) will not have improved, however, and some means of protection and support may be necessary. Encapsulation in polyester and cellulose acetate lamination are two options currently available for providing physical support to brittle documents. The problem facing the archivist is which option to choose.

Treatment decisions must be based on sound information regarding the state of the art of available procedures. It is important for the archivist to gather as much information as possible by reading current journals, consulting with conservators, and attending professional archival and conservation meetings. The archivist must become knowledgeable regarding exactly what the various procedures are intended to accomplish, the process and materials employed, potential dangers to archival records while they are undergoing treatment, and ease of reversibility. As far as possible, the archivist should be aware of the long-term effects of any treatment, whether it is "tried and true," and the extent of its current usage in established conservation laboratories and centers. Admittedly, this places a great burden on the archivist to know and learn many things that may at first seem difficult and foreign. But, it is an important responsibility, and one that must be taken seriously if archival materials are to receive proper care. This is not to say that the individual archivist must know how to carry out all of the procedures. But he or she must learn enough to qualify as a knowledgeable consumer of conservation services and a judicious partner with the conservator in making treatment decisions. It is the archivist who has final responsibility for preservation.

The following conservation techniques and procedures are described from the perspectives of function or intended goal, safety, and applicability to archival materials. Instructions appear in the Appendixes for basic conservation procedures that are considered appropriate for archivists with some training and experience. Other techniques should only be implemented by trained persons with the proper equipment.

Fumigation

The issues surrounding the topic of fumigation are complex. The topic has received increased attention in the conservation and archival literature of late, spurred in part by the museum community and greater public awareness of health-related and environmental problems associated with hazardous materials.[15] Federal statutes and regulations govern the use of insecticides, fungicides, and rodenticides. These specify labelling requirements, safety precautions, and conditions of use, to protect both the environment and the user. Any repository involved in fumigating collections (or contracting for such services) must be aware of all procedures and rules mandated by state and local law regulating the use of pesticides and fumigants which are applicable to the institution. Advice in these matters may be sought from the Environmental Protection Agency, Washington, D.C.; from state agencies responsible for controlling toxic substances; and from licensed professional fumigators.

[15]See: Stephen R. Edwards, Bruce M. Bell, and Mary Elizabeth King. *Pest Control in Museums: A Status Report (1980)*. Lawrence, Kans.: Association of Systematics Collections, 1981. This book should be considered required reading for all archivists.

It is advisable to have a staff member develop specialized knowledge in this area. Ideally, it should be the preservation officer or archivist responsible for overseeing the fumigation of collections. This individual should become a certified applicator of pesticides, not to perform such functions, but to ensure that the institution has the necessary knowledge to evaluate different pesticides, application techniques, and private firms offering these services. This is but another area in which it is necessary for the archivist to become a knowledgeable consumer of goods and contractual services in order to adequately care for collections.

When selecting a pesticide, only those registered for "museum use," "institutional use," or "use in public buildings" should be used. Fumigation must be properly planned to avoid releasing toxic fumes into staff or other populated areas, and must be done in compliance with pertinent regulations in the Occupational Health and Safety Act of 1970. At every step, precautions must be taken to avoid endangering human health and safety.

It is important to proceed cautiously with fumigation, and to fumigate only when necessary. Given the unknown effect of fumigants on record materials, the many questions raised over the problem of residual fumigant vapors, and potential health hazards, this action must be seen as an emergency response to a critical situation, and not as a part of ongoing curatorial care applied uniformly whether required or not. Fumigation must be seen as mandatory, however, if there is the slightest evidence of mold growth or insect activity. Several options are currently available.

Vacuum fumigators are effective, speed up the fumigation process, and are found fairly commonly in archival repositories and libraries. They are available in a range of sizes and some are outfitted with the capability of drying wet materials. One fumigant commonly used in vacuum chambers is ethylene oxide. Since it is flammable, toxic, and explosive, ethylene oxide is generally employed in a mixture with carbon dioxide or an inert gas. (Oxyfume 12, a mixture of 12 percent ethylene oxide and 88 percent freon-12 or Carboxide, 10 percent ethylene oxide and 90 percent carbon dioxide, are commonly used.) The process works by creating a vacuum in the chamber where collection items are placed; the machine then meters a specific quantity of fumigant, which thoroughly permeates the materials. The cycle lasts for up to twelve hours, after which the fumigant is expelled from the chamber and replaced by fresh air. Because of the toxic nature of ethylene oxide—which will kill mold, insects, larvae, and eggs in a vacuum chamber—precise adherence to manufacturers' specifications is advised in installing the equipment, which must include a proper exhaust and venting system

to evacuate the gas from the chamber after a cycle is completed. As a safety precaution, it is advised that upon completion of a cycle the air be washed up to four times to reduce the amount of residual gas that might remain in the chamber and to which operators would be exposed upon opening the door. In addition, the area in which the fumigator is located must be well ventilated to reduce the opportunity for gas buildup resulting from opening chamber doors or leaking pipes in the piping and exhaust system. All systems should be checked regularly by a safety engineer, and operating instructions for the specific equipment should be followed precisely. Ethylene oxide is currently under review by the Occupational Safety and Health Administration (OSHA). OSHA is proposing to amend its existing standard that regulates employee exposure to ethylene oxides from 50 parts ethylene oxide per million parts of air (50 ppm) as an eight-hour time-weighted average (TWA) down to a TWA of 1 ppm.[16] To ensure that all safety and use regulations can be met, it is advised that OSHA and state regulatory agencies be consulted before purchasing or operating a vacuum fumigator that uses ethylene oxide.

Vacuum fumigation chambers are not inexpensive, and it may not be feasible for a repository to purchase one. In some localities, it may be possible to initiate shared fumigation capabilities, either through the joint purchase and maintenance of a vacuum fumigator, or by renting time, so to speak, on a fumigator owned by a local agency. When seeking to share these resources, natural history museums should not be overlooked, as they often need to fumigate specimens. Other possible allies include local or state libraries, archives, art and history museums, and universities.

If the archives does not have an in-house vacuum fumigator and if there are no possibilities for shared resources, it will be necessary to resort to the services of commercial fumigation or exterminating companies. Searching for an appropriate firm can be problematic at best. Most local exterminators deal routinely with pests found around foodstuffs and with rodents or termites, and may wish to transfer this expertise—perhaps inappropriately—directly to archival materials. It may take a bit of trial and error to find a firm that will be both sensitive to the specialized needs of archival collections and willing to work with the archivist to find nondestructive solutions to the infestation. Local repositories or museums may be able to suggest the names of companies or individuals they have found

[16]Department of Labor. Occupational Health and Safety Administration. Docket No. H-200. "Occupational Exposure to Ethylene Oxide." *Federal Register,* 48:17284 (April 21, 1983).

satisfactory. Licensed professional fumigators will generally be more knowledgeable than local exterminators.

The archivist or preservation officer (who, ideally, will be a certified applicator of pesticides) will need to consult with the fumigator regarding the suspected type of infestation as well as the nature of the materials to be treated. The archivist must be satisfied that the chemicals the fumigator proposes using will be effective in eliminating the problem and have no adverse effects on paper, inks, or people. Part of the data-gathering process should include consultation with a conservator or conservation scientist if the fumigant proposed is unknown. Further, it is necessary to determine where the fumigation is to take place. If off-site, security and transportation issues will have to be resolved satisfactorily. If an appropriate location within the institution can be designated that provides security for the materials as well as necessary physical requirements for the fumigation cycle, all the better. Depending upon the process and fumigant employed, the fumigation may take place in a chamber, under a plastic sheet such as polyethylene (indoors or out), or, in the case of structural fumigation, within an entire building or room. The area or space designated must be capable of being sealed off completely to allow for effective fumigation and must be amenable to good exhaust and ventilation once the treatment cycle is completed to remove any residual chemicals or fumes. Fans may be used to direct contaminated air out through doors and windows. Care must be taken that the area designated for fumigation is well away from staff, offices, or casual traffic. A location specifically designated for archival fumigation will expedite future treatments, and also begin to incorporate this function in the minds of administrators as a necessary archival procedure.

Thymol has been commonly recommended in the conservation literature for treating mold-infested books and documents. Thymol is now known to pose serious health hazards and is no longer recommended. The chemical o-phenyl phenol is recommended as a substitute for thymol in every application (e.g., in fumigation chambers or as a mold inhibitor in paste). As a fungicide, o-phenyl phenol is twenty times more effective than thymol, is much less toxic, and is also cheaper and readily available.[17] Fumigation chambers employing o-phenyl phenol are capable of treating mold on a small scale (several volumes or a number of documents at a time) rather than large collections en masse. If such a chamber is to be used, it should be located in a well ventilated, isolated area, away from people, that can be exhausted to the out-of-doors after use. See Appendix B-12 for specific information on the hazards of both thymol and o-phenyl phenol, recommended precautions, and instructions for building a safe fumigation chamber.

After any fumigation cycle—no matter the process nor fumigant used—it is advisable to air materials thoroughly to rid them of any residual chemicals or fumes that could pose health hazards to staff handling collections. Documentation is also important. A fumigation record should be compiled, documenting the collection treated, the date, type of infestation, fumigant and process used, length of cycle, and operator or firm.

Freezing is another fumigation option that is now available. It is very desirable because no dangerous chemicals are involved. Freezing water-damaged records as a part of disaster recovery to inhibit mold growth is now common practice. Additional work is underway in this area to extend this method to other problems of infestation.

Photographs should never be fumigated. Because of the sensitivity of photographic emulsions to chemicals and fumes, photographic prints and negatives should not be subjected to fumigation. If photographs are mold-infested, the advice of a conservator should be sought regarding appropriate treatment.

Dry Cleaning, Washing, and Bleaching

Dirt and stains can disfigure documents and obscure text and image areas, sometimes rendering them illegible. Granular dirt that becomes imbedded in paper fibers can cause mechanical damage as fibers break down as they are flexed against the sharp cutting edges of dirt particles. Equally important, airborne solid pollutants may serve as nuclei for deteriorative chemical reactions as they settle on records. Cleaning paper documents with soft brushes and erasers will remove a great deal of loose surface dirt and keep it from becoming irretrievably imbedded in paper fibers. Surface cleaning will be successful in many instances, not only in improving the appearance of archival materials but in helping to prolong their useful life. Depending, however, upon a variety of factors, including the nature of the stain and the type of paper, some stains must be accepted as permanent damage. There are practical limits to what one should expect as a result of surface cleaning. Whether or not the results are terribly obvious to the naked eye, much good has been accomplished if dust, soot, and particulate matter have been removed from collection items. Since exposure to moisture or aqueous treatments will "set" some dirt and stains, dry

[17]Based on information received from Dr. Robert McComb, Research and Testing, Preservation Office, Library of Congress, via telephone conversation, May 19, 1983.

surface cleaning must precede wet treatments.

Washing will remove additional stains and discoloration as well as many soluble decomposition products that are present in paper as by-products of the ongoing process of deterioration. When washed, many documents appear fresh and new, and stains often disappear completely or are diminished. Water baths, which are preliminary to a number of other treatments, including some deacidification processes, are often seen as an asset because water reestablishes the hydrogen bonds that assist in holding paper fibers together. Thus, to a degree, water strengthens paper. Coated papers should never be washed, and paper containing water-soluble inks and colors should only be treated by a conservator. Wet paper is very fragile and must be supported during treatment; aqueous methods should not be attempted by untrained personnel (see Figure 10-1).

Solvents and enzymes are used to remove stains, but such treatment is generally reserved for works of art on paper rather than archival materials. Vacuum or suction tables are often used in such contexts to localize treatments and hasten the movement of solvents through paper.

Chemical bleaching will remove many stains, but it is a harsh and somewhat damaging treatment that is seldom recommended for archival records. Chemical bleaching is employed when cosmetic concerns are uppermost, as with works of art on paper. Sun bleaching is gaining credence among a number of art conservators, but, again, is not appropriate for archival materials given sheer numbers and the emphasis of archival conservation on preservation rather than restoration.

Figure 10-1. Oversized materials are especially difficult to handle during wet treatment. Here, two people carefully maneuver a wall map after washing. Photograph courtesy of the Northeast Document Conservation Center.

Deacidification

Acidity is the primary cause of paper deterioration. The acid catalyzed hydrolysis of cellulose (i.e., the aging reaction caused by acids in paper) is responsible for most of the deterioration, yellowing, and embrittlement of the paper found in archival and library collections. Recalling the pH scale (which ranges from 0 to 14), paper with a pH of 7.0 is neutral. Numbers below 7.0 represent increasing acidity, while numbers above this point represent increasing alkalinity. The degree of acidity increases by ten times for each whole unit decrease in pH below 7.0. A number of deacidification procedures have been developed that will bring paper from the acid state to one of alkalinity.[18] Deacidification processes are designed to neutralize the acids present in paper and deposit an alkaline buffer or reserve that will inhibit its return to the acidic state. The ideal deacidification procedure would allow mass treatment of archival materials, would be inexpensive, and would pose no dangers to people or papers. Much work has been done to develop a procedure that meets all of these requirements, and while many advances have been made, a practical mass process is not presently available. Deacidification processes are classified according to the method by which the neutralizing and buffering agents are introduced: aqueous (water), non-aqueous (non-water solvent), and vapor. Each has particular advantages and disadvantages.

William J. Barrow, an early leader in the field of paper research, developed an aqueous process of deacidification which is now known as the "Barrow two-step process." With this method, paper is generally first washed in a water bath. It is then immersed in a saturated solution of calcium hydroxide to neutralize the acid. Next, the paper is bathed in a saturated solution of calcium bicarbonate. This bath carbonates the residual calcium hydroxide that would otherwise harm paper, and deposits a calcium carbonate buffer. The aqueous Barrow two-step process also washes away stains resulting from prior use and aging, thus improving the appearance of many papers.

A one-step aqueous process was developed by James Gear and colleagues at the National Archives. This process involves a single soaking of paper in a solution of magnesium bicarbonate. The most common preparation technique is to bubble carbon dioxide through a suspension of magnesium hydroxide in water for two hours, let the residue settle, and decant the clear liquid. The resulting liquid is a saturated solution of magnesium bicarbonate. This one-solution process is less complex than the Barrow two-solution process; it, too, removes some of the aging stains in paper. In addition, the magnesium ions provide some protection against oxidative attack and foxing.

Aqueous deacidification methods, when properly conducted, are very effective, but they require special skills and are relatively labor intensive and thus expensive. Only single sheets may be treated, thus bound materials must be disbound, treated, and then rebound, which adds considerably to the cost of deacidifying them. Aqueous treatments are obviously not appropriate for materials containing water-soluble inks and colors; all questionable or unknown inks must be tested for solubility before treatment.

Non-aqueous deacidification processes use organic solvents rather than water as the solvent carrier of the alkaline buffering agent. Richard D. Smith, of Wei T'o® Associates, developed the most generally accepted process of non-aqueous deacidification. The original Wei T'o® deacidification process used magnesium methoxide dissolved in methanol and a chlorofluorohydrocarbon solvent. The solution initially forms magnesium hydroxide to neutralize the acid. The magnesium hydroxide subsequently combines with carbon dioxide from the air to form magnesium carbonate which is the same buffering agent as used in the one-step aqueous process. Improved non-aqueous deacidification solutions containing methoxy magnesium methyl carbonate and ethoxy magnesium ethyl carbonate are now available. Wei T'o® solutions can be applied to paper by spraying, dipping, soaking, or brushing; bound materials may be treated by spraying or brushing, making disbinding unnecessary. Before application, inks and colors should be tested for solubility in the solution. Wei T'o solutions should be used either in a fume hood or in a well-ventilated area, with the operator wearing a respirator and goggles.

A vapor phase deacidification process developed by W. H. Langwell in England initially seemed to be promising because of its ease and simplicity of application, and the fact that it could be carried out on a mass scale with negligible equipment costs. The process involved interleaving books and boxed documents with treated sheets from which an alkaline vapor evolved that raised their pH to an acceptable level. Interleaving sheets were saturated with volatile cyclohexlamine carbonate

---

[18]The term "deacidification" as commonly used encompasses those processes that neutralize acids in paper and deposit an alkaline reserve. However, it is a general and imprecise term that is not accepted by chemists. During sessions of the Deacidification Discussion Group held at the 1983 annual meeting of the American Institute for Conservation, the terms neutralization and alkalinization were proposed to replace deacidification. If the new terminology is adopted, "deacidified" papers will come to be known as "alkalized papers." This proposal is part of the overall trend toward developing a more precise terminology, and yet another area in which archivists must keep current.

(CHC), an organic chemical related to ammonia. Unfortunately, these vapor-phase deacidification sheets produce toxic vapors that do not have a permanent effect, and do not leave an alkaline buffer. Because their use would pose a health hazard, CHC-impregnated sheets are not recommended.

Other mass deacidification processes are in various stages of development. Smith developed a mass deacidification process for the Public Archives/National Library of Canada using liquefied gas, which has proved successful. Bound volumes are being treated with no discernible change in appearance. Cost per volume is approximately $4. This Wei T'o® system, though planned as a pilot process, is capable of treating 5,000 volumes per week if operated on a twenty-four hour per day basis.

The Library of Congress is working to perfect a vapor process using diethyl zinc. A vacuum chamber is required and experiments have been undertaken in cooperation with the National Aeronautics and Space Administration. It is projected that once the system is operational, the cost per volume will range between $3 and $5. Given the complexity and hazards of working with diethyl zinc (which is pyrophoric), and great equipment costs, this process will probably never be available in individual repositories. It does, however, hold great promise for regional conservation centers and cooperative conservation programs.

When embarking on any in-house program to deacidify archival materials, a number of factors must be evaluated. Initial set-up costs must be considered for equipment and supplies (such as sinks, drying racks, a fume hood, and chemicals), depending upon the system or systems to be employed and future plans. Equally important, staff must be properly trained. It is not enough to read articles or instruction sheets; there are simply too many things that cannot be conveyed in writing (e.g., how to deal with a variety of weak papers, fugitive inks, and dangerous chemicals). The safety of neither employees nor of records should be placed in jeopardy through the application of treatments that are not thoroughly understood. While extended training is not easy to obtain, internships with established conservation laboratories are sometimes possible. An experienced consultant also could be employed to review needs and systems, and to set up an in-house training program. The importance of proper training cannot be minimized. Things can and do go wrong when undertaking any conservation treatment. Qualified personnel will be able to anticipate problems and respond quickly in the face of imminent danger to materials. Testing is always required to ensure that the water or solvent used will not cause inks or colors to fade, feather, or completely disappear. Testing the pH of the paper before and after treatment is also necessary, first to determine if treatment is required, and then, if undertaken, to determine if it was successful.

Deacidification is generally not seen as necessary unless the pH of the paper falls below 6.0. This is largely a practical matter, given the masses of material with a much lower pH, which are thus in more desperate condition. For example, paper with a pH of 4.0 is 100 times more acidic than paper with a pH of 6.0. Neutralization and buffering processes should raise the pH of paper to the alkaline range, generally between 8.5 and 9.5. There is some concern regarding the problem of excessive alkalinity, although this issue is yet to be resolved by research.

While deacidification will stabilize, extend the useful life, and sometimes improve the appearance of paper records, it cannot restore life to brittle records. Following deacidification, appropriate methods of support may be required to render brittle documents usable.

Mending, Reinforcement, and Support

Mending documents with long-fiber Japanese paper and a starch adhesive is a time-tested way of repairing tears and breaks in paper, especially works of art on paper. Japanese paper is strong and starch adhesives are readily reversible. It is necessary, however, to build up skills in order to use this technique satisfactorily. Also, some papers are more amenable than others to long-fiber mending. Very brittle papers may be too weak to accept even the most gossamer of Japanese paper, while heavy coated sheets may be too stiff and board-like and offer a surface that is somewhat unaccepting of the Japanese paper. One of the benefits of mending with long-fiber Japanese paper is the tendency of the fibers almost to disappear on the surfaces on which they are placed; this will be less likely on slick modern or colored papers. Brittle papers that are essentially shattered into pieces are generally best reassembled using a different mending or support technique. While mending with Japanese paper can be somewhat time-consuming, strong, long-lasting, and safe repairs can be achieved using this method.

Voids and holes in paper may be successfully filled with paper pulp. This is done either by hand or with a leaf-casting machine. The latter works on a very simple principle and may be used either to fill in missing pieces of a document or to form custom "handmade" paper to the desired weight, color, and texture, which can then be used for mending and repair purposes. A document to be repaired on a leaf caster is placed on a screen above a tank containing the proper formulation of paper pulp and water. Through creation of a vacuum under the screen, the pulp is pulled down and deposited in the holes in the paper. In effect, paper is formed within the void of the sheet being repaired. Skill and experience are required to match paper pulp with the document to be repaired. The technique is time-consuming for single sheets and is currently being used primarily on items of high individual value. The process is most useful where there are multiple sheets of paper with similar characteristics. Once a reasonable pulp match is made, many sheets can be repaired quickly by the leaf-casting technique.

Mending with heat-set tissue is another alternative. Thin tissue paper is impregnated with a stable synthetic resin that softens and adheres when heated (to a much lower degree than that required for cellulose acetate lamination). The heat-set tissue is torn into narrow strips, which are then adhered over tears using a teflon-coated tacking iron. Such mends are reversible with mild solvents. While heat-set tissue is generally quick and easy to use, it is sometimes difficult to make it adhere properly. Heat-set tissue is especially suitable for some modern papers that are not amenable to repair with long-fiber Japanese paper because of their weight, texture, or coatings. Repairs using Japanese paper and starch paste, however, are generally preferred for mending materials of value. If heat-set tissue is to be used, the tissue recommended for archival purposes is that developed by the Library of Congress. It may be purchased commercially from Bookmakers (see supply list, Appendix F, for address).

A number of pressure-sensitive mending tapes are now available which are advertised to be of archival quality, acid-free, non-yellowing, and reversible. The limited experience with them to date suggests that these claims may not be entirely accurate. Until independent testing either confirms or refutes manufacturers' claims, it is recommended that these products not be used on materials of permanent value. It should go without saying that pressure-sensitive tapes designed for home and office use should never be used on archival materials, despite manufacturers' claims.

Tissuing and silking are two methods of reinforcing paper that are of interest primarily for historical reasons. Silk or tissue is attached with a starch paste to the back of the document, and sometimes to both back and front. Silk was popular because of its transparency, but it went out of favor when it was determined that its useful life (thirty to fifty years) was far too short a period for archival treatments. When done properly, tissuing is practically invisible and provides safe, durable reinforcement. Much skill in the application of the tissue is required, however, to ensure that documents will not later curl. While some oversized materials, such as maps and architectural drawings, are sometimes backed with strong Japanese paper, tissuing per se is no longer common. It has been replaced by other less costly and more easily applied means of providing reinforcement.

Heat-sealing lamination is a method of reinforcing paper that has been in use since the late 1930s. It was developed initially by the National Archives, though later refinements were added by the Barrow Research Laboratory. Documents are laminated in a "sandwich" layered in the following sequence: tissue, cellulose acetate, document, cellulose acetate, and tissue. Through the application of high heat and heavy pressure, the cellulose acetate is fused into the paper. In the lamination process developed at the National Archives, heat (approximately 300° F for about two minutes) and pressure are applied simultaneously to the "sandwich" using a large hydraulic flat-bed press. Later, Barrow developed a press using a pair of rollers. The "sandwich" is heated to 300° F for approximately twenty seconds, then is automatically fed between the rollers to form the lamination. The end-product of both processes is a thickened, plastic-like document with a somewhat frosted appearance. The original character of the document is, for all practical purposes, permanently altered. Legibility is generally not a problem, although light or faded inks may be more difficult to read.

Paper must be deacidified before lamination. Early examples of laminated paper that were not deacidified exhibit evidence of accelerated deterioration, in large measure the result of cellulose hydrolysis caused by the processing heat. In addition, the cellulose acetate is affected by the degradation products of paper, causing further breakdown of the entire lamination structure. Cellulose acetate is a permeable plastic film that will allow air to penetrate the document after lamination. Thus, acidic gaseous pollutants are able to adversely affect laminated documents that have not been neutralized and buffered.

There are a number of disadvantages associated with cellulose acetate lamination: (1) The heat and pressure involved in the process may be harmful to paper. (2) Further, not only will laminated paper continue to deteriorate, but the laminating materials themselves may deteriorate independently and may be adversely affected by the decomposition products of the paper. Thus, the entire system can become embrittled and eventually break down. (3) Reversing lamination is difficult at best, and is sometimes impossible. The solvents required to reverse the process may be damaging to paper and inks, and the time often required to reverse lamination is so great as to render it impractical. (4) The equipment needed is costly.

The advantages of heat-sealing lamination are: (1) The process lends itself to mass production. (2) The document is mechanically well-protected.

The selection of the proper laminating film is most important. The cellulose acetate should have the following characteristics: (1) the film must be stable, (2) it must remain flexible and resistant to abrasion, (3) it must be thin but have substantial strength, (4) it must be completely transparent, and (5) it must contain no additives or plasticizers that could migrate to the document and cause damage.

In the past, cellulose acetate lamination has often been applied indiscriminately as the only treatment option. Records were laminated that should not have been either because their condition did not warrant it, or because unique features of the paper were not considered. For example, the heat and pressure applied during the laminating process will flatten engravings and prints as well as any embossed seals. Once laminated, the authenticity of documents cannot be determined by physical means since paper fibers, watermarks, and inks can no longer be examined.

Despite the problems with lamination, there is a place for it in archival conservation treatment programs. There are some instances—as with shattered, brittle paper that is beyond traditional mending—when it is the only viable cost-effective solution. When used judiciously and done properly, cellulose acetate lamination can provide protection for the safe handling of fragile materials for reasonable periods of time. It is not recommended, however, for use on materials of high intrinsic value.

Polyester encapsulation is a relatively new, simple process developed at the Library of Congress. With this method of support, single documents are enclosed between two pieces of polyester, which are then sealed around the four edges with stable double-coated tape. Static electricity holds the documents in place within the capsule. Papers with loosely adhered pigments, such as pastels, charcoal, and some watercolors, should not be encapsulated because the static charge could lift or alter the media. There are a number of variations on this basic procedure, and machines that seal polyester capsules using ultrasonic welding or electromagnetic radiation are now available. Despite improvements in the method of constructing and sealing the capsules, however, the original principle remains unchanged. Polyester, a chemically and dimensionally stable inert plastic, provides the support. (Only polyester film containing no plasticizers, surface coatings, UV inhibitors or absorbents should be used.) Unlike cellulose acetate, it is not affected by the degradation products of paper. No adhesives or impregnates come into contact with the paper, thus its original character is not changed. Further, the process is easily reversed by simply cutting away the capsule.

Polyester encapsulation provides physical support but has no affect on the chemical stability of the paper. Therefore, as paper will continue to deteriorate after encapsulation, it is recommended that paper be deacidified before encapsulation if at all possible. If deacidification is not feasible, however, polyester encapsulation will still provide protection for brittle, heavily used, or valuable documents. Because it is stable, easily reversed, and introduces no harmful products into paper, polyester encapsulation is preferred over cellulose acetate lamination as a means of providing long-term protection for archival materials requiring support.

Both lamination and polyester encapsulation provide physical support and protection for documents, allowing them to be handled and flexed without danger of mechanical damage (i.e., breaking or tearing). Following these treatments, however, documents must still be protected from the hazards of a hostile environment: excessive heat and moisture, light, and polluted air. Manuscript ink, for example, will fade under exposure to strong light whether or not the document has been encapsulated or laminated.

11   Setting Up a Preservation Workshop

A work space should be set aside specifically for carrying out preservation treatments; it should be physically separated from areas where other archival functions are carried out. The workshop may be an entire room or a designated space within the archives processing area. The latter is entirely satisfactory as an initial step. What is important is that some space be set aside for hands-on conservation activity. The establishment of a work area represents the adoption of a positive conservation attitude and, as such, can be a useful tool in furthering the program, training staff, and convincing administrators of the value of a treatment program by the quality of work turned out. Simple procedures properly undertaken in-house will be far less expensive than sending the same work to an outside conservation laboratory.

A space measuring approximately nine feet by twelve feet provides a workable amount of space for a preservation workshop in which one or two people can work comfortably. However, less space—such as that surrounding a modest-sized worktable—will suffice if a larger area cannot be allocated initially. In general, though, it is best to start with sufficient space to permit flexibility and future expansion. Better laboratory practice is achieved when there is ample space for manipulation and placement of materials. In allocating new space or renovating existing quarters, future treatment and equipment needs should be considered so that the designated space, electrical outlets, and plumbing can accommodate a fume hood, sinks, and similar requirements.

The space selected for the preservation workshop must be secure. Archival materials will be in the shop for varying periods of time awaiting or undergoing treatment, and they must be as secure there as if they were in storage. Also, any document being worked on —perhaps being cleaned or mended—should not be subjected to unauthorized handling or examination by staff members who might be fascinated by the craft aspects of conservation treatment. Further, many people are intrigued by the tools and paraphernalia found in a preservation workshop—beautiful brushes and curious-looking metal implements, for example. These, too, must be protected against handling and casual borrowing.

Security is thus important to protect archival materials while they are in the workshop, to inhibit interruption of treatments, and to prevent tools and supplies from disappearing. If the preservation workshop is to be situated in a separate room, it should be fitted with locks to allow access limited to conservation personnel, the supervising archivist, and/or the preservation officer. If a preservation work area is to be carved out of existing space in the processing area, efforts should be made to place it outside of the main flow of staff traffic. Also, all staff should be warned against the damage that could result if any work in progress were disturbed.

The preservation workshop should be well illuminated. Natural daylight is often an advantage when doing careful work; if there are windows, however, they must be covered with ultraviolet-filtering sheets. Overhead fluorescent lights should be outfitted with UV filters as well. Supplemental light may be provided by incandescent adjustable lamps, which may be clamped to the edges of tables; these provide good direct illumination for close work.

Good working surfaces are another requirement in a preservation workshop. The number of tables or work stations will depend upon the number of staff expected to carry out treatments. At a minimum, however, a large sturdy table approximately four feet by six feet should be secured. This will allow one person to work on most formats found in the collection. The tabletop should be covered with Formica, which can be easily cleaned; if Formica cannot be acquired, a smooth wooden top treated with several coats of polyurethane varnish would also provide a suitable, easy to clean surface. Slotted steel angle-iron can be used for legs and the

support framework of work and auxiliary tables. The height of the table should allow individuals to work either in a standing position (which is most comfortable for many people, and necessary when working on large items), or sitting on a stool. If possible, the table should be situated to allow one to walk completely around it; again, this is an asset when working on oversized materials. It will be helpful if electrical outlets are built into the table on the two long sides, situated just under the tabletop. It is advisable to take advantage of the space underneath the table for storing supplies that must be kept flat (such as paper and mat board). The table may be outfitted with a range of shallow shelves; drawers to hold small tools and supplies also may be incorporated into the system. It is generally most economical to have a table built to individual specifications, taking into account the procedures to be undertaken in the shop, the number of staff involved, and the limitations imposed by the space. In addition to the worktable, it is helpful to have several smaller tables or countertops in the area where materials awaiting treatment or supplies may be placed to keep the worktable clear.

It is advisable, but not absolutely necessary, in the early stages of developing a treatment program, to have a sink and running water in the work area. Hands must be washed often when carrying out treatments so as not to soil archival materials, and water is also necessary for tasks such as making paste, washing brushes and implements, and wet-tearing Japanese mending paper.

The preservation workshop must be kept scrupulously clean at all times. Eating, smoking, and drinking should be forbidden. Debris and dirt resulting from carrying out treatments should not be allowed to accumulate, and tabletops and work surfaces should be cleaned as often as necessary. Tools and equipment also must be kept clean and in good working order. Brushes should be washed with a neutral soap (such as Orvus®) and hung to dry with bristles downward. Small holes may be drilled in brush handles, through which threads or cords can be looped to form hangers. Any metal equipment, such as book presses and the bed or frame of cutting shears, should be kept rust-free. If such equipment is rusty, a good cleaning with 4/0 dry steel wool followed by painting with a rustproofing paint is recommended. Blades on board shears or paper cutters obviously should not be painted. They should, however, be sharpened professionally at the first sign of dullness.

The appearance of the preservation workshop and the condition of the tools will convey a great deal about the approach taken to conservation within the institution. It is not likely that high-quality work will be produced in a workshop that is cluttered and dirty; in fact, archival materials might well be endangered in such a setting. On the other hand, good work and adherence to high standards are encouraged in surroundings that are neat, clean, and well organized. The relationship between conservation and craft may be seen in this context as well. Tools become an extension of the worker's hand, and tools that are kept clean and in good working order will help to get the job done right. The care expended on tools is very obvious and also contributes to the overall aura of the preservation workshop. Each worker should have a set of hand tools, both to encourage proper care and handling and because everyone uses tools somewhat differently and they quickly become personalized.

The layout of the workshop, whether it is a compact space in the processing area or a separate room, should allow for an efficient flow of work. Thus, all of the treatments to be carried out should be analyzed from the perspectives of their space requirements and necessary supplies. A good stock of supplies for all treatment procedures should be kept close at hand in cabinets or on shelves, while excess supplies may be kept in auxiliary storage. All conservation supplies should be kept clean and stored in an area that is cool, dry, and away from light. Depending upon access to the workshop by non-conservation personnel, it may be desirable to keep supplies in locked cabinets. Paper supplies and mat board, which must be stored flat, either may be stored in map cases or, as suggested above, on shelves constructed under worktables. Polyester may be easily dispensed using rolls that may be mounted on table tops, from wall mounts, or on shelves above the work surface. Pegboards may be hung on walls to hold brushes, rulers, and small tools.

Appropriate treatments to be undertaken initially in the preservation workshop include the following: humidification of rolled or folded documents, removal of foreign objects and harmful accretions (rusty metal fasteners, fly specks, etc.), surface cleaning, testing of surface pH and ink solubility, mending with long-fiber Japanese paper, polyester encapsulation, disassembly of framed units, treatment of leather bound volumes, and phased box construction. Instructions for these basic procedures are provided in Appendix B.

The supplies and equipment listed below are required to outfit a preservation workshop in which these basic procedures will be undertaken. Supplies and equipment are briefly described as to use (when not obvious); the quantity specified is based on the assumption that one person will be working in the facility. Bargain-priced tools are seldom a good investment and will cost more over a period of time in terms of replacement costs and unsatisfactory performance. Specialized hand-tools such as bone folders, paste brushes, microspatulas, and scalpels are generally satisfactory when purchased from a conservation supplier. High-quality common hand tools such as hammers, pliers, and utility knives should be purchased as well. The Sears, Roebuck and Co. line of Craftsman® tools is one excellent brand.

Suggested amounts of paper and other supplies will suffice for the initial set-up and also will go a long way in treating collections. The rate at which such expendable products will have to be replaced will depend on the amount and rate of work carried out. A repository may wish to set up treatment capabilities for one or two basic procedures, such as surface cleaning and polyester encapsulation. In such instances, it is possible to set up a work space and purchase supplies to accommodate only these tasks; additional procedures may be added at a later date as time, space, and staff capability permit. Sources of equipment and supplies are listed in Appendix F.

Equipment	*Quantity*
Table (4' x 6', with Formica top and storage shelves underneath)	1
Stool (wooden; legs may be cut to desired height)	1
Lights (clamp-on, adjustable, with incandescent bulbs)	2
Paper cutter (heavy-duty, tabletop, blade between 30″ and 36″)	1
Storage cabinet (metal, with shelves)	1
Vacuum cleaner (portable, tank type with wand receiver)	1
Equipment—optional	
Book dryer/exterminator	1
Book press (nipping press; minimum platen size: 14″ x 18″)	1
Encapsulating machine	1
Plastic garbage cans with lids (for use as a humidification chamber; one large and one small in one of the following combinations: 45 gal. and 20 gal. or 32 gal. and 10 gal.)	2

Hand Tools	Use	Quantity
Air bulb	surface cleaning	1
Bone folders (pointed for scoring, rounded for pressing and rubbing; not plastic)	mending; phased box construction	2
Brayer	encapsulation	1
Brushes		
paste (¼″ and 1″ diameter)	mending	2
surface cleaning		3
Chisel, round	phased box construction	1
Eye dropper	pH testing	1
Hammer	phased box construction	1
Knives, utility or mat with disposable blades (such as Stanley knife, No. 299 or 691)	phased box construction, cutting mats	2
Magnifier, Linen Tester (5x)	examination and manipulation	1
Microspatula (stainless steel)	mending, lifting	2
Needles (No. 3 darning)	tearing Japanese paper	1 packet
Pliers, nipping	disassembling frames	1
Punch, leather hole	phased box construction	1
Ruler (stainless steel)	measuring, wet-tearing Japanese paper	1
Ruling pen	Wet-tearing Japanese paper	1
Scalpel handle, #4		2
Scalpel blades, #23	cutting, lifting	4 dozen
Scissors, small and large		1 each
Staple remover		1
Straight edge (heavy stainless steel; aluminum tends to shave off when cutting against it)	cutting mat board	1
Triangle, metal	phased box construction	1
Tweezers	mending, removing foreign objects	1

Supplies	Use	Quantity
Absorene® wallpaper cleaner	surface cleaning	1 dozen 15-oz. boxes
Barrow Laboratory Paper Test Kit (or Tri-Test Spot Testing Kit)	determine presence of alum, groundwood, and acidity	1
Cotton swabs	testing ink solubility	2 boxes
EM Laboratory colorpHast® Indicator Sticks (non-bleeding, 0–14 range, 0–6.0 range)	testing surface pH	1 box each
Erasers		
Magic Rub®, vinyl (Faber Castell #1954, block type)	surface cleaning	1 dozen
Magic Rub® peel-off pencil	surface cleaning	2
Gloves, white cotton knit	surface cleaning	2 dozen

Grid	polyester encapsulation	1
"Lig-free"® board (.040 and .060 thick; pH 8.5-9.2)	phased box construction	20 boards
Linen tape (1 inch x 300 yards)	mat construction	1 roll
Mat board (with an alkaline reserve)		10 boards
Methyl cellulose	mending	1 lb.
Mounting corners (polyester)	mounting for exhibition	5 boxes
Neat's-foot oil and lanolin	leather treatment	1 gallon
One-Wipe® treated dust cloths	dusting	2 dozen
Opaline® dry cleaning pads	surface cleaning	2 dozen
Orvus®	cleaning brushes	1 quart
Paper		
Blotting paper, white (32″ x 40″, neutral pH)	drying	100 sheets
Bond (letter- or legal-sized, pH 8.5)	interleaving, photocopying	5 reams
Japanese mending paper		
—Tengujo	mending	10 sheets
—Kozo	mending	10 sheets
—Sekishu	mending, hinging	10 sheets
Silicone release paper	mending	20 sheets
Tissue (neutral pH)	wrapping	1 roll
Plate glass (32″ x 40″ x ½″)	flattening, drying	2 pieces
Polyester film (Mylar® Type D, Melinex® Type 516, or Scotchpar® Industrial Grade)	encapsulation	
—3-mil, 10″ x 12″		500 sheets
—5-mil		1 roll
Polyester web (40″ wide)	mending	1 yard
Polyethylene (buttons, 1″ diameter, 1/16″ thick, cut from sheets)	phased box construction	10 sheets
Potassium lactate solution	leather treatment	1 gallon
Rivets (ca. 5/16″ head)	phased box construction	2 packages
Skum-X® (Dietzgen)	surface cleaning	3 one-pound containers
Tape, double coated (3M Scotch Brand® #415, ¼″ wide)	encapsulation	10 rolls
Thread, heavy linen	phased box construction	1 spool
Wheat paste, dry powder #301	mending	2 lbs.
Wheat starch, Aytex-P	mending	2 lbs.

Miscellaneous

Adhesive containers (glass jars with tight-fitting lids)

Cloths, soft (cheesecloth or old terry towels)

Waste paper (unprinted newsprint, for pasting out; used once and discarded)

Weights may be made by covering bricks with kraft paper or bookcloth, or filling small containers with lead shot. Small metal weights are also available from metal or printing supply houses. Bottoms of weights should be covered with felt or blotting paper to provide cushioning; as they become soiled, these coverings should be replaced.

The start-up cost for setting up a preservation workshop will vary depending upon the range of procedures to be implemented and whether or not any equipment or supplies are already available in the institution. Archives within a college or university should explore the possibility of procuring supplies on an at-cost basis from departments that may utilize similar laboratory supplies and equipment. Many of the miscellaneous items can be acquired free or at little expense. The cost of setting up a preservation workshop should be included in the conservation budget; many expenditures represent one-time costs, while expendable supplies such as paper and boards will have to be included in the budget on a yearly basis. Experience with the amount of work produced within a given period will help to determine appropriate replacement rates for various supplies.

Appendix A
Glossary

acid

A chemical compound having a pH below 7.0 and capable of neutralizing alkalis. Acids damage paper and other organic substances by weakening their molecular bonds. In paper, this results in yellowing and brittleness. Acid is present in paper as a result of impure groundwood pulp, alum-rosin sizing and other additives introduced during the papermaking process, and atmosphere pollutants.

acid migration

The ability of acid to transfer from an acidic material to a less or non-acidic material. This takes place either through direct physical contact or through vapor action if acidic and less or non-acidic items are stored in the same container.

alkali

A base substance having a pH above 7.0 and capable of neutralizing acids.

alkaline reserve

Buffer or reserve of an alkaline substance added to paper to counteract acid. Usually 3 percent precipitated calcium or magnesium carbonate by weight of paper.

alum

Aluminum sulphate; sometimes known as papermaker's alum. Alum is used in combination with rosin to size papers; it helps the fibers to retain the size and also aids in dispersing the paper fibers in the vat. Alum is acidic when dissolved in water and is a primary source of acid in paper.

archival quality

Imprecise term pertaining to materials (generally supplies) that carries the connotation of permanence and high quality. Also used in the context of various processes, such as film processing. The term must be backed up with precise chemical and physical specifications.

board

Refers to mat board, binders board, etc. Thicker and heavier than paper stock, generally at least .012 inches thick. The term also refers to book covers.

cellulose

Complex carbohydrate; chief component of the cell walls of plants, wood, etc. Primary component of paper.

cellulose acetate

Clear, hard, and glossy acetate salt of cellulose. Used in heat sealing lamination and also as a film base. A hygroscopic material.

chain lines

In handmade paper, parallel watermark lines about one inch apart that correspond to the chain wires on a paper mold. The chain wires are slightly thicker than the laid wires, which run perpendicular and are attached to them. Chain lines are visible when held up to transmitted light, and generally run parallel with the grain direction. They are often simulated on machine-made paper.

chemical wood pulp

Paper pulp made by cooking wood chips with sulfate, sulfite, or soda to remove lignin. After cooking, the pulp is washed to remove the processing chemicals and other impurities. Permanent papers and boards can be made from chemical wood pulp.

coated paper

Paper with surface coatings (adhesives, clay, mineral pigments, etc.) to give it a smooth hard surface suitable for printing.

cockle

Pucker or wrinkle in paper, vellum, or other material, generally caused by high humidity or wetting. Also caused by nonuniform drying or shrinking.

deckle

Wooden frame (removable top half of paper mold) that confines the paper fibers when the paper mold is dipped into a vat of slurry. A deckle edge is formed around the four sides of a sheet of handmade paper as a result of paper fibers slipping between the deckle and frame of the mold. The deckle edge appears irregular and somewhat feathery; it is often produced artificially in machine-made paper. On a paper machine, the deckle is the rubber apron or restraint that confines the pulp as it flows on the moving screen.

durable   Degree to which paper retains original strength during sustained use.

emulsion   Image-bearing layer in photography. Photosensitive composition consisting generally of light-sensitive silver halides suspended in gelatin, coating surface of paper, film, etc.

footcandle   Term used in measuring light. One footcandle equals the illumination produced when the light from a point source of one candle falls on a source one foot away from the candle.

foxing   Small, usually brownish spots appearing on paper; attributed to action of fungi on trace metal (iron) in paper under humid conditions.

glassine   A dense, glazed, semi-transparent paper often used to make envelopes and sleeves for storing photographic negatives. Usually acidic.

grain direction   Direction in which most of the fibers in machine-made papers are aligned. Fibers tend to align in the direction the mat of fibers is moving on the papermaking machine. Paper tears more readily with than across the grain; when dampened, paper will stretch across the grain. Grain direction is generally parallel with chain lines. An easy way to determine grain direction is to gently fold a piece of paper (without creasing it) in somewhat of a bouncing motion, first across and then with its length. The direction in which it most easily folds or flexes is the grain direction. Handmade papers generally have a negligible grain direction.

groundwood pulp   Also known as mechanical wood pulp. Groundwood pulp is created by mechanical means only; it retains all of the impurities of wood (including lignin). Groundwood pulp paper is weak, impermanent, and acidic, and discolors upon exposure to light and air. Newsprint is the most common example of ground-wood pulp paper.

hydrolysis   Chemical action involving water. Decomposition in which a compound is split into other compounds by taking up the elements of water.

hygroscopic   Ability of a material to absorb or emit moisture in response to changes in the relative humidity.

intrinsic value   Term used to define or describe the qualities of archival materials. Records have varying degrees of intrinsic value based on such factors as uniqueness or value of informational content, age, physical format, artistic or aesthetic qualities, and scarcity. Determination of intrinsic value is closely linked to decisions regarding preservation and physical treatment. Materials having high intrinsic value generally warrant preservation in their original format, while records designated as having little or no intrinsic value often can be copied to preserve informational content.

laid lines   In handmade paper, closely-spaced parallel watermark lines that are visible when paper is held up to transmitted light. Created by the laid wires on a paper mold, which are perpendicular and attached to the chain wires. Laid lines are sometimes simulated on machine-made paper.

lightfast   Ability of a material to resist fading upon exposure to light.

lignin   Naturally occurring organic acid found in wood. A major cause of acidity in paper. Lignin is removed during chemical but not mechanical pulping.

mold   Microscopic vegetable plants that develop from spores (that are always present in the air) under conditions of high temperature and high relative humidity.

A paper mold is a rectangular wooden frame upon which the chain and laid wires are stretched. When dipped into a vat of slurry, water drains through the wires and the mat of fibers rests on the frame. The deckle sits on top of the mold and serves as the frame or surround, which restrains the paper fibers.

neutral Exhibiting neither acid nor base (alkaline) qualities; 7.0 on the pH scale.

oxidation Chemical reaction that converts an element into its oxide; to combine with oxygen.

pH scale Measurement used to describe hydrogen ion concentration. Scale ranges from 0 to 14, with 7.0 the point of neutrality. Numbers below 7.0 signify increasing acidity, while numbers ranging above 7.0 signify increasing alkalinity. The scale is logarithmic, thus each whole number increase or decrease represents a ten-fold change.

permanent Degree to which paper remains chemically stable and resists deterioration from either impurities introduced during the manufacturing process or the external environment.

polyester Flexible transparent plastic sheeting made of polyethylene terephthalate. Sold under a variety of trade names, including Mylar®, Melinex®, and Scotchpar®. When formulated with no coatings or additives, it is inert and chemically stable. Used to encapsulate documents and as a film base.

polyester web Synthetic fabric made from filaments of polyethylene terephthalate. Used to support paper during aqueous treatments and also as a non-stick surface through which moisture will pass during mending, drying, etc.

pulp Raw material from which paper is made; ground, cooked, or macerated cellulose fibers suspended in water.

relative humidity The amount of water vapor in the air, expressed as a percentage of the maximum that the air could hold at a given temperature. Relative humidity (RH) is temperature dependent; generally, as the temperature increases, the RH decreases, if no additional moisture were added to the air.

size Material used in interior or surface sizing of paper to give it water and ink resistant characteristics. Sizing agents include gelatin, rosin, glue, starch, and synthetic resins.

slurry Suspension of cellulose fibers in water from which paper is made.

watermark Image or symbol formed in a sheet of paper which is visible when the paper is held up to transmitted light. In handmade paper, the watermark forms as fewer fibers settle over a raised area woven into the mold, resulting in a greater translucency of the sheet in that area. Watermarks are simulated in machine-made paper by a device known as the dandy roll that impresses a design in the wet mat of fibers.

Appendix B
Basic Conservation Procedures:
Instructions

Many of these basic procedures may be integrated into archival processing and implemented either by archivists or technicians. If no staff member is trained in these techniques, appropriate training should be sought through internships, workshops and seminars, and, if possible, consultation with a conservator. The services of a technical conservation consultant can be a worthwhile investment in the design of a workshop or in setting up an in-house training program. These means of acquiring knowledge and training may be combined with reading manuals and extensive practice on archival discards and duplicates, or other materials having no value. It should go without saying that no matter who undertakes the hands-on work, no conservation treatment should be carried out on collection items until competency is achieved. No treatment at all is better than treatment that is poorly or inappropriately executed. Someone on the archives staff, such as the preservation officer or supervising archivist, should oversee the hands-on work, specify treatments, select appropriate supplies, and monitor and evaluate the quality of the work produced.

B1. Relaxing and Flattening Documents

Paper documents that have been kept tightly rolled or folded for a period of time tend to resist unfolding and are likely to break into pieces if they are forced open or forced to lie flat. Records that resist even gentle attempts at opening should be set aside until they can be relaxed by humidification (see Figure B1-1). Such paper retains a "memory" for its rolled or folded condition, and will resist attempts to change configuration unless relaxed.

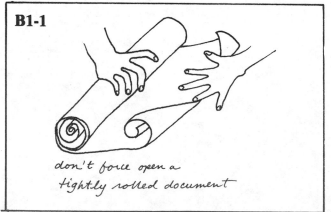

B1-1

don't force open a
tightly rolled document

Rolled or tightly folded papers are often brittle, depending upon age, type of paper, and storage conditions. The fibers of such papers have lost their natural moisture content, and any attempt to open the documents without replacing lost moisture may result in significant damage. Humidification reintroduces moisture and allows the paper fibers to move and flex without breaking. A relative humidity of between 80 and 90 percent is needed to humidify or relax documents, and a humidity chamber must be constructed that will allow materials to be exposed to this level of moisture under controlled conditions.

The exteriors of documents that have been rolled or folded for years may be quite dirty. These surfaces should be vacuumed under low pressure before humidification as moisture will set any loose surface dirt into the paper. Since records that require relaxing are likely to be quite brittle, any dusting and cleaning must be gentle; dusting with a soft brush may be all that is possible. Only the exteriors or outer surfaces should be lightly dusted or cleaned; no attempt should be made to open documents to allow further cleaning before humidification.

It is unlikely that water-soluble inks or colors will run or spread during the humidification process, since the materials do not come into direct contact with the water and the length of exposure to the humid conditions in the chamber is relatively brief. As a precaution, however, it is advisable to check any inks on the outside of rolled or folded packets for solubility in water (see Appendix B-4) before humidification. Inks that appear to be readily susceptible to water should be set aside until they can be referred to a conservator for treatment.

A humidification chamber can be fabricated out of an airtight, noncorrosive, rustproof enclosure. The easiest and most inexpensive approach is to purchase two plastic trash containers, a large one that will hold the water and a smaller one that will sit inside the large container and hold the documents to be humidified. A pair of trash containers in either of the following combinations will suffice: 45-gallon and 20-gallon, or 32-gallon and 10-gallon. A number of holes should be cut in the top of the sides of the small container to speed up circulation of the moist air. Since the holes are cut only in the top half, there is no danger of water seeping in and wetting the documents. Water, approximately two inches deep, should be placed in the bottom of the large or outer container. Sheets of blotting paper then should be placed standing upright in the water surrounding the small container to help convey the moisture up throughout the chamber. The large container must have a tight-fitting lid to keep the moisture inside the chamber; the inner container should be left open. The humid air

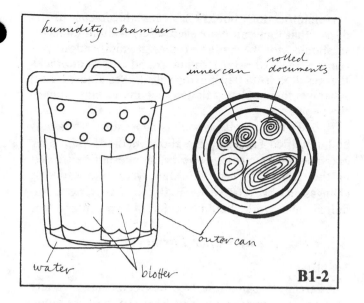

B1-2

acts as a gas and expands to fill the chamber (see Figure B1-2).

As far as possible, all strings, rubber bands, paper clips, and other metal fasteners (see Appendix B-2) should be removed from the documents to be humidified before placing them in the inner container. If long rolled documents require humidification, it is possible to increase the chamber height by inverting a second large trash can over the outer container as a lid. This effectively doubles the height of the chamber.

The humidity in the chamber will increase the moisture content of the documents and should relax the fibers so they can be opened safely without damage. The time required for this to take place will vary depending upon the type and weight of paper, degree of brittleness, how tightly the documents are rolled or folded, and the relative humidity generated within the chamber. Initially, the documents should be left in the chamber for a day and checked periodically to see whether they have relaxed enough to be safely opened. It is important not to force the documents open. It may take several days for the material to become sufficiently humidified to allow for their safe opening and flattening. During this period, the documents should be checked closely for any sign of mold growth.

A mold inhibitor should be used if the temperature in the chamber is over 70° F and materials are to be in the chamber for more than a twenty-four-hour period. Approximately one teaspoon of o-phenyl phenol should be dissolved in two to three tablespoons of ethyl alcohol, and this solution added to the water in the bottom of the outer container. Interior surfaces of the outer container can be wiped with the solution for further protection, although this should be done in a well-ventilated area, and neoprene or butyl rubber gloves should be worn.

When the documents are sufficiently humidified, they should feel pliable and exhibit little resistance to opening. It may take several days to reach this point, and it may be necessary to repeat the process at a later time if the documents have a tendency to return to the rolled position. Once removed from the humidity chamber, however, the documents must be dried between blotters and weighted under pressure to flatten them. Each document should be opened carefully on a flat, smooth surface and placed between two pieces of white blotting paper. A number of humidified documents of the same size may be layered between blotters, and then the whole stack placed under a glass weight. One-quarter-inch plate glass is ideal for the purpose, and is not overly expensive. All four edges should be sanded so the glass can be handled safely. Although somewhat heavy, a sheet of glass 32 inches by 40 inches will cover archival blotters, and its weight should be sufficient for most flattening needs. The glass allows for equal distribution of weight over the entire surface of the documents. Unless a very flat work surface is available, it may be wise to use two pieces of glass as a sandwich. If additional weights are needed, bricks covered in book cloth with a piece of felt lining the bottom as a cushion are ideal (see Figure B1-3). With oversized documents larger than the blotters and glass, it will be necessary to abut the blotters to cover the entire surface of the documents. Pieces of glass should then be abutted across the surface of the blotters to provide uniform weight.

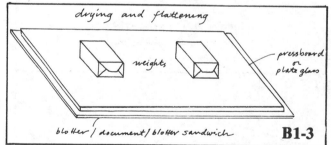

B1-3

After about fifteen minutes, the blotters should be replaced with dry, clean blotters to aid the drying process, and then the blotters should be changed at intervals of every several hours until drying is complete. The drying process is likely to take one to two days, depending upon the weight of the paper, the amount of moisture induced, and the relative humidity in the repository.

An old refrigerator also can be modified to use as a humidification chamber. Metal shelves should be replaced with a non-corrosive material, such as nylon window screening stretched on suitable wooden frames and fastened with stainless-steel staples. The rolled and folded documents can be placed on these nylon shelves. An enamel or stainless-steel tray filled with water should be placed in the bottom of the refrigerator and covered with nylon screening as a further precaution against documents falling into the water (see Figure B1-4). The refrigerator door provides a tight seal. Before use, the interior of the refrigerator should be cleaned with Lysol® (one cup of Lysol® Disinfectant in one gallon of water; rubber gloves should be worn). The humidification and drying procedure is the same as that outlined for using plastic trash containers.

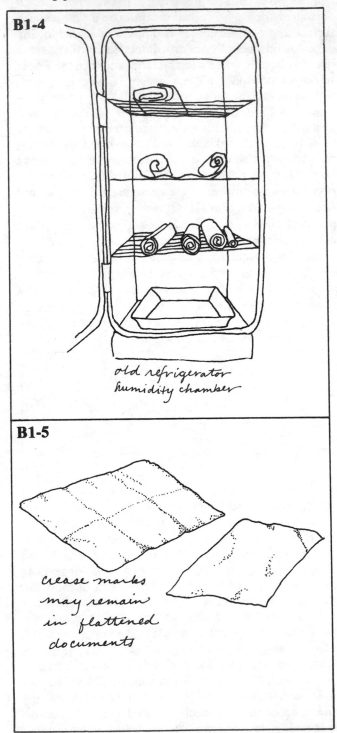

B1-4

old refrigerator
humidity chamber

B1-5

crease marks
may remain
in flattened
documents

Humidification should relax most documents to the degree that they can be opened safely without damage. It should not be expected that humidification will remove traces of prior fold marks and creases or cracks that resulted from paper being rolled. (See Figure B1-5.) Attempts to completely flatten such marks may damage the paper.

Rolled photographs as well as paper documents may be humidified following the above method. Vellum or parchment documents, however, should not be treated in this fashion. These skins are very responsive to changes in the relative humidity; if flattening is required, such work should be referred to a conservator.

B2. Removal of Paper Fasteners

Problems

As archivists can attest, records creators use a variety of innovative measures to attach related sheets of paper together. The integrity of such groupings must be respected while, at the same time, ensuring their preservation. Unfortunately, many of the means employed to attach sheets together are destructive over time.

Straight pins, staples, and paper clips often rust. Further, these and other metal attachments such as brads and clamps can serve as cutting edges against which brittle papers may break (see Figure B2-1).

Rubber bands harden and crack over time, often become encrusted on the surface of the paper, and introduce sulphur products, which can cause staining and cellulose breakdown.

String, cloth ties, and ribbons, sometimes used to hold packets of letters or dockets together, can cut into brittle papers and also can be highly acidic (see Figure B2-2). If such ties and ribbons are colored, this color may bleed onto the documents under humid conditions.

Adhesives, either dotted in corners or run in a line across the tops of sheets, may be highly acidic. If the adhesive has holding power over time and does not lose its tackiness and break down, the strong line of attachment also may serve as a cutting edge as the sheets are flexed (see Figure B2-3). Adhesives also can leave permanent stains and sometimes cause cockling.

Removal

Most metal objects may be carefully removed by hand, although extra caution will be required if the paper is brittle. (See Figure B2-4.) Some metal fasteners are so securely attached, however (such as grommets), that any effort to remove them would severely damage the surrounding paper. Such fixtures are best left in place. The use of staple removers is not generally recommended because of their tendency to tear paper; they can easily remove an entire brittle corner along with the

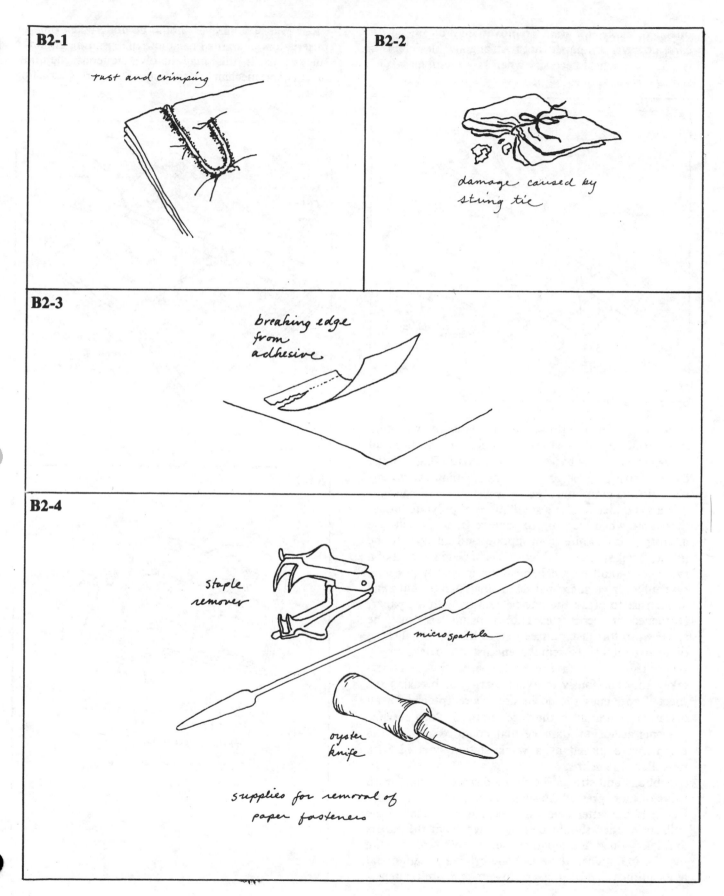

B2-1

rust and crimping

B2-2

damage caused by
string tie

B2-3

breaking edge
from
adhesive

B2-4

staple
remover

micro spatula

oyster
knife

supplies for removal of
paper fasteners

intended staple. (A staple remover may be used *with care,* however, on paper that is strong and flexible; this is often a practical necessity when faced with masses of archival records needing processing.)

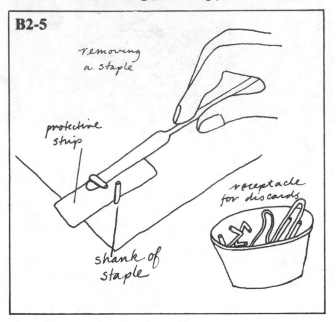

Working from the back, a microspatula may be used to carefully lift the shanks of staples or similar metal fasteners as well as paper clips (see Figure B2-5). Small oyster knives, which are less flexible than microspatulas, also serve this purpose quite well. As a precaution, it is a good idea to slip a small piece of polyester under the staple while working to remove it, to prevent the microspatula or knife from slipping and cutting into the paper. Encrusted rust, which could impede removal of a fastener, should be mechanically removed if possible, carefully using a microspatula or fingernail to chip away at the rust to break the line of contact with the paper. Hardened and encrusted rubber bands also may be removed in this fashion (see Figure B2-6). Any flicking or lifting motion to remove encrusted particles or fly specks from the surface of brittle paper must be undertaken very cautiously to avoid tearing or breaking the sheet. Paper cups should be used as receptacles for all discarded materials as they are removed. Such practice prevents accidental damage that could result if brittle papers were placed at a work station covered with miscellaneous debris.

Ribbons and strings should be discarded, along with locks of hair, pressed flowers, and the like. (See Figure B2-7.) If the latter items are deemed important to the collection, they should be segregated from the papers and maintained in a separate file. A cross-reference file may be maintained to record the original location and association value of pressed flowers and similar items.

Removal of adhesives should be undertaken only by conservators or trained personnel. Depending upon the adhesive used, this may involve aqueous methods, solvents, or mechanical techniques requiring exacting skills.

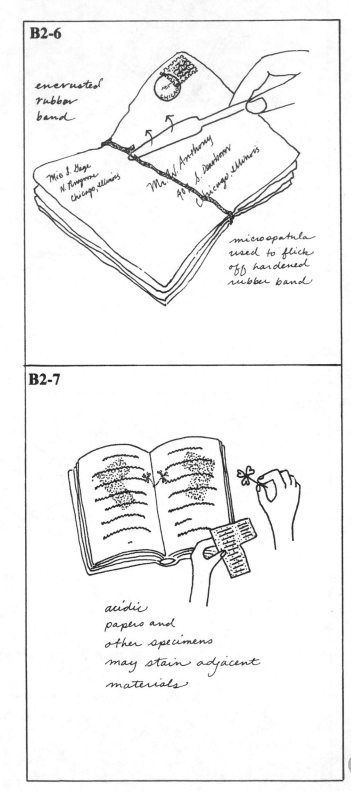

Appropriate Means of Attachment

Once damaging means of attachment have been removed, some method of maintaining the intellectual integrity or sequence of units of paper is often required.

Rust-proof staples are not recommended because they deface the material by adding holes; on brittle papers they also can function as a cutting edge. Further, during photocopying, the corners of stapled sheets may break off if the pages are folded back or, if staples are removed and replaced each time photocopying is required, a perforated line may result. Extremely brittle sheets are best left with no mechanical means of attachment; even lightweight plastic paper clips will exert too much pressure on them. Individual units may be segregated by filing them in separate folders, or separated within folders through the use of interleaving sheets. Another means of maintaining original order is to number the sheets sequentially on the backs using a soft lead (no. 2) pencil. Paper in good condition may be affixed together using paper clips made of inert plastic, although such clips do sometimes have a tendency to fly off. Another approach that has been successful is to use rust-proof stainless-steel paper clips. These are positioned on small strips or guards of paper that has an alkaline reserve (1 inch wide and 4 inches long), which are folded over the tops of the documents to support and protect them from the pressure of the clips (see Figure B2-8).

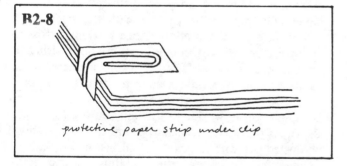

protective paper strip under clip

Photographs should never be clipped together or to other documents with any mechanical devices. The indentations left by paper clips will be permanent, and metal fasteners may crack or scratch photographic emulsions.

B3. Surface Cleaning of Paper Records

A clean work surface should be prepared and the following items assembled: brushes, crumbled erasers (Opaline® dry cleaning pads or Dietzgen's "Skum-X"®), Absorene® wallpaper cleaner, Magic Rub® block and stick vinyl erasers, cotton gloves, air bulb, weights, and blotting paper (see Figure B3-1). Soft flat brushes several inches wide (such as Oriental

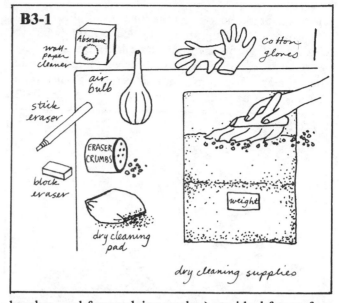

dry cleaning supplies

brushes used for applying washes) are ideal for surface cleaning; brushes with white bristles are best because it is easy to see when they become soiled. Brushes and other implements must be kept clean. It is advisable to have several brushes on hand so that a clean one is always available; dirty brushes should be washed with a neutral soap (such as Orvus®) and hung to dry. A good supply of white cotton gloves is also necessary; they should be discarded when they become dirty, although some gloves can withstand a limited number of launderings. Maintaining a clean work environment during surface cleaning is important. The time expended in periodic clean-up, removal of particles, etc., is a necessary investment.

Before beginning treatment, it is a good idea to remove jewelry (bracelets, rings, watches) that may scratch the surface of the paper or catch on paper fragments and cause tears.

Papers to be surface (i.e., dry) cleaned must be examined before treatment. Heavily coated papers (such as those often used in illustrated art books or glossy magazines) are very difficult to clean satisfactorily without leaving streak marks. Papers with edge tears or voids must be handled very carefully to avoid further damage. Extremely brittle papers cannot withstand any abrasive action. Obviously, care must be taken that the cleaning process selected does not remove or obscure penciled notations or other important non-permanent images on the paper. Pastel, pencil, charcoal, and watercolor renderings or drawings should not be cleaned using these methods; works of art on paper should be referred to a paper conservator. Photographic prints should not be subjected to these cleaning methods either. At a maximum, photographs may be gently dusted with a soft brush or air bulb; no abrasive methods should be used on the surfaces of photographs. The edges of photographic cardboard mounts may be cleaned using the methods described, but great care must be taken to avoid any abrasive action extending onto the photographs, and all eraser particles and crumbs must be removed completely. (See Figure B3-2).

B3-2

dry cleaning of photo. mount only

It is very easy to tear or otherwise weaken paper while attempting to clean it, and some stains and embedded dirt will not respond to dry cleaning techniques and must be accepted as permanent damage.

Dry cleaning should precede wet cleaning and any aqueous treatments (including mending) because the water can permanently set the dirt in the paper fibers. Stains that disfigure or obscure information and do not respond to dry cleaning methods may be referred to a conservator for washing or treatment with solvents.

The document to be cleaned should be placed on a clean piece of blotting paper and weighted to keep it from slipping (and thus possibly being damaged) during treatment. The blotting paper should be replaced as soon as it becomes soiled. Hands should be clean and cotton gloves worn to keep perspiration and oils from transferring to the document. Some people cannot work comfortably wearing gloves. If this is the case, a small square of blotting paper should be used as a "rest" for the hand that is helping to hold the document in position, and hands should be washed often to keep the working hand clean.

Treatment should begin with the least abrasive dry cleaning method and work through successively stronger methods as necessary. With all of the techniques, work should begin in the center of the paper and move out toward the edges. This will help to keep any edge tears from extending further in toward the center of the document.

First, a soft brush and crumbled eraser particles (such as Opaline® cleaner or Skum-X®) should be used to brush away loose dirt. The eraser particles will pick up

dirt that might otherwise streak or be worked into the paper fibers if a brush were used alone. A light hand with the brush will help keep dirty particles from becoming embedded in the paper. A rubber air bulb also may be used to blow away loose surface dirt and eraser crumbs. It is very important to keep eraser particles and crumbs from working themselves under the document being cleaned. (See Figure B3-3.) Any abrasive action over such hard particles could result in holes or tears being rubbed into the paper.

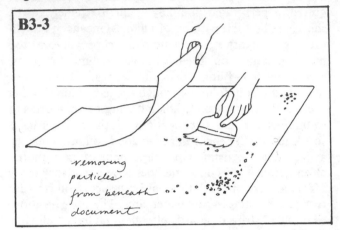

B3-3

removing particles from beneath document

The next gentlest approach is the actual working of the particles across the surface of the paper. Opaline® cleaner or Skum-X® may be sprinkled on the soiled paper and then gently rubbed with the pads of the fingers in a circular motion. Since working across the entire surface of a document can be quite tiring, an alternative is to use a Magic Rub® block eraser, instead of the fingers, in a gentle circular motion. The action of the block eraser on the Opaline® or Skum-X® crumbs is similar to the working of a ball bearing (see Figure B3-4). As the eraser particles become dirty, they should be dusted off with a clean, soft brush or air bulb. As Skum-X® particles are larger and thus easier to remove than Opaline® particles (which are more powdery), many people prefer working with the former. Opaline® dry cleaning pads should not be used directly on the paper as a "big eraser"; rather, the pad should be manipulated so that the particles fall out onto the surface of the paper (see Figure B3-5). If the pad is used directly, the fabric cover will quickly become dirty, thus helping to work the dirt into the paper fibers rather than lifting it away.

Large surface areas also may be cleaned with Absorene® wallpaper cleaner, using a small wad of it like a kneadable eraser and discarding it when it becomes dirty. The Absorene® should not be used to "scrub" the paper, but rather should be blotted across the surface of the paper in a gentle rolling motion. (See Figure B3-6.) When not in use, the Absorene® should be kept

B3-4

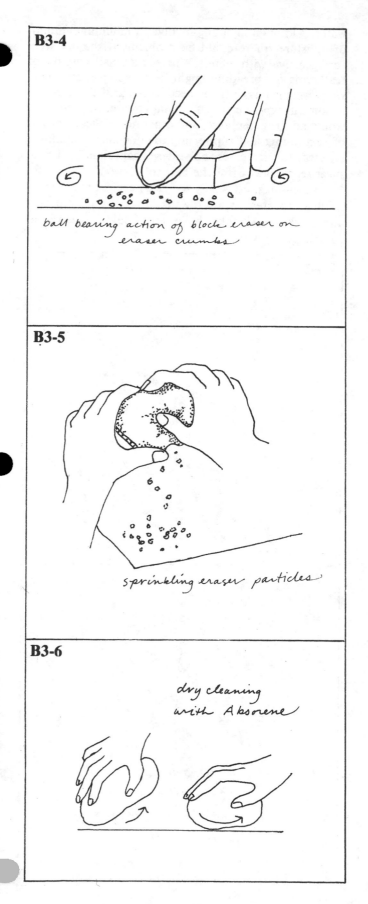

ball bearing action of block eraser on eraser crumbs

B3-5

sprinkling eraser particles

B3-6

dry cleaning with Absorene

in a tightly-sealed glass jar to keep it from drying out; if it does become dry, a small amount of water may be worked into it to make it moist and pliable again. If it becomes too dry, it forms crystals, which can be abrasive. Also, care must be taken to remove all traces of the Absorene® cleaner from the surface of the paper. (Other brands of wallpaper cleaner are not recommended. As with all commercial products, it is important to keep a close watch on the label listing component ingredients to ensure that harmful or unknown elements are not introduced over time.)

If the preceding methods do not clean the paper satisfactorily, a Magic Rub® vinyl eraser may be used next. A light hand is needed so that the paper fibers are not raised. Beginning in the center of the paper, short, one-directional strokes should be worked outward to the edges (see Figure B3-7). Pencil or stick erasers, such as Faber-Castell's peel-off Magic Rub® , which can be sharpened to a point, are useful for cleaning areas close to non-permanent images. The use of Magic Rub® erasers will likely result in the most dramatic differences in the appearance of the paper; much visible dirt will be removed. Once begun, however, the process must continue consistently over the entire surface of the paper to avoid streaks and unsightly splotches. Cleaning with Magic Rub® erasers is thus the most time-consuming of the dry cleaning processes; once initiated, the promise to stick with the job until it is completed is implicit.

Magic Rub® vinyl erasers are recommended for surface cleaning. Other brands and types of erasers may be too abrasive and may damage the surface of the paper. If erasers become dirty during use, they should be rubbed on a piece of waste paper to remove the dirty area and expose a clean surface. Care must be taken that all eraser particles are completely removed from documents after cleaning. Particles left on paper can cause problems over time: eraser crumbs can become gummy, causing sheets to stick together.

B3-7

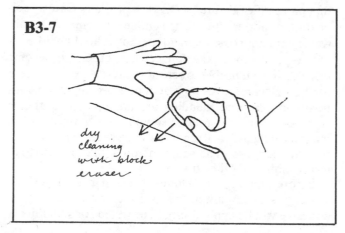

dry cleaning with block eraser

Both sides of a document should be cleaned. The purpose of dry cleaning is to remove abrasive, potentially acidic particles that can become permanently embedded in the fibers of the paper. Thus, to be effective, gritty dirt on both sides of a document must be removed. Concern must extend beyond marks or dirt that can be visually disfiguring to the invisible mechanical and chemical damage that can result from dirt that remains on the paper. To enhance the preservation of archival materials, both the front and back of documents must be cleaned, even if information is recorded on only one side.

Surface cleaning can be very time-consuming, especially if one is to work from gentle brushing successively through cleaning with a Magic Rub® eraser. Treatment limits may have to be set, based upon the degree of dirt present, the value of the records, and staff resources. In some instances, it may be sufficient to limit the cleaning to the use of Opaline® or Skum-X®; in other cases it may be justified to go further. In this as in other areas of preservation activity, priorities must be established based on need and resources.

B4. Testing for Ink Solubility

Before attempting any treatments involving water or other solvents, all inks on a document must be tested for solubility. If there are several different inks on a single document, each must be tested. If there is any evidence of ink solubility or feathering with the application of a given solvent, it should not be used.

The testing procedure is very simple. A small drop of water is placed on an unobtrusive part of a letter or line of ink; a period or part of an ascender or descender on letters such as "f" or "g" are good letters to test, since any spreading or feathering of the ink will not likely obscure any information (see Figure B4-1). The water may be applied with a small pointed brush (an eyedropper can deposit too much water). After several seconds, the drop of water is picked up with a small piece of blotting paper. (See Figure B4-2.) If there is any trace of color on the blotter, the ink is soluble, to some degree, in water, and aqueous treament methods should not be used. As some inks take longer than others to become soluble, it is advisable to repeat the test a second time if the first attempt gives no reaction, especially if aqueous treatments beyond mending are anticipated. Both the spot tested and the blotter should be examined with a magnifying glass. A linen tester is an excellent magnifier for this purpose. The same methods may be used for testing solvents other than water.

Before mending with long-fiber Japanese paper and wheat paste, any ink in the torn area over which moist adhesive will be applied should be tested for solubility in water. Although mending involves a minimum amount of moisture, there could be problems if the ink were very reactive with water. Whereas a small amount of feathering or spreading might be acceptable, especially when weighed against the need to repair the document, in some instances even a minimal amount of feathering would not be acceptable, and other non-aqueous means of reinforcing and supporting the document should be selected. In such cases, polyester encapsulation without sheet repair may offer the best solution.

Colored inks, especially red and purple, are generally soluble in water, as are the inks found in felt-tip pens and markers. All inks, however, should be viewed as soluble until tested.

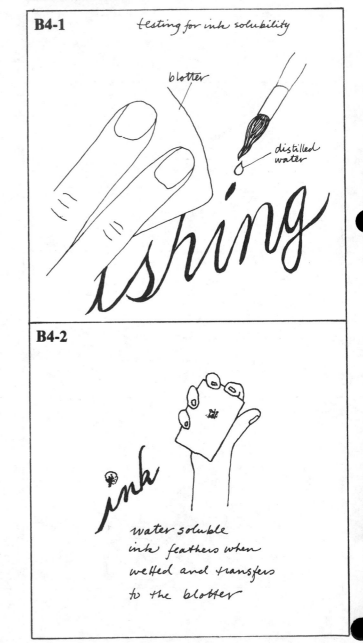

B4-1   testing for ink solubility

blotter

distilled water

B4-2

ink

water soluble inks feathers when wetted and transfers to the blotter

B5. *Testing the pH of Paper*

A number of methods available for testing the pH of paper do not require laboratory facilities or sophisticated technical training. These methods provide indications of the surface pH of the paper. The pH indicators respond chemically with a color range when brought into contact with specific levels of acidity or alkalinity. They are easy to use, and are accurate enough to indicate whether a paper is neutral or decidedly or mildly acidic or alkaline. Test results with coated papers are not entirely satisfactory using the methods to be described, since the coatings tend to obscure the true character of the interior of the paper. Coatings may also dissolve with the application of water or other solvents.

Within an archival context, these techniques are most useful for checking the quality of archival supplies, such as boxes, folders, interleaving sheets, and mat board, to determine whether or not the product meets specifications and the manufacturer's claims regarding pH level. The surface layer of such supplies may be scraped away with a microspatula or scalpel to allow testing of the interior pH level of the products. Archival documents may be tested as well to help determine their quality, condition, and need for treatment. These tests also provide a quick and easy means of checking a collection *after* deacidification to determine whether or not the neutralization and buffering processes successfully brought the paper to the required pH level.

Several of the testing methods leave a permanent mark or stain on the paper and thus are not desirable for direct use on archival materials. The EM Laboratory colorpHast® Indicator Sticks are non-bleeding and leave no stain on the paper being tested. For this reason, they are recommended for use on archival papers and other materials of value. ColorpHast® Indicator Sticks are strips of plastic impregnated with indicating agents, which respond with a color change to indicate the pH of the paper being tested. Care must be taken to avoid touching the sensitive portion of the stick. ColorpHast® Indicator Sticks are available in the following ranges: 0–14, 0–6, 5.0–10, 7.5–14, 0–2.5, 4.0–7.0, and 6.5–10; the smaller the range, the more accurate the reading. The test procedure is as follows:

(1) Slip a small piece of polyester under the area of the paper to be tested.

(2) Place a drop of distilled water on the area to be tested (see Figure B5-1). Do not test areas close to ink or a coloring agent. If the spot being tested contains ink, the results cannot be assumed to be accurate for the paper as the pH of the ink may have altered the results. Paper does not necessarily have a uniform pH over its entire surface. Areas near the margin are likely to be more acidic due to handling. Thus, for greater accuracy, it may be advisable to check the paper in several spots and compare results.

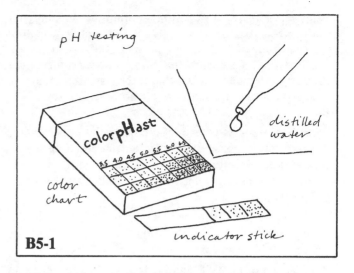

B5-1

(3) Lay the active end of the pH indicator paper in the droplet and move it back and forth slightly to ensure that the entire sensitive portion is wetted (see Figure B5-2).

(4) Place a second piece of polyester over the pH indicator stick and cover with a light weight to ensure that the test stick and the paper are in firm contact (see Figure B5-3).

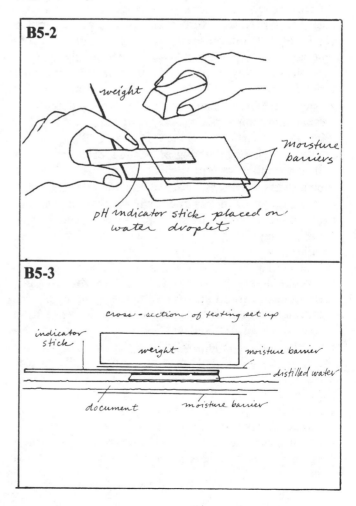

B5-2

B5-3

(5) After three to five minutes, remove the polyester and the test stick and determine the pH value by matching the colors of the wet indicators to the color chart on the EM box. To ensure that the indicator squares are properly oriented with the chart, the test stick should be held so that the non-sensitive portion is at the top of the box.

(6) Blot up any water remaining on the paper tested; place the paper between dry blotters under a light weight to complete drying. Small water marks sometimes remain on the paper, even with the application of a tiny drop of water.

(7) Paper with pH values below 7.0 are acidic; deacidification should definitely be considered for papers having a pH below 6.0.

(8) A pH of about 8.5 indicates that the paper has an alkaline reserve.

ColorpHast® Indicator Sticks are quite precise given the fact that several color indicators appear on each test strip, depending upon the test range selected. The multiple indicator response increases the degree of accuracy. The test sticks may be used to test the pH of solutions, such as paste, as well as papers. They are especially useful for testing colored or toned papers, for which it is difficult to differentiate color changes if spot tests are used. ColorpHast® Indicator Sticks have a limited shelf life; they should be kept in an airtight container and replaced every two years. Theoretically, pH indicator sticks are simple to use and accurate. In actual practice, the distilled water used may not have a pH of 7, but rather, for example, a pH of 6.5 because of dissolved carbon dioxide. The pH of the water will thus alter the test results.

Other methods of testing pH leave a permanent stain and are qualitative rather than quantitative. That is, they indicate whether or not the paper is acidic, neutral, or alkaline, more or less in a yes or no fashion, without providing precise readings of pH level within narrow ranges. They are primarily useful for testing archival supplies.

The Barrow Laboratory Paper Test Kit (now also marketed as the Tri-Test Spot Testing Kit) contains three indicator solutions for testing the presence of acid, groundwood, and alum. A thin line of a given solution is drawn on an uninked portion of the paper and allowed to dry; the resulting color is then checked against the spot test color chart that accompanies the kit (see Figure B5-4). The color chart is contained in a detailed instruction booklet, which also describes the testing procedures developed by William J. Barrow. It is recommended that the indicator solutions be refrigerated to prolong their useful life. These tests are simple and positive. They are recommended for testing archival

paper supplies and whenever a minor line stain can be tolerated on archival records.

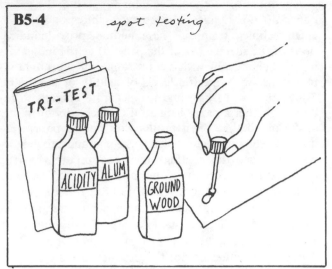

Other products, such as the Archivist's Pen® and pHydrion Insta-Chek® Surface pH Pencil, also rely on a color change to indicate the presence of acid. Each product comes with instructions. As these, too, leave a permanent stain, they are recommended for use on archival supplies rather than collection materials.

B6. Paste Preparation

Wheat starch paste is a strong, tacky adhesive that dries clear and is reversible with a small amount of water. It is highly recommended for mending valuable records. Methyl cellulose is less tacky and strong, dries clear (sometimes with a slight shine), but has good working qualities and has the additional attribute of a long shelf life. Methyl cellulose is suitable for minor mending and patching (especially when a document is to be encapsulated after mending), but because of its relatively weak bonding strength it should not be used for hinging or backing except when mixed with a stronger adhesive. Dry wheat starch and methyl cellulose powder have a long shelf life; they will keep almost indefinitely when stored in air-tight containers in a cool, dark place.

The proportions recommended for each of the following pastes will make up small batches, enough to be used over a period of several days without having excessive waste (see Figure B6-1).

Cooked Wheat Starch Paste

Cooked wheat paste is the preferred adhesive for mending, hinging, and backing valuable materials. Starch (rice and wheat) adhesives have long been used for mounting and repairing works of art on paper, and have thus withstood the test of time. Wheat starch (extracted from wheat flour) is available from conservation

B6-1

paste preparation supplies

PASTE

and archival suppliers. *Wheat flour* used for baking, wallpaper paste, etc., should not be substituted for *wheat starch.*

| Wheat starch (Aytex-P) | 2 Tablespoons (about 20 grams) |
| Distilled or filtered tap water | ½ cup |

Place the water in the top half of an enamel or stainless-steel double boiler, add the wheat starch and let soak for approximately twenty minutes; stir occasionally. No heat is applied during this soaking period, when the starch granules are swelling. Water is then placed in the bottom half of the double boiler, and the mixture is cooked over medium heat for about twenty minutes, stirring constantly with a clean wire whisk or wooden spoon (which should be used for no other purpose). The heat source may be a hot plate or gas or electric stove. The paste will thicken and become translucent. After cooking, the paste should be strained through cheesecloth or a small square of nylon window screening, and then placed in a clean glass jar and allowed to cool. When ready to use, it may be necessary to add a bit of water to bring the paste to the proper working consistency (similar to thick cream).

Cooked starch paste should be stored in an air-tight container in a cool, dark place. It should be watched closely for mold growth and discarded at the first sign of a sour smell or the appearance of any small dark spots or flecks, which may indicate the beginning of mold activity. As the paste decomposes, it loses its adhesive strength.

A few drops of concentrated o-phenyl phenol solution may be added to the cooked wheat starch as a mold inhibitor to extend its shelf life to several weeks. O-phenyl phenol crystals should be dissolved in one teaspoon of ethyl alcohol to the point of saturation. Using a glass rod as a stirrer, o-phenyl phenol should be added slowly to the ethyl alcohol until no more crystals will dissolve. The solution should be stored in a dark glass bottle and labelled "Poison."

Two to three drops of the o-phenyl phenol solution may be stirred into the cooked paste during the last few minutes of cooking. The paste must still be watched for mold activity and discarded at the first sign of contamination. In most archival settings, the addition of o-phenyl phenol is not necessary if only enough paste is prepared as can be used within a few days.

Pre-Cooked Wheat Starch Paste

Pre-cooked wheat starch is also available, and while some people prefer traditional cooked pastes, it is quite satisfactory for use on archival materials. It is easy to prepare, requires no heat source, and provides a strong lasting bond. It is reversible with the application of a small amount of water.

| Dry wheat paste No. 301 | 2 Tablespoons (about 20 grams) |
| Distilled or filtered tap water | ½ cup |

Slowly add powder to cold water, stirring constantly until the mixture is smooth. Some people find it helpful to use a small flour sifter to add the dry powder to the water as a means of discouraging the formation of lumps. More water or powder may be added as necessary to obtain the desired consistency, although such additions can result in a lumpy paste. With practice, the correct proportions can be mixed immediately to form a smooth adhesive. If necessary, however, the paste can be strained through cheesecloth or a square of nylon window screening to remove any lumps. It should be placed in a clean jar with a tight-fitting lid, stored in a cool, dry place, and discarded at the first sign of mold contamination. Since the water tends to separate out of solution, the paste needs to be stirred occasionally as it is used. Prepared wheat paste has a shelf life of two to three days.

Given the ease of preparing this paste, it is not recommended that o-phenyl phenol be added to it as a fungicide. Rather, small batches of the adhesive should be made as required, and discarded after a day or two.

This particular adhesive tends to be slightly acidic. Its pH may be checked with EM Laboratory colorpHast® Indicator Sticks. Acidity may be countered by adding a small amount of calcium carbonate to the mixture (10 percent by weight of the dry wheat powder). Thus, about two grams of calcium carbonate would be added to the above recipe.

Methyl Cellulose Adhesive

| Methyl Cellulose Powder No. 6 | 1½ Tablespoons (about 7 grams) |
| Distilled or filtered tap water | 1 cup |

Add powder to cold water and stir thoroughly until smooth. Let stand for 30 minutes and stir again. Add more water or powder to obtain desired consistency. Put into a clean storage jar. Methyl cellulose has a long shelf life; it is not susceptible to mold infestation and, thus, it is not necessary to add o-phenyl phenol as a mold inhibitor. To keep from contaminating or dirtying the preparation, it is advisable to pour out the required amount into a small dish as needed, rather than using it directly out of the storage container.

Starch pastes and methyl cellulose are the only adhesives recommended for use on archival materials. They are sufficiently strong, dry, clear, and are readily reversible. Commercial adhesives, including gummed and "archival" pressure-sensitive tapes, should be avoided. Polyvinyl acetate emulsions, which are used in bookbinding, should never be used for paper repair.

B7. Mending with Long-Fiber Japanese Paper

Prepare a clean work surface and assemble materials: long-fiber Japanese paper, wheat starch paste or methyl cellulose, brushes, bone folder, microspatula, tweezers, blotting paper, polyester web, silicone release paper (or wax paper), and weights.

Handmade Japanese paper is available in an incredibly wide range of weight and color. Papers made from the inner bark of the mulberry tree, however, are especially suitable for mending because they have very long fibers that make a strong and fairly invisible mend. The mulberry paper selected for mending should be unsized and close in color and weight to the damaged document. Sekishu (natural or white) and Kozo are both good medium-weight mending papers; Tengujo is suitable for light-weight documents. Since papermaking in Japan is becoming increasingly mechanized, quality should not be taken for granted, nor should the assumption be made that just because it is Japanese paper, it is necessarily handmade. Japanese papers should be evaluated (as should all papers used in an archival context) and their pH should be checked before use.

Surface cleaning should precede mending; extra care will be required with torn and weakened documents. Before mending, it is important to examine the torn or broken areas of the document. Tears must be properly aligned before mending to avoid cockling of the document or disfigurement of the text. After mending, the document should lie flat without wrinkles. In many cases, tears have broad or overlapping edges, that is, two flat areas with an obvious top and bottom (see Figure B7-1). It is possible to reinforce mends of such tears by applying a small amount of paste on these flat surfaces *before* applying the Japanese paper. (In some instances, application of mending strips to such tears is thus unnecessary.) Straight tears may be mended with thin strips of Japanese paper torn to the proper length and width; curved tears will require the preparation of

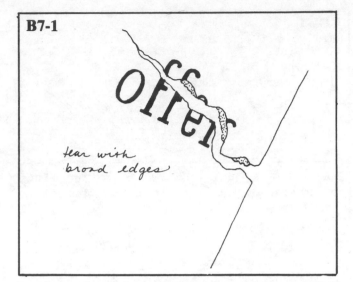

B7-1

tear with broad edges

mending strips torn to match the shape of the tear. With very long tears, it is better to apply a series of short slightly overlapping strips, to avoid both stretching the Japanese paper and the cockling of the mend when it dries.

To maximize the attributes of long-fiber Japanese paper, its edges need to be "feathered" before it is applied to the tear. A mending strip with soft fibrous edges provides strength and eliminates the damage that can be caused by a strip of straight-edged paper, which can function like a cutting edge on brittle documents. A feathered edge also will tend to disappear on the surface of a document and be less noticeable than a harsh straight edge of a cut mending strip. To the degree possible, feathering should match the paper surface to which it is to be applied. A large number of exposed fibers would thus be suitable when mending handmade paper, while fewer fibers would be appropriate when repairing machine-made paper. The technique of tearing Japanese paper to a suitable width with a feathered edge requires patience and practice. Once skill is developed, however, the action is simple and quick.

Before proceeding, the paper should be checked to see if it has a noticeable grain direction as the paper will tear more easily with the grain than across it. Strips of feathered Japanese paper may be made as follows: working on top of a blotter or other absorbent paper, the Japanese paper is painted with a line of water along the edge of a ruler set at approximately 1/8 inch in from the edge of the paper. Either a small round brush or a ruling pen may be used to paint the line of water. The paper should not be flooded with water; this would result in a pulpy mass, which would be impossible to tear into strips. To help avoid the problem of excessive water, some people use a very thin solution of methyl cellulose in water. This is somewhat thicker and less

B7-2

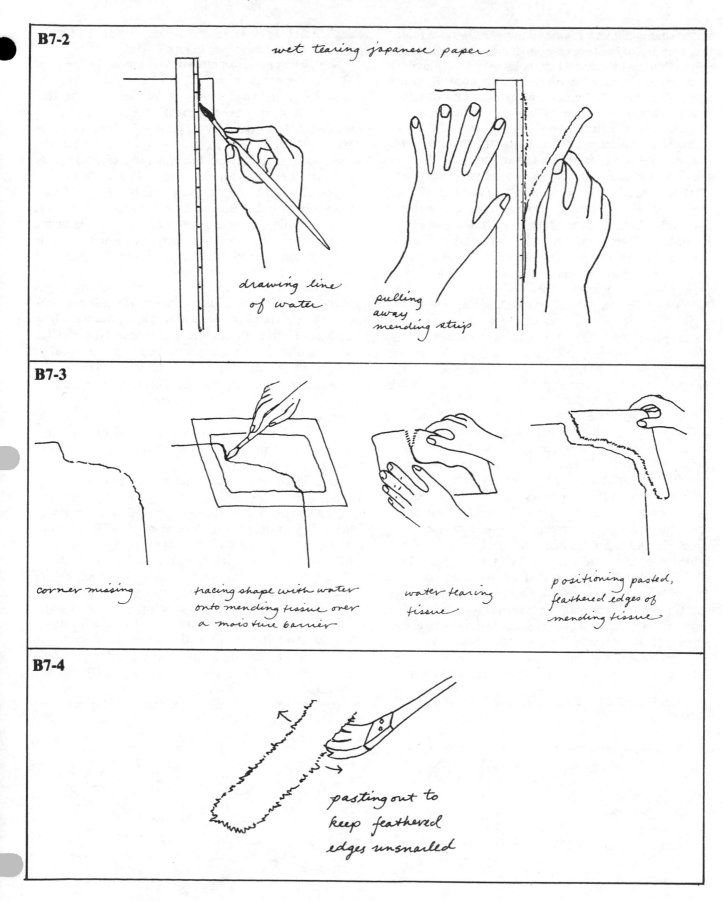

wet tearing japanese paper

drawing line
of water

pulling
away
mending strip

B7-3

corner missing

tracing shape with water
onto mending tissue over
a moisture barrier

water tearing
tissue

positioning pasted,
feathered edges of
mending tissue

B7-4

pasting out to
keep feathered
edges unsnarled

runny than plain water. Once dampened, a bone folder is run on top of the Japanese paper along the edge of the ruler to impress the line; then, holding the ruler in place as a guide, the paper is carefully torn away from the sheet. The strip will not come away in one motion; it is best to work down the strip in almost a pinching action to gently pull the fibers away (see Figure B7-2).

It is also possible to dry-tear strips of Japanese paper. One method of dry-tearing is to run the point of a needle along the edge of a ruler set on the paper at the appropriate width. The needle will demark a line of separation without cutting the paper fibers, thus allowing the feathering of the edges when the strip is gently pulled away from the sheet. Care must be taken to avoid cutting the fibers by pressing too hard with the needle.

To tear rounded or curved mending strips, a piece of glass is placed over the torn document. A piece of Japanese mending paper is then placed on top of the glass. The outline of the tear will be visible and may be traced either with a brush dipped in water or with a needle; the glass protects the document from this action. Once the shape of the tear is thus outlined on the Japanese paper, a strip of the proper shape and width may be torn away by hand. (See Figure B7-3.)

Once the Japanese paper has been torn to the proper width (generally about 1/8 inch) and slightly longer than the tear, it is ready to be pasted-out with wheat starch paste or methyl cellulose, using as little adhesive as possible. The adhesive also should be as thin and dry as feasible while still being tacky and workable; if too much moisture (i.e., wet adhesive) is applied during the mending process, the drying time is increased considerably and the document will likely cockle. When brushing on the paste, care must be taken that the long fibers do not become snarled or gummed up. (See Figure B7-4.) Pasting-out should be done on a waste sheet (such as unprinted newsprint), which is then discarded; the actual mending should be done on top of a piece of silicone release paper (or wax paper) to keep the document and mending strip from adhering to other surfaces. A quicker alternative is to paste-out a marble surface and lay down several mending strips at a time to pick up the adhesive (see Figure B7-5).

Next, using a microspatula or tweezers and a finger to lift and support the mending strip (see Figure B7-6), the Japanese paper should be carefully laid on the tear (which has already been aligned), making sure that the feathered edges extend across the width of the tear. (See Figure B7-7.) Care must be taken not to stretch the strip. A bone folder or a brush may be used to lightly press or tamp the strip in place and to work out the feathered edges of the mending strip (see Figure B7-8). Edge tears may be reinforced by wrapping a few fibers of the mending paper around to the reverse side of the document (see Figure B7-9). Once the mending strip is in place and tamped down, a small piece of polyester web should be placed over the strip. Then, a small piece of blotting paper should be used to pick up any excess adhesive or moisture. The polyester web will not stick either to the mend or the blotting paper, but will allow moisture to pass through to the blotter. The mended document should then be placed between two pieces of polyester web and under weighted blotters to dry. After a little time has elapsed, the polyester web may be removed and dry, weighted blotters substituted to complete the drying. Once the mend has dried, any excess Japanese paper extending over the edges of the document may be trimmed off with scissors or a straightedge and blade.

Tears need only be mended on one side of a document. Although careful mending with the appropriate weight and color of Japanese paper will be nearly invisible, it is advisable to place the mend on whichever side of the document will obscure the least text. To avoid dirty or "muddy" mends, paste and all implements should be kept scrupulously clean. Tools should be washed with a mild soap and thoroughly rinsed.

To gain facility, workshop personnel must practice this technique on papers of no value. Untrained persons should never attempt to work on valuable documents, and records exhibiting complex breaks and tears should be set aside until they can be referred to qualified personnel.

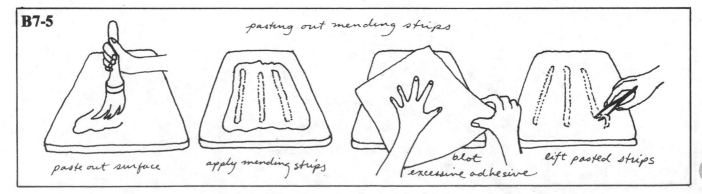

B7-5

pasting out mending strips

paste out surface

apply mending strips

blot excessive adhesive

lift pasted strips

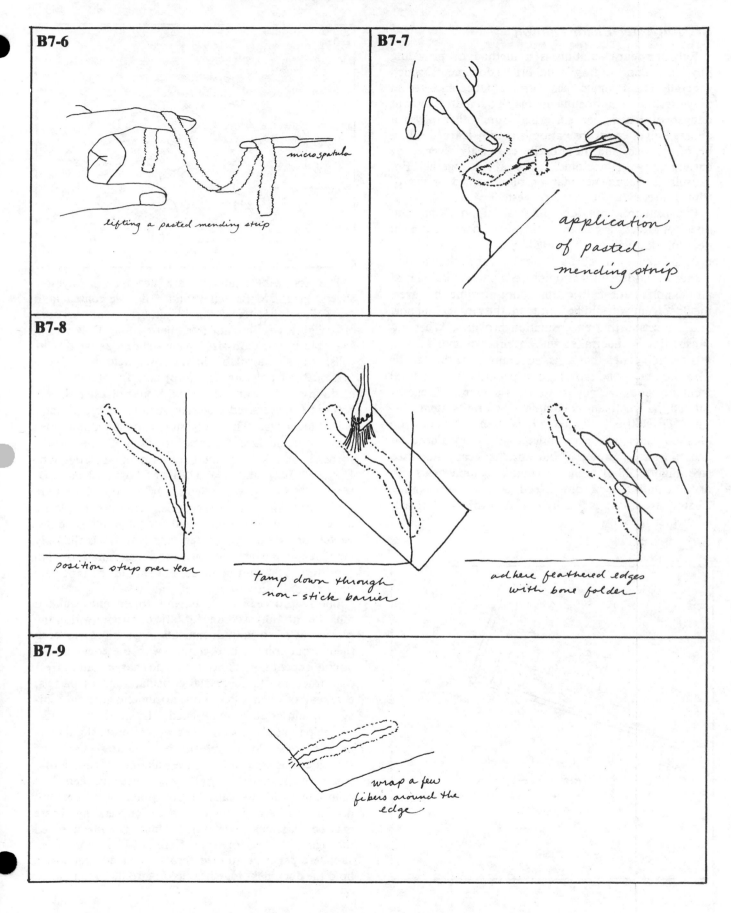

B7-6

microspatula

lifting a pasted mending strip

B7-7

application
of pasted
mending strip

B7-8

position strip over tear

tamp down through
non-stick barrier

adhere feathered edges
with bone folder

B7-9

wrap a few
fibers around the
edge

B8. *Polyester Encapsulation*

Polyester encapsulation is a method of providing physical support to fragile and brittle documents, which generally are in single-sheet format. Once enclosed in polyester, archival documents may be handled without danger of tearing or suffering from other physical abuse. Polyester encapsulation is readily learned with a bit of practice, and the procedure is easily reversed by cutting away the tape holding the capsule together. Encapsulated documents may be photocopied or microfilmed directly through the polyester.

Encapsulation provides physical support only and does not affect the chemical stability of paper; chemical deterioration will not be halted by enclosing paper records in a polyester capsule. For this reason, it is recommended that deacidification precede encapsulation if at all possible. If deacidification is not possible, however, the document will still benefit from the physical support and protection that encapsulation provides. When encapsulation is undertaken without prior deacidification, it is recommended that a visible reminder of this fact be incorporated in the capsule to help ward off the natural feeling of complacency that once a document is encapsulated, its treatment is complete. A brief statement—"not deacidified"—typed or written in pencil on alkaline paper will serve notice that the document has been physically protected but not chemically stabilized (see Figure B8-1). Such a notice complements the documentation kept on collections and conservation treatments, and is especially useful in the event of personnel changes.

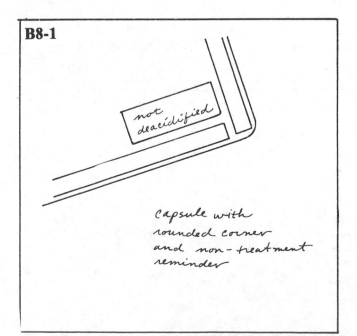

capsule with rounded corner and non-treatment reminder

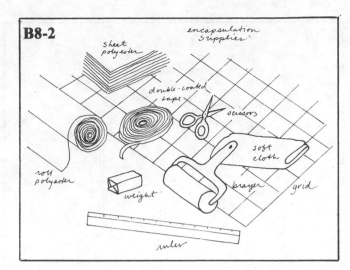

The following materials are necessary: Polyester sheets, grid, 3M Scotch Brand® double-coated tape No. 415, soft lint-free cloth, weight, brayer, and scissors or straightedge and blade (see Figure B8-2). Polyester is available in standard-sized precut sheets as well as in rolls; it is also available in various weights and thicknesses. 3-mil polyester is appropriate for standard- to medium-sized documents, while 5-mil polyester should be used for oversized materials such as maps, posters, and blueprints. The polyester should contain no plasticizers, surface coatings, or UV inhibitors or absorbers, and should meet goverment specifications L-P-00670B(2) and L-P-377B. Mylar® Type D, Melinex® Type 516, or Scotchpar® Industrial Grade Polyester Film are acceptable. No other plastic materials should be substituted for polyester. The 3M Scotch Brand® double-coated tape No. 415 is the only tape recommended for use in encapsulation. No substitutions should be made, nor should the tape ever be applied directly to archival materials.

Before proceeding, documents to be encapsulated must be carefully examined. Static electricity within the capsule helps to hold documents in position and keep them from coming into contact with the edges of the double-coated tape. Since the static charge could affect or attract any loose or flaky media, such as pastels, charcoal, or thick watercolors, documents with such images should not be encapsulated. The static charge also will help to hold a document that is suffering slight tears in one piece. Major breaks or fractures, however, should be mended before encapsulation to ensure that pieces do not come away after enclosure and then float randomly within the capsule. Encapsulation reduces but does not entirely eliminate the need for mending. There may be occasions when major mending can be avoided through the use of tiny "bridges" of long-fiber Japanese paper positioned across a tear at intervals to hold the document together (see Figure B8-3). As stated

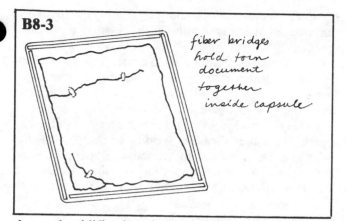

B8-3

fiber bridges hold torn document together inside capsule

above, deacidification should precede encapsulation if feasible; all other necessary treatments, such as mending and surface cleaning, should be carried out before encapsulation as well. Dirt that is not removed prior to encapsulation will not only be unsightly and move about within the capsule due to the static charge, but the particles also can become embedded in the paper fibers as pressure is applied to the capsule when forcing out the air.

Once documents have been examined for their suitability for encapsulation and have undergone all appropriate treatments, the actual process can commence. Two pieces of polyester should be cut; these should be one inch larger on all sides than the document to be encapsulated. It is helpful to work on a grid so that the polyester and the document can be properly squared, which will result in a neat and pleasing product.

One piece of polyester should be placed on the grid and squared. It should be wiped with a soft lint-free cloth to remove any dirt and also set up the static charge (see Figure B8-4). Caution: the surface of polyester scratches readily, and care must be taken to avoid rubbing on it too hard, even with a soft cloth. Next, the document is placed on the piece of polyester, and it too is aligned or squared using the grid as a guide. There should be a one-inch margin of polyester extending around all four sides of the document. Once properly aligned, a clean weight should be placed on top of the document to keep it in position.

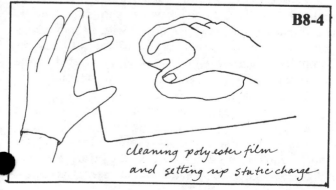

B8-4

cleaning polyester film and setting up static charge

The double-coated tape is next applied on the polyester around all four sides of the document, approximately 1/8 inch away from its edge. The grid should be used as an aid in positioning the tape in straight lines. The tape may abut at three corners with a gap of 1/16 inch left at the fourth corner for air circulation. At this stage, the brown protective paper is left *on* the tape.

The second piece of polyester is then wiped with a soft cloth and placed clean side down on the document, making sure that it is exactly aligned on top of the first piece of polyester. The weight is then carefully pulled away from its position on top of the document and placed on top of the second piece of polyester. Care must be taken to avoid moving the document while manipulating the polyester. At this point, the weight is holding the entire capsule in position (see Figure B8-5).

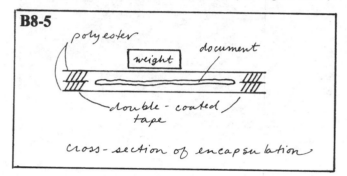

B8-5

polyester · *document*

weight

double-coated tape

cross-section of encapsulation

Using a brayer or soft cloth, excess air should be pushed out of the package by going over its entire surface. Then, carefully lifting one corner of the top piece of polyester, the strips of protective paper should be pulled off the tape along two sides of the document (see Figure B8-6). The polyester should be gently adhered along the lines of exposed tape. The brayer or soft cloth should be used again to remove any air pockets or bubbles. At this point, the slip of paper indicating that the document has not been deacidified should be slipped in at the back of the document if appropriate.

The protective paper from the two remaining sides should then be pulled away from the tape, and the polyester pressed into firm contact with it. The entire surface of the capsule should be gone over again with the brayer or soft cloth to remove any remaining air (see Figure B8-7).

Finally, the capsule should be trimmed using either a straightedge and blade or a paper cutter, leaving a margin of approximately 1/16 inch away from the tape around all four sides. This margin of polyester prevents dirt from accumulating on the edges of the tape. The last step is to round the four corners of the capsule, using scissors, a fingernail clip, or the much more expensive "corner rounder." The latter is available from archival suppliers. If the corners of the capsule were left

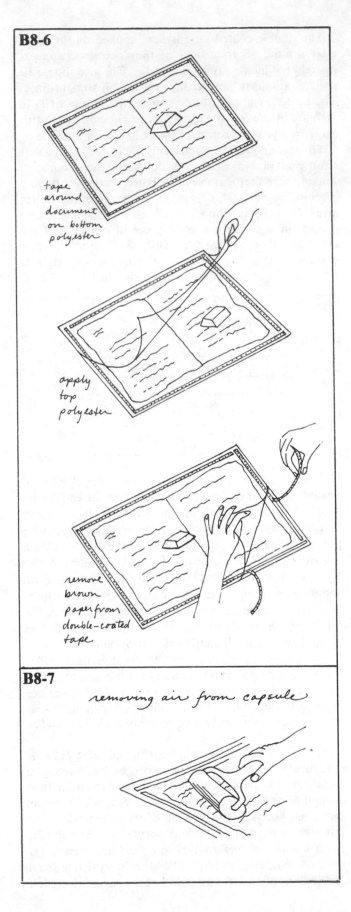

B8-6

tape around document on bottom polyester

apply top polyester

remove brown paper from double-coated tape

B8-7

removing air from capsule

square, the sharp edges could tear or otherwise damage unprotected documents with which they may come into contact.

Other methods besides double-coated tape have been devised to seal the four edges of polyester capsules. Some people have used sewing machines to quickly stitch together the pieces of polyester. More sophisticated are the machines that bond two sheets of polyester together via either ultrasonic welding or electromagnetic radiation. The result is an attractive, flat, and unobtrusive weld. While encapsulating machines are expensive, they are feasible for major programs that undertake a large amount of encapsulating. See Appendix F for suppliers of these machines.

Polyester sheets may be used in a number of other ways besides encapsulation to support and protect fragile documents. Polyester folders may be made by sealing one or two edges of two sheets of polyester together with double-coated tape (see Figure B8-8). A

B8-8

capsule sealed on 2 edges

number of these polyester folders can be kept on hand and used as needed in carrying out reference functions; unprotected fragile documents can easily be slipped into a folder before being given to a researcher. If necessary, extra support can be provided by placing a piece of two-ply museum board in the folder with the document. Polyester easily creases with the use of a bone folder, and a variety of small envelopes or slings can be devised to contain documents for exhibition and storage purposes. Polyester also can be cut to the proper dimensions and creased to form protective book jackets (see Figure B8-9). Folded items, such as pamphlets, can be encapsulated, and polyester books with post bindings can be constructed as well. See the Library of Congress pamphlet, *Polyester Film Encapsulation,* listed in the bibliography (Appendix D), for instructions in a number of these techniques.

Photographs may be encapsulated if desired. Given the availability, however, of ready-made polyester and other inert plastic sleeves that are designed expressly for photographic prints and negatives, the effort to encapsulate such materials by hand does not seem warranted.

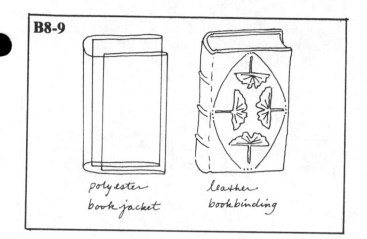

B8-9

polyester
book jacket

leather
bookbinding

B9. Treatment of Leather Bound Volumes

The necessary materials are: potassium lactate solution, neat's-foot oil and lanolin, saddle soap, One-Wipe® treated dust cloths, Endust®, soft brushes, pads of cheesecloth or terry toweling, cotton swabs, waxed paper, sponge, rubber gloves, glass dishes, and a vacuum cleaner (see Figure B9-1). A large, flat work surface should be covered with clean blotters or wrapping paper, which can be replaced as it becomes soiled.

Treatment with potassium lactate solution and neat's-foot oil and lanolin is recommended as a preservative for leather bookbindings. Potassium lactate reintroduces into the leather protective buffering salts that either were washed out of the leather during processing or were not present initially. Also, potassium lactate neutralizes strong mineral acids that may be present in the leather due to pollution in the surrounding air. The application of potassium lactate is generally followed by treatment with neat's-foot oil and lanolin. This leather dressing lubricates the leather and keeps the fibers supple and flexible. It is important to proceed cautiously with this treatment to ensure that the treatment is desirable and acceptable and that only appropriate materials are treated.

The treatment described is appropriate only for vegetable-tanned leathers. Alum-tawed, vellum, or parchment skins should never be subjected to such treatment, nor should chamois or suede-type leathers. Chrome-tanned leathers should be excluded as well. Care also must be taken to avoid treating imitation leathers. Book cloth or vinyl embossed with a grain can often fool the untutored eye. Clues may be provided by worn areas, however, especially at corners or endcaps where the surface of the material may have worn away to expose the texture or fibers of cloth or other covering material. When in doubt regarding the nature of the covering material, do not proceed until expert advice can be obtained.

Examination is the first step (see Figure B9-2). Volumes covered fully or partially with vegetable-tanned leather should be separated from bindings covered in other materials. This includes books bound in full leather as well as half and quarter bindings (i.e., those with leather on the spine and corners or on the spine only). Once volumes covered in vegetable-tanned leathers have been isolated, they must be evaluated to determine whether or not this treatment is appropriate given their condition. A leather treatment program should begin while bindings are still in good condition. Once leather has deteriorated to the stage known as red rot, it is beyond help from this treatment. At this stage the leather is powdery and brownish-red in color, and tends to rub off easily. Volumes showing evidence of red rot should be boxed or placed in a polyester book jacket until rebinding is feasible. Fine or designer bindings generally should not be treated with potassium lactate and neat's-foot oil, especially if there are onlays or inlays of various types and colors of leather; these will likely darken during treatment, thus altering the binding from design and aesthetic viewpoints. Extremely valuable or rare volumes should be set aside until advice can be obtained regarding the appropriateness of the treatment. All light-colored leather will darken somewhat during treatment, but this is primarily a concern with fine or extremely valuable bindings. Many financial ledgers and law books found in archival collections are covered in calf, which is often light in color. In such instances, the slight darkening of the leather is generally acceptable.

Leather that is scuffed or scratched may be treated, but any areas exhibiting breaks or extremely thin leather must be avoided so that the solutions will not soak through the boards, spine, or hinge areas and stain and damage the end sheets and text block. Boards that are overly wetted may warp. Tears or voids in the leather should be avoided as should broken hinges, exposed spines, or broken endcaps. Boards that are completely detached from the book may be treated, especially if there is any likelihood of the volume being eventually restored. Solutions should be applied lightly over areas with gold tooling so as not to overly moisten and lift the gold away.

Cleaning should precede treatment with potassium lactate solution and neat's-foot oil and lanolin. Volumes may be dusted with a soft brush and One-Wipe® treated dust cloths. A brush is most satisfactory for cleaning the edges of the volumes. The binding should be held tightly closed to avoid working the dirt into the interior of the text block, and the brushing motion should be away from the book rather than toward the spine. One-Wipe® cloths may be used to pick up

B9-1

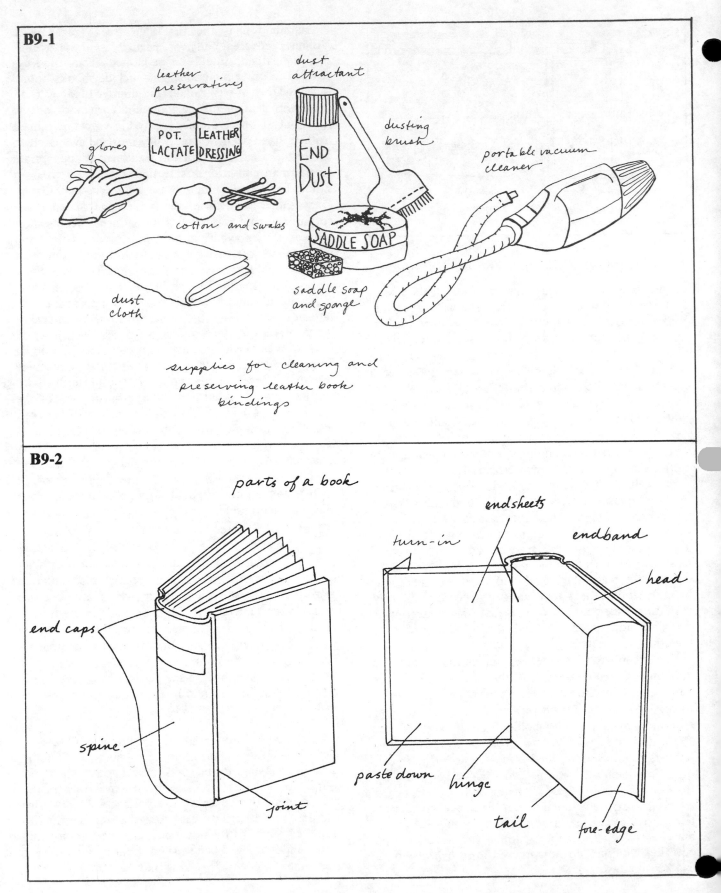

leather preservatives

dust attractant

gloves

POT. LACTATE   LEATHER DRESSING

dusting brush

portable vacuum cleaner

END Dust

cotton and swabs

SADDLE SOAP

dust cloth

saddle soap and sponge

supplies for cleaning and preserving leather book bindings

B9-2

parts of a book

endsheets

turn-in

endband

head

end caps

spine

joint

paste down

hinge

tail

fore-edge

surface dirt from the front and back covers as well as the spine and book edges. Endust® is another product recommended for cleaning books. It should be sprayed onto a piece of soft cloth, allowed to dry, and then used to clean the exterior of the binding. Caution is recommended in the use of Endust®, however, to avoid having the spray settle on items where it is not wanted. As cloths and brushes become dirty, they should be replaced with a clean supply.

Depending upon the amount of loose dirt present, it may be advisable to use a vacuum cleaner, especially if bindings and shelves have not been cleaned for a long period. A portable hand vacuum cleaner is satisfactory. The suction should not be so strong as to damage the materials being cleaned, and a piece of nylon screening or cheesecloth should be placed over the nozzle to prevent any fragments of the bindings or scraps of paper from being sucked into the vacuum cleaner. Vacuuming is especially helpful for cleaning the tops of volumes, where a great deal of dirt and dust often settle. After vacuuming, the individual volumes may be dusted with brushes and treated cloths (see Figure B9-3).

If the leather is very dirty, cleaning with saddle soap (such as Propert's brand) may be advisable. A small amount of water or potassium lactate should be used to work the soap to a somewhat dry lather. Using a small sponge or soft cloth, the saddle soap should be worked over the surface of the leather, avoiding red rot, tears, and breaks, as well as paper or cloth portions of the binding. Once dry, the soap should be gently buffed away with a soft cloth. Caution: with some leathers having a very noticeable grain or deep pores, the saddle soap may have a tendency to remain in these areas, leaving a white residue. Before proceeding with saddle soap, it is advisable to test it on a small area. Also, overmoistening of the leather must be avoided. If the saddle soap is too wet and runny it can soak the boards, causing warping, and also can cause the leather to darken excessively.

After cleaning, the next step is the application of potassium lactate solution. This solution, which is bright yellow in color, will stain paper as well as hands. It contains a fungicide, paranitrophenol. Thus, it is advisable to wear thin rubber gloves when working with it. Also, it is extremely important to avoid getting any potassium lactate on paper or book cloth, including paper sides, paper labels, or the endsheets or interior of the text. As a precaution, the text block should be wrapped with waxed paper to avoid accidents until facility is gained in this procedure. Liquids around valuable books always pose potential danger. Two pieces of waxed paper should be cut: one the width of the book and slightly more than double its height, and the other the height of the book and sufficient to wrap around the text block from the back hinge to the front hinge. The sheets are then placed inside the back cover, extending from the hinge area out over the edges of the text block. Then the text block is wrapped as one would cover a gift box, folding the excess paper up over the edges of the text. The waxed paper should be held in place by taping it to itself where it overlaps inside the front cover (see Figure B9-4). Once facility is gained with this treatment, such wrapping is unnecessary. One hand should always be kept clean when carrying out this treatment. Then, if an accident occurs, the book can be rescued quickly and safely with no danger of staining.

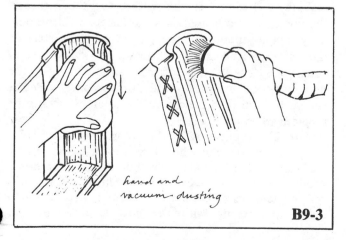

hand and vacuum dusting

B9-3

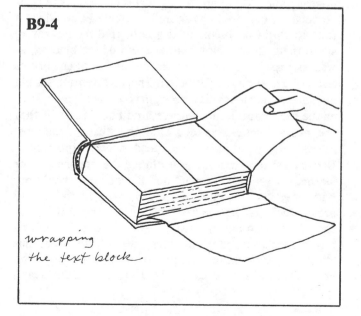

B9-4

wrapping the text block

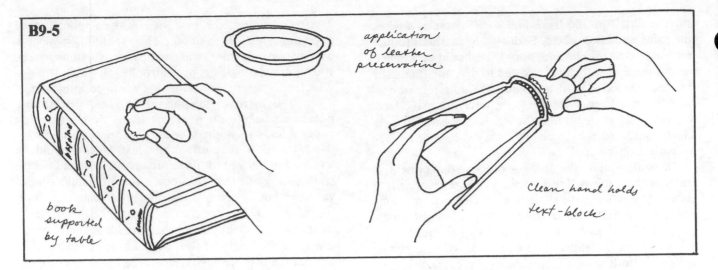

B9-5

application of leather preservative

book supported by table

clean hand holds text-block

Before proceeding with the application of the potassium lactate solution, a small spot in an unobtrusive area (such as the bottom edge of the back cover) should be tested to determine whether any darkening occurs. If the degree of darkening is unacceptable, this step should be omitted.

To avoid contaminating or dirtying the primary supply, a small amount of potassium lactate solution should be poured into a glass bowl or dish with a flat bottom; a heavy ashtray is ideal. A small pad of cotton, cheesecloth, or terry toweling should be dipped into the solution, wrung out until it is almost dry, and gently applied over the entire surface of the leather. A light patting motion is correct; the potassium lactate should not be rubbed or scrubbed into the leather (see Figure B9-5). Two light coats of potassium lactate solution are better than one heavy coat; if too much is applied initially, it will soak right through the leather, possibly warping the boards and staining the endsheets. Oversized or especially weak bindings should be treated one side at a time to avoid problems of trying to find a safe way to stand them to dry. Non-leather areas of the binding, as well as tears or holes in the leather and broken corners and joints, should be avoided. Special attention should be paid to the most vulnerable parts of the binding, such as the head cap, joint, corners, and book edges, if they are intact. These areas on a binding withstand the most abuse and wear and thus need special protection. Because of the danger of staining the endsheets, the leather turn-ins on the front and back covers should not be treated. A cotton swab may be used to treat small areas, such as that surrounding a paper label. Gold-tooled areas should be treated lightly. Areas exhibiting red rot should be avoided. Once leather has reached this stage of deterioration, the potassium lactate will do no good, and will only cause the leather to darken and harden.

It is important to watch how the potassium lactate penetrates into the leather as it is applied. If it sits on the surface, that may be an indication that the volume was recently oiled or that the leather was waxed or varnished at some point (see Figure B9-6). If the potassium lactate does not penetrate but beads up on the surface of the leather, the excess should be wiped off and the application discontinued. Any beading will cause spotting after it eventually dries. No attempt should be made to treat varnished or waxed books.

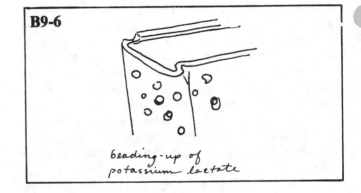

B9-6

beading-up of potassium lactate

As the potassium lactate is worked over the surface of the book, the cloth used as an applicator will become dirty. The solution will pick up dirt from the surface of the leather as well as a small amount of leather dye in some cases. The latter is generally so minimal as to be no cause for concern. As the cloth becomes soiled it should be turned to a clean position, and it should be replaced when necessary.

After the application of the potassium lactate solution, the volumes must be allowed to dry. The recommended waiting periods vary, but twenty-four hours should suffice, given local variations in relative humidity. The volumes should be completely dry to the touch before proceeding with the next step. Small and medium-sized volumes that are intact and in good condition may be placed in a standing position to dry, with the covers slightly open to allow them to stand upright. Oversized volumes should be left flat on the table to allow the wet side to dry. (See Figure B9-7.)

B9-7

after leather treatment, small books can stand upright, but large ones should be laid flat to dry.

Once dry, the volumes are ready for the application of neat's-foot oil and lanolin. A small amount of the mixture should be poured into a small glass container. Using a pad of cheesecloth or terry toweling, the entire surface of the volume should be treated, working in a gentle, circular, patting motion. A very light coat of the mixture should be applied. Weakened areas of the leather, broken joints, holes, and areas of red rot should be avoided. The neat's-foot oil and lanolin will not harm the areas affected by red rot, but the leather is thin in such areas and the oil will likely soak right through to the boards. Leather turn-ins should be avoided to keep from staining the endsheets. Depending upon whether or not the leather has ever been treated before, it may readily soak up the mixture. If the mixture does seem to penetrate quickly, two *light* coats should be applied. The volume should be left to dry for twenty-four hours, and then buffed gently with a clean, dry cloth to remove any excess.

Leather treatment should be repeated every two to five years, depending upon the condition of the volumes and the environmental conditions to which they are subjected. In highly polluted areas, the period between treatments should fall within the shorter range. Also, if the leather appears to be drying out, the treatment should be repeated. Documentation is very important.

An ongoing written record should be kept indicating when specific volumes were treated and by whom. A card file is one easy way to record this information.

Formulas for potassium lactate solution and neat's-foot oil and lanolin are listed below. They may either be formulated in-house or purchased, although most institutions will find it most convenient to purchase directly from a conservation supplier. No other formulations or ingredients are recommended. Avoid products that do not specify contents or that contain additives such as wax, lacquer, or microwaxes. The British Museum Leather Dressing formula, which is often recommended in the conservation literature, is not suitable for use under many climatic conditions found in the United States.

Potassium lactate solution	
Potassium lactate, U.S.P.	7.00%
Paranitrophenol	0.25%
Distilled water	92.75%
Neat's-foot oil and lanolin	
Neat's-foot oil	60%
Lanolin, anhydrous	40%

Treatment with potassium lactate solution and neat's-foot oil and lanolin is currently under review in the conservation field. While still recommended as a means of preserving leather bindings, it is important to proceed cautiously and knowledgeably. All materials should be evaluated before treatment, and the archivist should keep current with the conservation literature to be aware of the latest thinking on the subject.

B10. Examining and Removing Framed Material Under Glass

This procedure should be undertaken with all framed materials that come into the archives (documents, certificates, letters, photographs, and works of art). Examination is an important step in conservation treatment, and when dealing with framed items it is essential for a number of reasons. The document may be in an advanced state of deterioration that is not fully evident because of the frame and mat assembly. Also, most matting is done with unstable materials (such as newsprint, cardboard, raw wood, etc.) that will accelerate the deterioration of the artifact. Inappropriate mounting techniques and adhesives can cause staining as well as physical stress. Direct contact between the document and the cover glass, which is common, can lead to the build up of excessive moisture, condensation, and possible mold growth. In the case of photographic materials, ferreotyping can also result. Equally important, information that could help to identify or date the item may

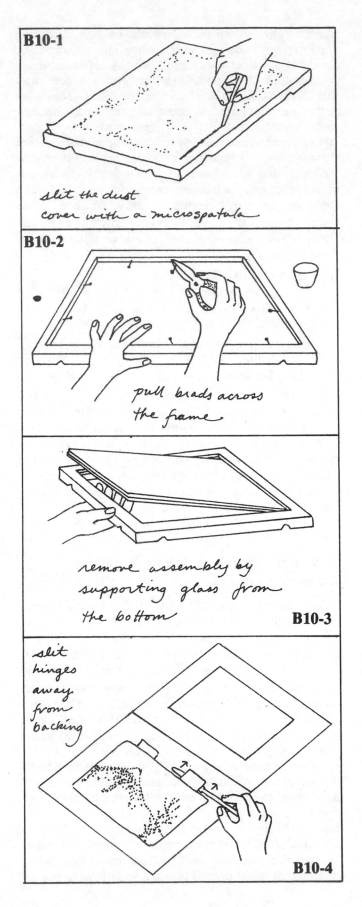

B10-1

slit the dust
cover with a microspatula

B10-2

pull brads across
the frame

remove assembly by
supporting glass from
the bottom
B10-3

slit
hinges
away
from
backing

B10-4

be obscured by the frame and mat construction.

The following tools should be assembled: nipping pliers, microspatula, scalpel and blade, brushes, air bulb, and vacuum cleaner. Clean white blotters should be placed on the table to serve as a work surface, and a paper cup should be placed nearby to serve as a receptacle for all hardware and tacks.

The frame should be placed face down on the blotter. All protruding screw eyes and wires should be removed. If there is a great deal of loose dirt, the frame should be vacuumed or dusted to prevent the accumulation from sifting inside the unit as work continues.

If there is a a a dust cover (i.e., paper adhered to the back of the frame), it should be removed by carefully slitting the paper along the rabbet with the microspatula (see Figure B10-1). The dust cover should be examined on both sides, and discarded if it has no value. Any written notations should be recorded. All loose stuffing (newspaper, advertisements, etc.) under the dust cover should be examined and discarded if it has no value.

The next layer will generally be a stiff backing (such as cardboard, mat board, or wood—which was used extensively in the 19th century). Any dirt that has sifted down to this level should be removed with a brush or air bulb. Brads or tacks holding the backing in place should be removed with the nipping pliers. The brads should be pulled away *across* the frame, toward the operator, to reduce the chance of accidental damage to the document (see Figure B10-2). As each tack or brad is removed, it should be dropped into the paper cup. Any loose hardware on the work surface could pose a hazard to the document or the frame.

Once all the hardware has been removed, the entire assembly (i.e., backing, mat, document, and glass) should be raised from the frame by supporting the glass from the bottom (see Figure B10-3). Then, with the glass resting on the blotting paper, the remaining layers should be carefully removed. Finally, the document should be gently lifted away from the glass. If the document is matted or otherwise mounted rather than floating loose in the frame, this structure should be evaluated, considering the quality of the materials and the method of attachment. All harmful materials should be discarded after first examining them for information regarding the item. Documents that are hinged to a mat may be slit away from the backing by inserting a microspatula or scalpel between the hinge and the mat, taking care to avoid the document (see Figure B10-4). Items that are glued into mat structures should be left intact. Removal of hinge extensions and adhesives should be carried out by qualified personnel.

A large number of framed items received in a repository do not have great intrinsic value as framed units. Once such items have been removed from their frames, their condition should be evaluated and any necessary treatments (such as cleaning or mending) should be carried out. The items should then be stored flat in conservation-quality enclosures. Items having high intrinsic value because of their historical significance or their association value may need to be returned to their original frames following necessary treatment. (For information on safe matting procedures, see: Merrily A. Smith, comp., *Matting and Hinging Works of Art on Paper*. Washington, D.C.: Library of Congress, 1981.)

B11. Regular Phased Box Design

(ONE-BOARD CONSTRUCTION)

Operational Sequence

I. MEASURE THE PHASED BOX

    A. Determine the height of the side walls
    B. Determine the outer limits of the flaps

II. CUT OUT THE PHASED BOX

III. CREASE AT THE FOLD LINES

IV. ATTACH THE TIES AND BUTTONS

    A. Attach the ties
    B. Attach the buttons

I. Measure the Phased Box

See diagram 2. Place the book in the middle of the inside of the board. Roll the book to the left and right and up and down to ensure the board is large enough. Place the book in a position which will allow sufficient margins for the flaps and place a weight on it. Using an upright triangle, mark the position of all the outer edges of the book on the board with broken lines. Make a second set of solid marks 1/16 inch out from the broken lines. (This allows clearance for the ridge which will be created by the crease. Figure 1 shows a creasing machine.) Working with a straight edge and triangle, connect the second set of marks, making sure that all lines are perpendicular and parallel.

Reprinted with the permission of the Preservation Office, Library of Congress, from: *Boxes for the Protection of Rare Books: Their Design and Construction,* Margaret R. Brown, compiler and editor. Washington, D.C.: Library of Congress, 1982.

A. DETERMINE THE HEIGHT OF THE SIDE WALLS

See diagram 3. Even though the book's height is constant, the walls of the phased box will vary because allowance must be made for the various flaps that fold over and take up space.

Head Wall A — Height equals the height of the book

Tail Wall B — Height equals the height of the book plus 1 thickness of board

Fore Edge Wall C — Height equals the height of the book plus 2 thicknesses of board

Spine Wall D — Height equals the height of the book plus 3 thicknesses of board

Mark these measurements on the board and draw lines forming walls A, B, C, and D. (Remember that the creases do take up a small amount of space. Allow for this.)

B. DETERMINE THE OUTER LIMITS OF THE FLAPS

See diagram 4.

Flap 1 — Length equals the length of the base board minus 1 thickness of board

Flap 2 — Length equals ⅓ the length of the base board

Flap 3 — Width equals the width of the base board minus 1 thickness of board

Flap 4 — Width equals the width of the base board

Mark these measurements on the board and draw lines on which to cut.

II. Cut Out the Phased Box

Using a leather hole punch (⅛-inch diameter), punch a hole at each of the four corners of the base board.

Using board shears or a knife and a straight edge, cut out all the outside edges of the phased box.

Round the outside corners with a round chisel or corner punch.

III. Crease at the Fold Lines

Transfer the marks for fold lines on either side of walls A, B, C, and D to the outside of the board. Crease the board at these fold lines. Eight creases are formed. When folded inward, these creases will form a rounded edge on the outside.

IV. Attach the Ties and Buttons

See diagram 5. The phased box is held together by two waxed thread ties which wrap around the buttons on the outside. Rivet two threads onto fore edge flap 4 approximately 1½ inches from the edge at the head and tail. Rivet two plastic discs directly across from the riveted ties in the center of side wall C. Pull over the waxed threads and wrap them around the buttons, thereby closing the box. This firmness keeps the book from being distorted by atmospheric changes.

A. ATTACH THE TIES

Place the cut and creased phased box face down with flap 4 in front of you. Punch two holes at the fore edge. The placement of the holes depends on the size of the flap. A usual placement is 1½ inches from the head and the tail and 1 inch in from the fore edge.

Make a simple half hitch with the thread and place it over the male part of the rivet. Draw the thread through the hole as you place the rivet on top and push it together to hold it in place. Then turn over the phased box and hammer the rivet together. Cut away the short end of the thread at the rivet. Hammer on a firm surface. The end grain of a square block of wood is ideal, if your table or bench is not firmly anchored.

B. ATTACH THE BUTTONS

After both ties have been attached, place the book in the phased box and fold over the flaps. With the box closed, draw the waxed thread straight over the fore edge and place a pencil mark on the center of side wall C to indicate the placement of the button. Remove the book.

Working from the outside of the box, punch holes at the pencil marks. Slip the male part of the rivet under the board and put it in the hole. On the outside, place the disc over the male rivet and place the female rivet on top of it. Hammer the rivet together.

The construction of the regular phased box (one-board construction) is now completed. See diagram 6.

DIAGRAM 1   Board Marked and Cut for Regular Phased Box Design

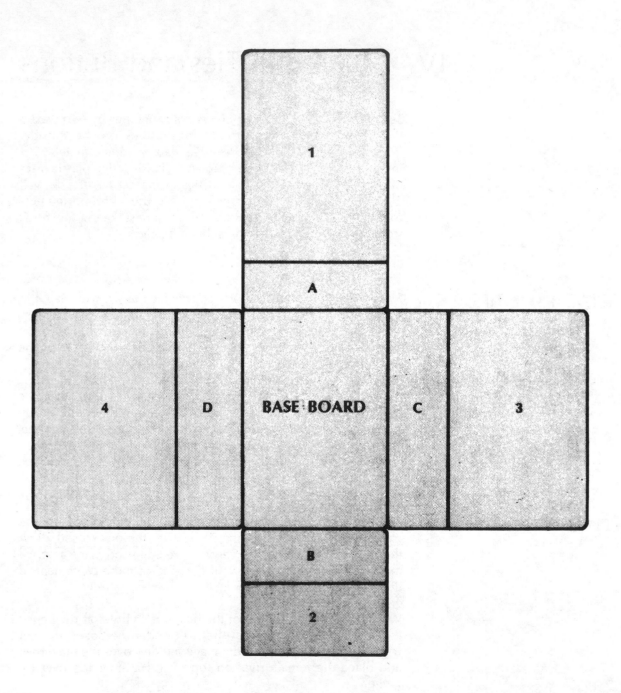

DIAGRAM 2 **Mark the Base Board Area of the Box**

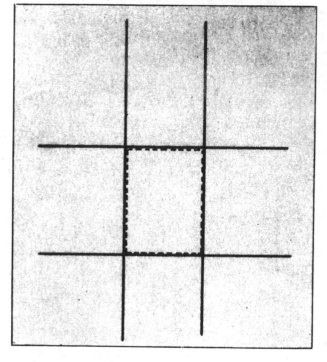

DIAGRAM 3 **Determine the Height of the Side Walls**

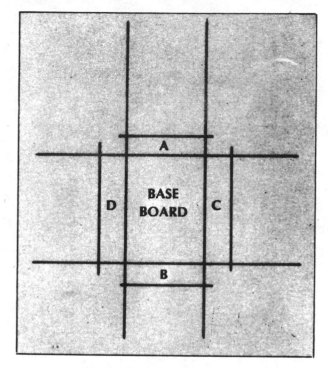

DIAGRAM 4 **Determine the Outer Limits of the Flaps**

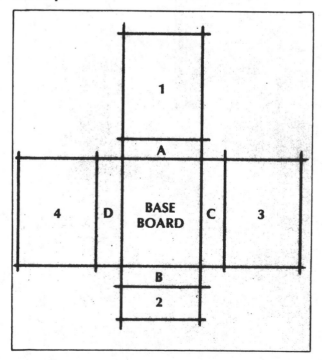

DIAGRAM 5 **Attach the Ties and Buttons**

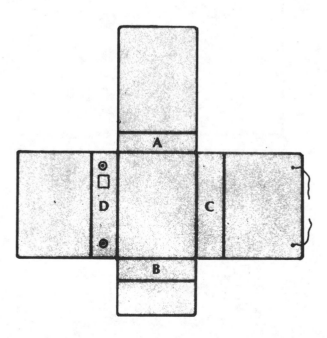

DIAGRAM 6 **Completed Regular Phased Box (One-Board Construction)**

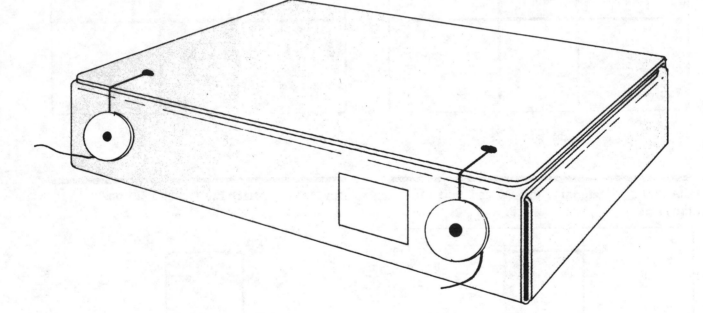

B12. Thymol and o-Phenyl Phenol: Safe Work Practices

By Deborah Nagin, M.P.H. and Michael McCann, Ph.D., C.I.H.

Molds, mildew and other fungi are of major concern to paper and book conservators because of the damage these organisms can do to manuscripts, books, and paper works of art. This is particularly a problem in those museums, libraries and archives where inadequate environmental controls create conditions of high relative humidity and high temperatures which are especially conducive to the growth of mold and mildew.

The two most common fungicides used to control mold and mildew are thymol (isopropyl-*meta*-cresol) and o-phenyl phenol (*ortho*-phenyl phenol, Dowicide 1). These fungicides are used in fumigation and humidification chambers, in alcohol solutions, and in starch paste adhesives.

Hazards of Thymol and o-Phenyl Phenol

Both thymol and o-phenyl phenol belong to a general family of phenols which also includes such compounds as phenol (carbolic acid), creosote, cresol and pentachlorophenol. Phenols typically are irritating to the skin, eyes and upper respiratory system, and can affect the central nervous system, circulatory system, liver and kidneys. Usually they are toxic by all three routes of entry: skin absorption, inhalation and ingestion.

Thymol

Thymol is found in a crystalline or flake form at room temperature, but readily sublimes to a vapor form when heated above 120°F (49° C). It can be absorbed through the skin, by inhalation or by inadvertent ingestion (e.g. by eating or smoking with contaminated hands). It can cause eye irritation. The major hazard to conservators, however, is by inhalation. Symptoms of acute overexposure include gastric pain, nausea, vomiting, and central nervous system overactivity (e.g. talkativeness). Very high levels of exposure could result in convulsions, coma and cardiac or respiratory arrest. This is unlikely to occur, however, because thymol has a very pungent and irritating odor which means it has good odor warning properties.

Very little is known about the long term effects of thymol. From the general properties of phenols, however, liver and kidney damage, and dermatitis might be expected.

In actual use by conservators, common complaints have included headaches, respiratory irritation and a pungent and clinging odor. More serious complaints have also been reported.

o-Phenyl Phenol

Like thymol, o-phenyl phenol is a solid at room temperature. It is not absorbed through the skin and is not a skin irritant. It is much less toxic than thymol but can cause eye irritation with symptoms ranging from redness and swelling to corneal injury depending upon the level of exposure. Inhalation of the powder could cause upper respiratory irritation and chronic exposure could cause kidney damage. However this is unlikely to occur under normal conservation practices. Reactions from spraying o-phenyl phenol, would be of more concern due to possible inhalation of the spray.

Note that the sodium salt of o-phenyl phenol (Dowicide A) can be irritating to the skin in aqueous solutions of 0.5% or greater.

Fumigation With Thymol Chambers

The commonest method of fumigating with thymol involves placing dishes of thymol crystals in a chamber with the material to be fumigated, and then heating the thymol crystals with a 15-20 watt light bulb until it vaporizes. The material being fumigated is exposed to the thymol vapors for three days up to a week before being removed.

Thymol chambers are usually homemade and can vary from plastic bags to very complex air-tight chambers. Usually they consist of a wooden box with a door, possibly windows, shelves and light bulbs as a heat source.

The most hazardous step in thymol fumigation occurs after the fumigation is finished (unless the thymol chamber is not air-tight, in which case there is exposure to thymol vapors during the entire fumigation process). When the thymol chamber is opened to remove the fumigated material, thymol vapors can escape into the room. If the chamber is left open, residual thymol crystals can vaporize to provide an additional source of exposure. If there were depositions of thymol crystals on the paper or book being fumigated, then handling the paper could result in skin exposure.

Precautions

1. Ensure that the thymol chamber is totally enclosed and sealed when fumigating in order to prevent the escape of thymol vapors into the room.

2. If the thymol chamber is made of wood, paint the inside with epoxy paint to prevent absorption of thymol by the wood walls. Do not use varnishes or other coating which might be affected by the thymol vapors.

3. If the thymol crystals are overheated (e.g. using light bulbs over 20 watts), then excess thymol will vaporize and deposit on chamber walls and the paper being fumigated. This will make removal of thymol vapors more difficult.

Note: According to Dr. Robert McComb, Research and Testing, Preservation Office, Library of Congress, o-phenyl phenol is less toxic and more effective than thymol, and should be substituted for thymol in every application.

4. When the fumigation is completed, remove the thymol vapors with a local exhaust ventilation system before opening the thymol chamber and removing the fumigated work. This will prevent exposure to the thymol vapors during and after removal of the work. Flushing the thymol chamber with air for one hour should be sufficient. After removal of the work, close the openings in the thymol chamber.

The accompanying diagrams show a possible local exhaust ventilation system for a thymol chamber. Air enters the chamber through an opening at the top and is removed through a duct at the bottom. The shelves in the chamber must be slotted or perforated to allow circulation of air and thymol vapors.

The ducting should be 4 inch diameter, circular galvanized steel with soldered joints. A larger diameter might be necessary if the fan inlet is larger.

The fan should be located outside the building or in the window so that the ducting is under negative pressure. Make sure that the exhausted thymol vapors cannot enter other offices or expose other people. The fan should be a forward curved centrifugal fan ("squirrel cage" type) of the smallest air flow capacity available. For a chamber under 30 cubic feet, a flow of 10 cubic feet per minute is sufficient. The fan should have a nonsparking, brushless induction motor.

The air intake for the thymol chamber should be the same size as the exhaust ducting and equipped with a sliding door or cover to seal the chamber during fumigation. The opening to the ducting can have a similar cover if desired, however the leakage of thymol vapors through the fan should minimal.

For more information on ventilation, see the COH Ventilation Data Sheet.

5. Wear neoprene or butyl rubber gloves when handling thymol crystals or when handling recently fumigated work which might be contaminated with thymol crystals. In case of skin contact flush with plenty of water. In case of eye contact rinse with water for at least 15 minutes and contact a physician.

6. While a local exhaust ventilation system is being installed or for emergencies, wear a NIOSH-certified respirator with an organic vapor cartridge when opening the thymol chamber and during possible exposure to thymol vapors. If the thymol vapor concentration is high enough to cause eye irritation, a full face respirator (gas mask type) should be worn.

Note that respirators must be fitted properly and adequately maintained. For more information see COH Respirator Data Sheet.

7. Do not eat, smoke or drink in the lab area in order to avoid possible accidental ingestion of chemicals. Wash hands after work or at breaks.

Humidification Chambers

Thymol is often used in high humidity chambers to inhibit biological growth. The levels of thymol required are much lower and therefore the hazard is greatly decreased although conservators have complained of a residual thymol odor on the treated material.

Precautions

1. Because of the lower thymol concentration, a humidification chamber does not have to be equipped with local exhaust ventilation. Obviously a humidification chamber with local exhaust ventilation does make it easier to air out the work to remove residual thymol deposits.

Good dilution air ventilation in the room can be sufficient. This should not be of the recirculating type, however, since that could transport thymol vapors to the rest of the building or cause the thymol vapors to reenter the room. The exhaust air should be directly vented to the outside.

2. Close the chamber after removal of treated material to prevent escape of residual thymol in the humidification chamber.

3. Wear butyl rubber gloves when handling thymol. In case of skin contact rinse with plenty of water; in case of eye contact rinse eyes for at least 15 minutes and contact a physician.

Thymol/Alcohol Baths

Another fungicidal treatment for paper is to pass the sheets of paper through a bath containing thymol dissolved in alcohol. The thymol-treated paper is then hung up to dry on a rack.

The main risks of exposure to thymol come from possible skin contact with the thymol while preparing and using the thymol bath, and possible inhalation of thymol vapors during drying of the treated paper.

The other main hazards comes from possible exposure to alcohol. Methyl alcohol (methyl hydrate) is not recommended by conservators for technical reasons, but should also not be used because of its hazards. Methyl alchohol can be absorbed through the skin or inhaled to cause central nervous system damage and optic nerve damage. It may cause blindness if ingested. It also has poor odor warning properties.

Ethyl alcohol (denatured alcohol, industrial alcohol) is much safer than methyl alcohol. It is not absorbed through the skin and is much less toxic by inhalation or ingestion. High concentrations are irritating to the eyes, nose and throat.

In addition to the health hazards, alcohols are flammable.

Precautions

1. Wear neoprene or butyl rubber gloves when preparing the thymol bath, immersing the paper in the thymol bath, and while handling the thymol-treated paper. In case of skin contact wash with plenty of water; in case of eye contact rinse eyes for at least 15 minutes and contact a physician.

2. The mixing of the thymol crystals with ethyl alcohol should preferably be done under a laboratory hood. Small amounts however could be mixed in the open if the room has good dilution ventilation. As discussed previously the room should have a separate exhaust.

3. Keep the thymol bath covered when not in use or drain it to prevent evaporation of solvent and thymol.

4. The thymol treated paper should be dried in a laboratory hood or in a drying rack equipped with local exhaust ventilation. An enclosed drying rack could be ventilated in a similar manner to the thymol chamber described earlier.

5. Do not allow smoking, open flames or sources of sparks or static electricity in the area where the alcohol is being used.

6. Use o-phenyl phenol rather than thymol whenever possible because of its lower toxicity.

Thymol-impregnated Sheets

A method of treating mildew-infested books involves impregnating blotting paper with 10% solution of thymol in alcohol, drying the blotting paper, and then placing the blotting paper between the pages of the book. The thymol-treated blotting paper is allowed to remain in the book for some weeks.

The hazards of the thymol/alcohol bath have been described in the previous section. Some evaporation of thymol will occur

THYMOL CHAMBER

EXTERIOR VIEW

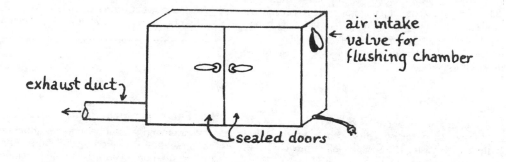

← air intake valve for flushing chamber

exhaust duct ⟶

sealed doors

INTERIOR VIEW

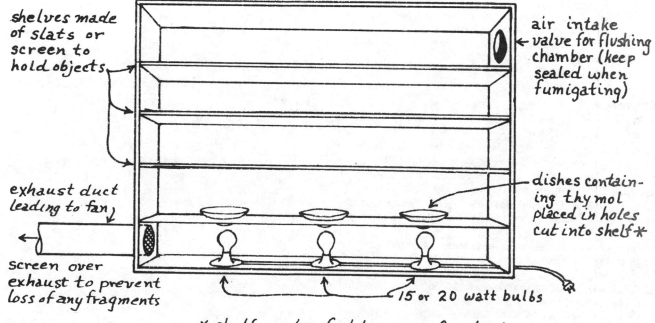

shelves made of slats or screen to hold objects

← air intake valve for flushing chamber (keep sealed when fumigating)

exhaust duct leading to fan

dishes containing thymol placed in holes cut into shelf ✳

screen over exhaust to prevent loss of any fragments

15 or 20 watt bulbs

drawing by Monona Rossol

✳ shelf made of slats or perforated material to allow air flow to the exhaust (Dishes could be supported on tripods instead.)

from the impregnated blotting paper. In addition the thymol in the blotting paper could be absorbed through the skin.

Precautions

1. See previous section for precautions in preparing and using thymol/alcohol baths.

2. Wear neoprene or butyl gloves when handling the thymol-impregnated blotting paper.

3. The book with the thymol-treated blotting paper should be placed in a laboratory hood or similar storage with local exhaust ventilation while being treated. After removal of blotting paper, the book should be aired out to remove residual thymol.

4. Use o-phenyl phenol rather than thymol whenever possible because of its lower toxicity.

Starch Paste

Both thymol and o-phenyl phenol are used as additives to starch paste adhesives. Crystals are dissolved in ethyl alcohol and added to the starch paste. The sodium salt of o-phenyl phenol is sometimes used in aqueous solutions.

Precautions

1. Wear neoprene or butyl rubber gloves when handling the fungicides. In case of skin contact, wash with plenty of water; in case of eye contact, rinse for at least 15 minutes with water and contact a physician.

2. The thymol or o-phenyl phenol should be mixed in a room with good dilution ventilation, as described earlier.

3. Use o-phenyl phenol rather than thymol whenever possible due to the lower toxicity of o-phenyl phenol.

References

1. The Repairing of Books, Sidney Cockerell, 2nd edition, Sheppard Press, London (1960)

2. "A Simple and Practical Fumigation System for Works on Paper." Barry Byers, Abbey Newsletter (in press, 1982)

3. Clinical Properties of Commercial Products, M. Gleason, et. al., 4th Edition, Williams and Wilkins Co., Baltimore (1976).

4. Occupational Diseases: A Guide to Their Recognition, Revised Edition, National Institute for Occupational Safety and Health (NIOSH) (1977).

5. Dangerous Properties of Industrial Materials, N. Irving Sax, 5th Edition, Interscience Publishers, New York (1978).

6. Condensed Chemical Dictionary, 10th Edition, Revised by G.G. Hawley, Van Nostrand Reinhold Company, New York (1981).

7. Work is Dangerous To Your Health, J. Stellman and S. Daum, Vintage Paperbacks, New York (1973).

8. Encyclopedia of Occupational Health & Safety, International Labor Organization, McGraw Hill, New York (1972).

9. Material Safety Data Sheet, Dowicide 1 Antimicrobial (o-Phenyl Phenol), Dow Chemical Company.

10. Material Safety Data Sheet, Thymol, Fisher Scientific Company.

Summary of Safe Work Practices for Thymol

1. Use local exhaust ventilation when handling and using thymol.

2. Wear neoprene or butyl rubber gloves when handling thymol.

3. In case of skin contact, wash with plenty of water; in case of eye contact rinse with water for at least 15 minutes and contact a physician.

4. Do not eat, drink or smoke when handling and using thymol. Wash hands after work and before eating.

For Further Information

Written and telephone inquiries about health hazards in fumigation will be answered by the Information Center of the Center for Occupational Hazards. The Information Center has a variety of written materials on this subject for dissemination. Permission to reprint this data sheet may be requested in writing from the Center. Enclose a self-addressed stamped envelope for our publications list. Write: Center for Occupational Hazards, 5 Beekman Street, New York, NY 10038. Telephone 212-227-6220.

This data sheet was prepared with financial assistance from the New York State Council on the Arts.

Appendix C
Evaluating the Conservation Literature

A large number of books and articles on conservation has been published in recent years. The conservation literature runs the gamut from highly technical materials written by and for professional conservators to "how-to" articles written at the most basic level for a lay audience (primarily book and manuscript collectors). In between is a growing body of professional literature on archival and library conservation, directed toward administrators, archivists, librarians, and curators.

In reading and evaluating the applicability of this literature to archival conservation, a number of factors must be considered. The date of any publication in this rapidly changing field is important. Recent research, new techniques, and ongoing evaluation of treatment procedures must be taken into account as one reads much of the early literature. This is not to say that all data in early publications is suspect, but, rather, that it must be read in light of present knowledge. Thus, a conservation manual written in the 1940s should not be accepted blindly in its entirety, given all of the advances that have come about in the intervening years.

Another element to consider in evaluating the conservation literature is the source—that is, the author and publisher. Is the author recognized and knowledgeable in the field? Is the publisher reputable? Vanity publications, "major" new works that emanate from unknown sources, or those that have not likely undergone peer review should be regarded with skepticism. The intended audience must be considered as well. Articles and books directed toward private collectors are not necessarily applicable to institutional collections. A number of articles in the past have advocated "home remedies" or "kitchen chemistry," which, if implemented, could have disastrous results, and should not be given credence by anyone.

Somewhat confusing the issue is the fact that reputable authors may take entirely different stances on the same subject or point. To a degree, this is to be expected, given the fact that the conservation profession is relatively new. Much is still in flux and further research is required to settle a number of issues definitively. For example, in reading articles on leather treatment, one will come across varying recommendations regarding the appropriate length of time to wait between applying potassium lactate solution and the application of neat's-foot oil and lanolin. The recommended waiting period ranges from one to twenty-four hours, all from reputable sources. In this instance, the resolution of the quandary is relatively easy: the neat's-foot oil should not be applied until the potassium lactate is thoroughly dry to the touch. The amount of time this will take will vary, depending upon the amount of moisture in the air, the amount of solution applied, and the porosity of the leather.

Good common sense should always be employed when reading the conservation literature. If recommendations do not appear to be in conformance with accepted conservation practice and theory, they obviously should not be followed. When in doubt, consult with a conservator, an archivist with a conservation specialty, or a conservation center. In this, as in other areas, the archivist must be a knowledgeable consumer. It is important to read widely and thoroughly, and to proceed with caution.

Appendix D
Bibliography

Basic Bookshelf

It is recommended that archivists build a basic conservation library that can be readily consulted. The following titles are suggested as a central core, which can be complemented as necessary by specialized titles. Current prices are given where applicable to indicate the cost of building this basic conservation collection.

Books

Bohem, Hilda. *Disaster Prevention and Disaster Preparedness*. Berkeley: Office of the Assistant Vice President—Library Plans and Policies, Systemwide Administration, University of California, April, 1978.

Suggests a comprehensive list of factors and options to be considered when establishing a disaster preparedness plan. Available from the Office of the Assistant Vice President—Library Plans and Policies, No. 7 University Hall, University of California-Berkeley, Berkeley, CA 94720. ($3.50)

Clapp, Anne F. *Curatorial Care of Works of Art on Paper*. 3d rev. ed. Oberlin, Ohio: Intermuseum Conservation Association, 1978.

Excellent manual covering causes of paper deterioration, environmental controls, and treatment procedures from a curatorial perspective. Includes a bibliography and source list of supplies and materials. Some treatment techniques are fairly sophisticated. Order from: Intermuseum Conservation Association, Allen Art Building, Oberlin, OH 44074. ($5)

Cunha, George M. and Dorothy Grant Cunha. *Conservation of Library Materials: A Manual and Bibliography on the Care, Repair and Restoration of Library Materials*. Vol. I. 2d ed. Metuchen, N.J.: Scarecrow Press, 1971.

Examines the scope of the problem and its causes, the nature of library materials, preventive measures, and repair, restoration, and testing procedures. ($16.50; Vols. I and II, $30)

Eastman Kodak Company. *Preservation of Photographs*. Kodak Publication #F-30. Rochester, N.Y.: Eastman Kodak Company, 1979.

Good coverage of routine procedures for photographic preservation; excellent source of information on the material nature of photographs. Suggested chemical and wet treatments should not be attempted by persons without photographic darkroom experience. ($5.50)

Eastman Kodak Company. *Storage and Preservation of Microfilms*. Kodak Pamphlet D-31. Rochester, N.Y.: Eastman Kodak Company, 1981.

Provides basic information on recommended environmental conditions, processing, and inspection procedures. Available free by writing: Eastman Kodak Company, 343 State Street, Dept. 412-L, Rochester, NY 14650.

Edwards, Stephen R., Bruce M. Bell, and Mary Elizabeth King, comps. *Pest Control in Museums: A Status Report (1980)*. Lawrence, Kansas: Association of Systematics Collections, 1981.

Recommended required reading for all archivists and manuscript curators. Covers federal statutes and regulations governing the use of pesticides, institutional policies, technical data on pesticides used in museums, illustrated information on common insect pests, and sources of further information. Order from: A.S.C., Museum of Natural History, University of Kansas, Lawrence, KS 66045. ($15)

Horton, Carolyn. *Cleaning and Preserving Bindings and Related Materials*. LTP Publications #12. Chicago: American Library Association, 1967.

Describes a practical step-by-step approach to the care and treatment of books. Includes simple repair techniques. ($10)

Library of Congress. *Polyester Film Encapsulation*. Washington, D.C.: Library of Congress, 1980.

Discusses the physical and chemical properties of polyester film, compares polyester encapsulation and cellulose acetate lamination, and gives illustrated instructions for making a polyester capsule, polyester book, etc. ($2.50)

McWilliams, Jerry. *The Preservation and Restoration of Sound Recordings*. Nashville: American Association for State and Local History, 1979.

Covers history, storage requirements, cleaning, and proper playback techniques, with basic information on restoration procedures. ($8.95; $7 to AASLH members)

Waters, Peter. *Procedures for Salvage of Water-Damaged Library Materials*. 2d ed. Washington, D.C.: Library of Congress, 1979.

A basic text that should be reviewed before establishing a disaster plan. Outlines procedures to follow after water damage to paper, books, and photographs. Includes a list of individuals available to provide disaster assistance and advice. ($4.50)

Weinstein, Robert A. and Larry Booth. *Collection, Use and Care of Historical Photographs.* Nashville: American Association for State and Local History, 1977.

Provides detailed information on identification, storage, handling, and use of photographic materials. Some of the preservation and restoration techniques described are quite complex and should be left to conservators. Also, recent research conducted on photographic materials should be consulted before undertaking physical treatment. ($16; $10.50 to AASLH members)

Articles

Banks, Paul N. "Environmental Standards for Storage of Books and Manuscripts." *Library Journal* 99 (February 1, 1974): 339–343.

Excellent brief review of temperature, humidity, light and air quality requirements. Includes information on shelving, exhibition, and disaster control.

Banks, Paul N. "Preservation of Library Materials." *Encyclopedia of Library and Information Science,* 23:180–222. New York: Marcel Dekker, Inc., 1978.

Presents an overview of the field suggesting numerous philosophical, ethical, technical, and practical problems that require resolution.

Wessel, Carl J. "Deterioraton of Library Materials." *Encyclopedia of Library and Information Science,* 7:69–120. New York: Marcel Dekker, Inc., 1972.

Provides a detailed summary of factors that affect the preservation of library and archival materials.

Newsletters

The Abbey Newsletter: Bookbinding and Conservation. Ellen McCrady, Editor, School of Library Service, 516 Butler Library, Columbia University, New York, NY 10027.

The best source of current information on supplies, materials, seminars, and new publications. Status reports are often given on developing procedures and techniques. (6 issues/year, $15)

Art Hazards News. Center for Occupational Hazards, 5 Beekman St., New York, NY 10038.

Source of current information on the use and hazards of materials used in conservation treatments and fumigation. The Art Hazards Information Center—a project of the Center for Occupational Hazards—will answer written and telephone (212-227-6220) inquiries on the hazards of arts and crafts materials and suitable precautions. (10 issues/year, $13)

Conservation Administration News (CAN). Robert H. Patterson, Editor, University of Tulsa, McFarlin Library, 600 South College Avenue, Tulsa, OK 74104.

Provides information on library and archival conservation programs, training opportunities, new publications, and grant funds for preservation activities. (4 issues/year, $18)

Bibliographies

Banks, Paul N. *A Selective Bibliography on the Conservation of Research Library Materials.* Chicago: Newberry Library, 1981.

Topical arrangement covering such subjects as technology and structure of record materials, inherent vice and environmental enemies, preventive maintenance, and treatment procedures. ($10)

Cunha, George M. and Dorothy Grant Cunha. *Conservation of Library Materials: A Manual and Bibliography on the Care, Repair and Restoration of Library Materials.* Vol. II, 2d ed. Metuchen, N.J.: Scarecrow Press, 1972.

Organized by subject to correspond with the arrangement of the text in Vol. I. 4,882 entries. ($16.50; Vols. I and II, $30)

Cunha, George M. and Dorothy Grant Cunha. *Library and Archives Conservation: 1980s and Beyond.* Vol. II: Bibliography. Metuchen, N.J.: Scarecrow Press, 1983.

A supplement to the 1972 bibliography listed above. 5,871 entries arranged by subject. ($28.50; Vols. I and II, $39.50)

Selected Readings

In addition, the following books, articles, and newsletters will provide useful information for planning and administering a program for the conservation of archival materials.

Books and Reports

American National Standards Institute. *Method for Evaluating the Processing of Black and White Photographic Papers with Respect to the Stability of the Resultant Image.* New York: ANSI, 1974. (PH 4.32-1974)

American National Standards Institute. *Methylene Blue Method for Measuring Thiosulfate and Silver Densitometric Method for Measuring Residual Chemicals in Films, Plates, and Papers.* New York: ANSI, 1978. (PH 4.8-1978)

American National Standards Institute. *Practice for Storage of Black and White Photographic Paper Prints*. New York: ANSI, 1974. (PH 1.48-1974)

American National Standards Institute. *Practice for Storage of Processed Safety Photographic Film*. New York: ANSI, 1981. (PH 1.43-1981)

American National Standards Institute. *Practice for Storage of Processed Photographic Plates*. New York: ANSI, 1981. (PH 1.45-1981)

American National Standards Institute. *Requirements for Photographic Filing Enclosures for Storing Processed Photographic Films, Plates and Papers*. New York: ANSI, 1978. (PH 1.53-1978)

American National Standards Institute. *Specifications for Photographic Films for Archival Records, Silver-Gelatin Type, on Cellulose Ester Base*. New York: ANSI, 1976. (PH 1.28-1976)

American National Standards Institute. *Specifications for Photographic Films for Archival Records, Silver-Gelatin Type, on Polyester Base*. New York: ANSI, 1976. (PH 1.41-1976) For a complete list of ANSI specifications, write: American National Standards Institute, 1430 Broadway, New York, N.Y. 10018.

Baker, John P. and Marguerite C. Soroka, eds. *Library Conservation: Preservation in Perspective*. Stroudsburg, Penn.: Dowden, Hutchinson and Ross, 1978.

A selection of thirty-four readings from the period 1946–1976 organized to address philosophical and administrative aspects of conservation.

Barrow, W.J., Research Laboratory. *Physical and Chemical Properties of Book Papers 1507–1949*. Permanence/Durability of the Book—VII. Richmond, Virginia: W.J. Barrow Research Laboratory, 1974.

Barrow, W.J., Research Laboratory. *Polyvinyl Acetate (PVA) Adhesives for Use in Library Bookbinding*. Permanence/Durability of the Book—IV. Richmond, Virginia: W.J. Barrow Research Laboratory, 1965.

Barrow, W.J., Research Laboratory. *Spot Testing for Unstable Modern Book and Record Papers*. Permanence/Durability of the Book—VI. Richmond, Virginia: W.J. Barrow Research Laboratory, 1969.

Barrow, W.J., Research Laboratory. *Spray Deacidification*. Permanence/Durability of the Book—III. Richmond, Virginia: W.J. Barrow Research Laboratory, 1964.

Barrow, W.J., Research Laboratory. *Strength and Other Characteristics of Book Papers 1800–1899*. Permanence/Durability of the Book—V. Richmond, Virginia: W.J. Barrow Research Laboratory, 1967.

Barrow, W.J., Research Laboratory. *Test Data of Naturally Aged Papers*. Permanence/Durability of the Book—II. Richmond, Virginia: W.J. Barrow Research Laboratory, 1964.

Barrow, W.J., Research Laboratory. *A Two-Year Research Program*. Permanence/Durability of the Book. Richmond, Virginia: W.J. Barrow Research Laboratory, 1963.

Brown, Margaret R., compiler and illustrator. *Boxes for the Protection of Rare Books: Their Design and Construction*. Washington, D.C.: Preservation Office, Library of Congress, 1982.

Bruer, J. Michael. *Toward a California Document Conservation Program*. San Jose: California Library Authority for Systems and Services, October 1, 1978.

Documents conservation needs, objectives, and proposed action in three areas of concern—education, training, and research; planning, needs assessment, and funding; operations and services. Available from CLASS, 1415 Koll Circle, Suite 101, San Jose, CA 95112. Price is $8 for CLASS members, $10 for others.

Buchanan, Sally, Phillip Leighton, and Leon Davies. *The Stanford-Lockheed Meyer Library Flood Report*. Stanford: The Stanford University Libraries, May 1980.

Canadian Conservation Institute, *Technical Bulletins*. Available without charge from the Canadian Conservation Institute, 1030 Innes Road, Ottawa, Canada K1A 0M8. Titles include:

Macleod, K.J. *Relative Humidity: Its Importance, Measurement, and Control in Museums*. Technical Bulletin 1, 1978.

Macleod, K.J. *Museum Lighting*. Technical Bulletin 2, 1978.

LaFontaine, R.H. *Recommended Environmental Monitors for Museums, Archives, and Art Galleries*. Technical Bulletin 3, 1978.

LaFontaine, R.H. *Environmental Norms for Canadian Museums, Art Galleries, and Archives*. Technical Bulletin 5, 1979.

Rempel, Siegfried. *The Care of Black and White Photographic Collections: Identification of Processes*. Technical Bulletin 6, 1979.

LaFontaine, R.H. and Patricia A. Wood. *Fluorescent Lamps*. Technical Bulletin 7, 1980.

Rempel, Siegfried. *The Care of Black and White Photographic Collections: Cleaning and Stabilization*. Technical Bulletin 9, 1980.

Casterline, Gail Farr. *Archives and Manuscripts: Exhibits*. Basic Manual Series. Chicago: Society of American Archivists, 1980.

Cunha, George M. *Conserving Local Archival Materials on a Limited Budget.* Technical Leaflet #86. *History News* (November, 1975). Nashville: American Association for State and Local History, 1975.

Cunha, George M. and Dorothy Grant Cunha. *Library and Archives Conservation: 1980s and Beyond.* Vol. I. Metuchen, N.J.: Scarecrow Press, 1983.

Cunha, George M. and Norman Paul Tucker, eds. *Library and Archives Conservation: The Boston Athenaeum's 1971 Seminar on the Application of Chemical and Physical Methods to the Conservation of Library and Archival Materials, May 17-21, 1971.* Boston: The Library of the Boston Athenaeum, 1972.

Darling, Pamela W. and Duane E. Webster. *Preservation Planning Program: An Assisted Self-Study Manual for Libraries.* Washington, D.C.: Association of Research Libraries, Office of Management Studies, 1982.

Darling, Pamela W. *Preservation Planning Program Resource Notebook.* Washington, D.C.: Association of Research Libraries, Office of Management Studies, 1982.

Dolloff, Francis W. and Roy L. Perkinson. *How to Care for Works of Art on Paper.* Boston: Museum of Fine Arts, 1971.

General Services Administration. Public Building Service. *Protecting Records Centers and Archives from Fire: Report of the General Services Administration Advisory Committee on the Protection of Archives and Records Centers.* Washington, D.C.: GPO, April, 1977.

Hunter, Dard. *Papermaking: The History and Technique of an Ancient Craft.* 3rd ed. New York: Dover Press, 1978.

Most complete work on the history and technique of papermaking; a classic (originally issued by Knopf in 1943).

Keck, Caroline K. *Safeguarding Your Collection in Travel.* Nashville: American Association for State and Local History, 1970.

Kyle, Hedi. *Library Materials Preservation Manual. Practical Methods for Preserving Books, Pamphlets and Other Printed Materials.* Bronxville, N.Y.: Nicholas T. Smith, 1983.

Lessard, Elizabeth. *Cyanotypes: A Modern Use for an Old Technique.* Technical Leaflet #133. *History News* (December, 1980). Nashville: American Association for State and Local History, 1980.

Describes an inexpensive way to contact print a collection of glass plate and film negatives.

Library of Congress. *Preservation Leaflets.* Washington, D.C.: Library of Congress, 1975-

Available free from LC's Preservation Office, this is a continuing series of "basic information" leaflets intended for those with limited background and experience in conservation of books and documents. Titles include:

> *#1—Selected References in the Literature of Conservation*
> *#2—Environmental Protection of Books and Related Materials*
> *#3—Preserving Leather Bookbindings*
> *#4—Marking Paper Manuscripts*
> *#5—Preserving Newspapers and Newspaper-Type Materials*

Library of Congress. *A National Preservation Program: Proceedings of the Planning Conference.* Washington, D.C.: Library of Congress, 1980.

Martin, John H., ed. *The Corning Flood: Museum Under Water.* Corning, N.Y.: The Corning Museum of Glass, 1977.

Materazzi, Albert R. *Archival Stability of Microfilm —A Technical Review.* Washington, D.C.: GPO, 1978. Available from ERIC, ED 171 255.

Discusses silver halide, diazo, and vesicular film and provides a basic introduction to sensitometry. Archival considerations of micrographics are explained in terms of their use properties and image stability.

Matthai, Robert A., ed. *Protection of Cultural Properties During Energy Emergencies.* 2nd ed. New York: Arts/Energy Study Association and American Association of Museums, 1978.

Middleton, Bernard C. *The Restoration of Leather Bindings.* Chicago: American Library Association, 1972.

Morris, John. *Managing the Library Fire Risk.* 2nd ed. Berkeley: Office of Risk Management and Safety, University of California, 1979.

Morrison, Robert C., Jr., George M. Cunha, and Norman P. Tucker, eds. *Conservation Administration: The 1973 Seminar on the Theoretical Aspects of the Conservation of Library and Archival Materials and the Establishment of Conservation Programs, October 1-5, 1973.* North Andover, Mass.: The New England Document Conservation Center and the Library of the Boston Athenaeum, 1975.

Morrow, Carolyn Clark. *A Conservation Policy Statement for Research Libraries.* Occasional Paper #139. Urbana-Champaign: University of Illinois Graduate School of Library Science, July 1979.

Morrow, Carolyn Clark. *Conservation Treatment Procedures: A Manual of Step-by-Step Procedures for the Maintenance and Repair of Library Materials*. Littleton, Colorado: Libraries, Unlimited, Inc., 1982.

Focuses on book repair procedures and means of providing protective encasement. Useful appendixes, including a dexterity test, equipment and supply list, and suggestions for determining the appropriate level of in-house treatment.

National Archives and Records Service. *Intrinsic Value in Archival Material*. Staff Information Paper 21. Washington, D.C.: National Archives and Records Service, 1982.

Suggests an approach for evaluating archival records to determine whether or not they need to be retained in their original format or if copies will suffice. Concepts discussed applicable to setting conservation treatment priorities.

National Archives and Records Service. Preservation Services Division. *Preparation of Solutions of Magnesium Bicarbonate for Deacidification of Documents*. Washington, D.C.: NARS, 1979.

National Conservation Advisory Council. *Conservation of Cultural Property in the United States*. Washington, D.C.: National Conservation Advisory Council, 1976.

A general review of the status of conservation in this country, with recommendations for the future in terms of education, training, and research. Represents judgments from the museum, historic building preservation, and library and archival communities. All NCAC publications listed here are available free from NCAC, c/o A & I 2225, Smithsonian Institution, Washington, DC 20560.

National Conservation Advisory Council. *Conservation Treatment Facilities in the United States*. Washington, D.C.: National Conservation Advisory Council, 1980.

Includes the AIC *Code of Ethics and Standards of Practice*.

National Conservation Advisory Council. *Report of the Study Committee on Libraries and Archives*. Washington, D.C.: National Conservation Advisory Council, 1978.

Details conservation needs and recommendations in seven areas—surveys; education and training; research and scientific support; publications; regional or cooperative treatment centers; reproduction; and standards.

National Fire Protection Association. *Archives and Records Centers 1980*. NFPA 232AM. Boston: National Fire Protection Association.

National Fire Protection Association. *The National Fire Code*. Boston: National Fire Protection Association, 1938-

National Fire Protection Association. *Protection of Libraries and Library Collections 1980*. NFPA 910. Boston: National Fire Protection Association, 1980.

Noble, Richard. *Archival Preservation of Motion Pictures: A Summary of Current Findings*. Technical Leaflet #126. *History News* (April, 1980). Nashville: American Association for State and Local History.

Plenderleith, H.J. and A.E. Werner. *The Conservation of Antiquities and Works of Art: Treatment, Repair and Restoration*. 2d ed. London: Oxford University Press, 1971.

While this volume is somewhat dated and the suggested treatments (some of which are no longer acceptable) are concerned largely with art-on-paper, this is the standard source of information on leather, papyrus, parchment, and paper. Provides excellent information on examination of prints, drawings, and manuscripts, in addition to considerations of the environment.

Preserving Your Historical Records. Proceedings of the Symposium Held at Drake University, October 20–21, 1978, sponsored by the College for Continuing Education of Drake University, Kansas City Federal Archives and Records Center, Iowa Historical Materials Preservation Society, and the Iowa Local Historical and Museum Association. Edited by Toby Fishbein and Alan F. Perry, July 1980.

Available without charge while the supply lasts, from: Archives Branch, Federal Archives and Records Center, NARS, 2306 E. Bannister Road, Kansas City, MO 64131.

Roberts, Matt T. and Don Etherington. *Bookbinding and the Conservation of Books. A Dictionary of Descriptive Terminology*. Washington, D.C.: Preservation Office, Library of Congress, 1982.

Russell, Joyce R., ed. *Preservation of Library Materials*. New York: Special Libraries Association, 1980.

Proceedings of a seminar sponsored by the Library Binding Institute and the Princeton-Trenton chapter of the SLA held at Rutgers University, July 20–21, 1979.

Smith, Merrily A., comp. *Matting and Hinging Works of Art on Paper*. Washington, D.C.: Preservation Office, Library of Congress, 1981.

Stolow, Nathan. *Conservation Standards for Works of Art in Transit and on Exhibition.* New York: Unipub (United Nations Educational, Scientific and Cultural Organization), 1980.

Sung, Carolyn Hoover. *Archives and Manuscripts: Reprography.* Basic Manual Series. Chicago: Society of American Archivists, 1982.

Swartzburg, Susan. *Preserving Library Materials.* Metuchen, N.J.: Scarecrow Press, 1980.

Trinkaus-Randall, Gregor. *Effects of the Environment on Paper: A Review of Recent Literature.* Technical Leaflet #128. *History News* (July, 1980). Nashville: American Association for State and Local History, 1980.

Walch, Timothy. *Archives and Manuscripts: Security.* Basic Manual Series. Chicago: Society of American Archivists, 1977.

Willson, Nancy, ed. *Museum and Archival Supplies Handbook.* 2nd ed. Toronto: Ontario Museum Association and the Toronto Area Archivists' Group, 1979.

Winger, Howard W. and Richard Daniel Smith, eds. *Deterioration and Preservation of Library Materials.* Chicago: University of Chicago Press, 1970.

Papers presented at the thirty-fourth annual conference of the Graduate Library School of the University of Chicago, August 4-6, 1969. Also appears in: *The Library Quarterly* 40:1-200 (January, 1970).

Williams, J.C., ed. *Preservation of Paper and Textiles of Historic and Artistic Value II.* Washington, D.C.: American Chemical Society, 1981.

Sections on paper range from basic maintenance to new developments in mass deacidification and the repair of works of art on paper.

Articles

Baas, Valerie. "Know Your Enemies," *History News* 35:40-41 (July, 1980).

Identification and habits of common insects and the damage they can cause to library materials.

Banks, Paul N. "Cooperative Approaches to Conservation," *Library Journal* 101:2348-2351 (November 15, 1976).

Barrow, W.J. "Black Writing Ink of the Colonial Period," *American Archivist.* 11:291-307 (1948).

Barrow, W.J. "Migration of Impurities in Paper." *Archivum* 3:105-8 (1953).

Berger, Pearl. "Minor Repairs in a Small Research Library," *Library Journal* 104:1311-1317 (June 15, 1979).

Bohem, Hilda. "Regional Conservation Services: What Can We Do for Ourselves?" *Library Journal* 104:1428-1431 (July, 1979).

Brahm, Walter. "A Regional Approach to Conservation: The New England Document Conservation Center," *American Archivist* 40:421-427 (October, 1977).

Buck, R.D. "A Specification for Museum Air Conditioning," Part I, *Museum News,* Technical Supplement No. 6, 43:4 (December, 1964).

"Colloquium on Preservation," *Oklahoma Librarian* 30:11-41 (October, 1980).

Contains articles by George Cunha ("Organizing for Conservation"), Pamela Darling (" 'Doing' Preservation, With or Without Money"), Lawrence Robinson ("Preservation of Nonprint Materials") and Sally Buchanan ("Disaster Prevention and Action").

Darling, Pamela W. "A Local Preservation Program: Where to Start?" *Library Journal* 101:2343-2347 (November 15, 1976).

Darling, Pamela W. "Developing a Preservation Microfilming Program," *Library Journal* 99:2803-2809 (November 1, 1974).

Darling, Pamela W. "Preservation: A National Plan at Last?" *Library Journal* 102:447-449 (February 15, 1977).

Report of the National Preservation Program Planning Conference held at LC in December 1976.

Darling, Pamela W. and Sherelyn Ogden. "From Problems Perceived to Programs in Practice: The Preservation of Library Resources in the U.S.A., 1956-1980," *Library Resources and Technical Services* 25:9-29 (January/March, 1981).

Gilbert, Edward R. "A Conservation Primer: The Preservation of Library Materials in Tropical Climates." *Bulletin of the Florida Chapter, Special Libraries Association,* 14:110-127 (July, 1982).

Harris, Carolyn. "Mass Deacidification: Science to the Rescue?" *Library Journal* 104:1423-1427 (July, 1979).

Haynes, Ric. "A Temporary Method to Stabilize Deteriorating Cellulose Nitrate Still Camera Negatives," *PhotographiConservation* 2:1-3 (September, 1980).

Hendriks, Klaus. "The Preservation of Photographic Records," *Archivaria* 5 (Winter, 1977-78): 92-100.

Knapp, Sharon E. "Microfilming Manuscript Collections: A Preliminary Guide for Librarians," *Southeastern Librarian* 28:16-20 (Spring, 1980).

London, Sol. " 'Outer Space' Saves 40,000 Water-Soaked Books," *Records Management Quarterly* 13:38-39.

Mason, Philip P. "Archival Security: New Solutions to an Old Problem," *American Archivist* 38:477–492 (October, 1975).

Orraca, Jose. "Shopping for a Conservator," *Museum News* (January/February, 1981): 60–66.

Patterson, Robert H. "Organizing for Conservation: A Model Charge to a Conservation Committee," *Library Journal* 104: 1116–1119 (May 15, 1979).

Lists ten "charges" which serve as a framework for beginning a conservation program.

Pobboravsky, Irving. "Daguerreotype Preservation: The Problems of Tarnish Removal," *Technology and Conservation* 3:40–45 (Summer, 1978).

Poole, Frazer G. "Preservation" in *Archive-Library Relations*, ed. by Robert L. Clark, Jr. New York: R.R. Bowker Co., 1976, 141-154.

Poole, Frazer G. "Some Aspects of the Conservation Problem in Archives," *American Archivist* 40:163–171 (April, 1977).

Powers, Sandra. "Why Exhibit? The Risks Versus the Benefits," *American Archivist* 41:297–306 (July, 1978).

Rhoads, James B. "Alienation and Thievery: Archival Problems," *American Archivist* 29:197–208 (April, 1966).

Seamans, Warren A. "Restoring and Preserving Architectural Drawings: An Economical Method for Treating Embrittled Documents," *Technology and Conservation* 3:8–10 (Winter, 1976).

Smith, Richard D. "The Deacidification of Paper and Books," *American Libraries* 6:108–110 (1975).

Discusses Smith's proprietary process of magnesium methoxide non-aqueous deacidification.

Smith, Richard D. "Progress in Mass Deacidification at the Public Archives," *Canadian Library Journal* 36:325–332 (December, 1979).

Spaulding, Carl M. "Kicking the Silver Habit: Confessions of a Former Addict," *American Libraries* 9:653–665 (December, 1978).

Spawn, Willman. "After the Water Comes," *Pennsylvania Library Association Bulletin* 28:243–251 (November, 1973).

Waters, Peter, *et al.* "Does Freeze Drying Save Water Soaked Books or Doesn't It? Salvaging a Few 'Facts' From a Flood of (Alleged) Misinformation," *American Libraries* 6:422–423 (July-August, 1975).

Newsletters and Journals

AIC Newsletter and Journal of the AIC. (Publications of the American Institute for Conservation of Historic and Artistic Works, Martha Morales, Executive Secretary, The Klingle Mansion, 3545 Williamsburg Lane, NW, Washington, DC 20008).

History News. (American Association for State and Local History, 708 Berry Rd., Nashville, TN 37204). "Conserva-tips," a monthly column, has featured the following articles in recent months:

"During a Fuel Crisis . . . Safeguards for Collections," January, 1980, p. 56.

"How to Flatten Old Documents," March, 1980, p. 45.

"Museum Lighting," April, 1980, p. 46.

"How to Prevent Mildew," June, 1980, p. 58.

"Paper and Plastic Preservers for Photographic Prints and Negatives," October, 1980, pp. 42–45.

"Care of Video Tapes," December, 1980, p. 39.

"Emergency Storage for Nitrate Films," January, 1981, pp. 38–41.

"Conservation Records," February, 1981, p. 48.

The AASLH also publishes Technical Leaflets which are issued with *History News* on a periodic basis and are often devoted to conservation topics.

Library and Archival Security. (The Haworth Press, 149 Fifth Ave., New York, NY 10010).

The New Library Scene. (Library Binding Institute, P.O. Box 217, Accord, MA 02018).

National Preservation Report. (Preservation Office, Library of Congress, Washington, DC 20540).

Supersedes *Newspaper and Gazette Report.*

PhotographiConservation. (Graphic Arts Research Center, Rochester Institute of Technology, One Lomb Memorial Drive, Rochester, NY 14623).

Picturescope. (Quarterly Bulletin of the Picture Division, Special Libraries Association, P.O. Box 50119, F Street Station, Tariff Commission Building, Washington, DC 20004.)

Technology and Conservation. (The Technology Organization, Inc., One Emerson Place, Boston, MA 02114). Available free upon application, specifying conservation responsibility.

Bibliographies

Audiovisuals for Archivists. Timothy L. Ericson, comp. Chicago: Society of American Archivists, 1982.

A majority of the slide/tape, motion picture, and video presentations in this 8-page compilation relate to some aspect of conservation: storage, handling, the environment, or basic conservation procedures.

Evans, Frank B., comp. *Modern Archives and Manuscripts: A Select Bibliography.* Chicago: Society of American Archivists, 1975.

Parts 9 and 10 cite sources of conservation information. Other sections cite information sources for preserving specific types of recording media, i.e., cartographic records, sound recordings, still pictures, etc.

Harrison, Alice W., Edward A. Collister, and R. Ellen Willis. *The Conservation of Archival and Library Materials: A Resource Guide to Audiovisual Aids.* Metuchen, N.J.: Scarecrow Press, 1982.

Over 500 annotated entries.

Hunter, John E. *Emergency Preparedness for Museums, Historic Sites, and Archives: An Annotated Bibliography.* Technical Leaflet #114. *History News* (April, 1979). Nashville: American Association for State and Local History, 1979.

Morrow, Carolyn Clark and Steven B. Schoenly. *A Conservation Bibliography for Librarians, Archivists, and Administrators.* Troy, N.Y.: Whitson Publishing Co., 1979.

1,367 entries, of which 172 are briefly annotated. Subject index.

Orth, Thomas W. *A Selected Bibliography on Photographic Conservation, January, 1975–December, 1978.* Rochester, N.Y.: Graphic Arts Research Center, Rochester Institute of Technology, 1979.

Reese, Rosemary, comp. *Care and Conservation of Collections,* Vol. II of *A Bibliography on Historical Organization Practices,* ed. by Frederick L. Rath, Jr. and Merrilyn Rogers O'Connell. Nashville: American Association for State and Local History, 1977.

Chapter 5 is devoted to environmental factors in conservation (193 citations); Chapter 6 covers conservation of documentary materials (259 citations). ✿

Appendix E
Audiovisual Sources: A Selected List

The following audiovisual programs are ideal for use in training and orienting staff in conservation practices and procedures. Materials available from a single source are grouped together. Unless specified, the presentations are available for both purchase and rental.

Title	Format/Length	Source
"Environmental Controls"	slide/tape-18½ min.	Conservation Specialist
"Storage and Handling"	slide/tape-13 min.	Nebraska State Historical
"Surface Cleaning"	slide/tape-10½ min.	Society
"Encapsulation"	slide/tape-8 min.	1500 R Street
		Lincoln, NE 68508
		(402-471-3270)
"Keeping Harvard's Books"	slide/tape	Book Conservator
		Harvard University Library
		Andover-Harvard Theological
		Library
		45 Francis Avenue
		Cambridge, MA 12138
		(617-495-5770)
"The Care and Handling of Books"	slide/tape-28 min.	Conservation Department
		Yale University Library
"Simple Repairs for Library Materials"	slide/tape-17 min.	New Haven, CT 06520
		(203-436-4509)
"The Restoration of Books: Florence 1968"	16-mm film-45 min. (available for loan only)	Preservation Office
		Library of Congress
		Washington, DC 20540
		(202-287-5213)
"The Curatorial Examination of Paper Objects"	slide/tape-32 min.	Audiovisual Loan Program
		Office of Museum Programs
"Cleaning of Prints, Drawings and Manuscripts: Dry Methods"	slide/tape-17 min.	Smithsonian Institution
		2235 Arts and Industries Bldg.
"The Hinging and Mounting of Paper Objects"	slide/tape-36 min.	Washington, DC 20560
		(202-357-3101)
"The Removal of Pressure-Sensitive Tape from Flat Paper"	videotape-20 min.	
"Paper: Matting and Framing"	slide/tape-20 min.	Educational Division
"Curatorial Care: The Environment"	slide/tape-17½ min.	American Association for State and Local History
		708 Berry Road
		Nashville, TN 37204
		(615-383-5991)
"The Fragile Record: Preserving Our Documentary Heritage"	slide/tape or videotape-20 min.	Wisconsin Conservation Service Center
		State Historical Society of Wisconsin
		816 State Street
		Madison, WI 53706
		(608-262-8975)

Appendix F
Conservation Supplies and Equipment

This list is arranged by type and function of material and equipment. Archival storage materials are included as well as devices for monitoring the environment and supplies needed to set up a conservation workshop and carry out basic conservation procedures. While the list of suppliers is broad, due to space limitations it is not definitive. Inclusion in the list does not signify SAA endorsement, nor does exclusion indicate censure. Suppliers' and manufacturers' names and addresses are provided at the end of the list; please refer to the appropriate reference number.

Item	Source
Absorene® wallpaper cleaner	1, 33
Adhesives	
Methyl cellulose	22, 29, 33
Wheat paste, dry powder #301	33
Wheat starch, Aytex-P	33
Archival Storage	
folders, boxes, envelopes,	10, 18, 20,
document cases, flat storage	22, 27, 33,
boxes, etc.	36
Boards	
binder's board	17
Lig-free® board (for phased boxes)	10
mat board	4, 10, 22, 36
Bone folders	8, 22, 33
Book dryer/exterminator	40
Book press	17, antique stores, used printing equipment companies
Brayer	22, 36, art supply stores
Brushes	
Paste	9, 33, art supply stores
Surface cleaning	2, 9, 39, art supply stores
Cheesecloth	department or hardware stores
Chisel, round	hardware stores, tool supply houses
Cotton swabs	drug or grocery stores
Cutting board	art supply stores
Encapsulating machine	10, 25, 36
Environmental monitoring equipment	
Gas detector kits	7
Humidicator paper	9, 22
Hydrogen sulfide indicator cards	24
Hygrometer	9, 14, 31
Hygrothermograph	9, 14, 31
Light meter	
Ultraviolet	23
Visible	photographic supply stores
Sling Psychrometer	22, 31, 34
Sulfur dioxide test papers	16
Thermometer	14
Water Alert®	11, 36

Erasers, Magic Rub® , vinyl	33, art supply stores
Eye dropper	33, art supply stores
Fumigation chamber, portable	3
Fumigation chamber, vacuum	37
Garbage cans, plastic	department or hardware stores
Gloves, white cotton	22, 33, photographic supply stores
Grid (for aligning polyester and documents)	20, 36
Hammer	hardware stores
Knives	
Mat	22, 33
Scalpel handle (#4) and blades (#23)	9, 33
Utility (Stanley #299 or 691)	22, 33, hardware stores
Linen tape	9, 10, 22, 36
Magnifier, Linen Tester (5x)	9
Map cases	19, 22
Microspatula	8, 9, 33
Mounting corners (polyester)	22, 36
Neat's-foot oil and lanolin	33
One-Wipe® treated dust cloths	33, hardware and grocery stores
o-phenyl phenol	33
Opaline® dry cleaning pads	13, 33, art supply stores
Orvus®	9, 33
pH Testing	
Archivist's® Pen	22, 36
Barrow Laboratory Paper Test Kit	5
EM Laboratory colorpHast® Indicator Sticks	9, 22, 29, 33, 36
Tri-Test Spot Testing Kit	22
Paper	
Blotting, neutral pH	22, 36
Bond, with an alkaline reserve	10, 20, 36
Japanese mending	2, 4, 22, 29, 33, 39
Silicone release paper	9, 33
Tissue, neutral pH	20, 22, 36
Paper clips	
Inert plastic	9, 36
Stainless steel	9, 10, 36
Paper cutter (board shear)	17, 22, art supply stores, used printing equipment companies
Photographic storage materials	
Sleeves, envelopes, slide organizers, albums, boxes, etc.	10, 15, 20, 22, 26, 28, 36
Plate glass	glass distributor
Pliers, nipping	hardware stores
Polyester, sheets or roll	9, 10, 12, 20, 21, 22, 35, 36
Polyester web	12, 33, 36
Polyethylene, sheets	9
Potassium lactate	33

Punch, leather	hardware stores
Rivets	6
Ruler (stainless steel, calibrated)	8, 33, art supply stores
Ruling pen	art supply stores
Sandpaper (#400)	hardware stores
Scissors	33, art supply stores, department stores
Skum-X® (Dietzgen)	33, art supply stores
Straightedge (heavy stainless steel, non-calibrated)	33, hardware stores
Tape, double-coated (3M Scotch Brand® #415)	9, 10, 20, 22, 35, 36
Thread, heavy linen	8, 9, 36
Triangle, metal	33, art supply stores
Tubes, neutral pH	10, 36
Tweezers	9, 14, 36, art supply stores
Ultraviolet (UV) filtering shields	
Filtering sleeves for fluorescent tubes	10, 22
Low UV emission fluorescent tubes	38
Plexiglas® UF3, sheets	10, 22, 30
Vacuum cleaner, portable	36

1. Absorene Manufacturing Company
   1609 North 14th Street
   St. Louis, Missouri 63106
   (314-231-6355)

2. Aiko's Art Materials Import
   714 North Wabash
   Chicago, Illinois 60611
   (312-943-0475)

3. H.W. Anderson Products, Inc.
   45 East Main Street
   Oyster Bay, New York 11711

4. Andrews/Nelson/Whitehead
   31-10 48th Avenue
   Long Island, New York 11101
   (212-937-7100)

5. Applied Science Laboratory
   2216 Hull Street
   Richmond, Virginia 23224
   (804-231-9386)

6. Art Handicrafts Company
   3512 Flatlands Avenue
   Brooklyn, New York 11234
   (212-252-6622)

7. Bendix Corporation
   National Environment Instruments Division
   P.O. Box 520, Pilgrim Station
   Warwick, Rhode Island 02888

8. Bookmakers
   2025 Eye Street, NW, Room 307
   Washington, D.C. 20006
   (202-296-6613)

9. Conservation Materials, Ltd.
   340 Freeport Boulevard
   Box 2884
   Sparks, Nevada 89431
   (702-331-0582)

10. Conservation Resources International, Inc.
    1111 North Royal Street
    Alexandria, Virginia 22314
    (703-549-6610)

11. Dorlen Products
    7424 West Layton Avenue
    Greenfield, Wisconsin 53220
    (414-232-4840)

12. E. I. DuPont de Nemours & Co., Inc.
    Fabrics and Finishes Department
    Industrial Products Division
    Wilmington, Delaware 19898

13. Durasol Drug and Chemical Company
    1 Oakland Street
    Amesbury, Massachusetts 01913

14. Fisher Scientific Company
    711 Forbes Avenue
    Pittsburgh, Pennsylvania 15219
    (412-562-8300)
    (check telephone directory for local distributors)

15. Franklin Distributors Corporation
    P.O. Box 320
    Denville, New Jersey 07834

16. Gallard-Schlesinger
    584 Mineola Avenue
    Carle Place
    Long Island, New York 11514
    (516-333-5600)

17. Gane Bros. and Lane, Inc.
    1400 Greenleaf Avenue
    Elk Grove Village, Illinois 60007
    (312-593-3360)

18. Gaylord Bros., Inc.
    Box 4901
    Syracuse, New York 13221
    (800-448-6160)

19. Hamilton Industries
    1316 18th Street
    Two Rivers, Wisconsin 54241

20. Hollinger Corporation
    P.O. Box 6185
    3810 South Four Mile Run Drive
    Arlington, Virginia 22206
    (703-671-6600)

21. I.C.I. America Inc.
    Plastics Division
    Wilmington, Delaware 19897

22. Light Impressions Corporation
    439 Monroe Avenue
    P.O. Box 940
    Rochester, New York 14603
    (800-828-6216)

23. Littlemore Scientific Engineering Company
    Railway Lane, Littlemore
    Oxford, England

24. Metronics Associates, Inc.
    3201 Porter Drive
    Palo Alto, California 94304

25. William Minter
    1948 West Addison
    Chicago, Illinois 60613
    (312-248-0624)

26. Photofile
    2000 Lewis Avenue
    P.O. Box 123
    Zion, Illinois 60099
    (312-872-7557)

27. Pohlig Bros., Inc.
    P.O. Box 8069
    Richmond, Virginia 23223
    (404-644-7824)

28. Printfile, Inc.
    Box 100
    Schenectady, New York 12304

29. Process Materials Corporation
    301 Veterans Boulevard
    Rutherford, New Jersey 07070
    (201-935-2900)

30. Rohm and Haas, Plastics Division
    Independence Mall West
    Philadelphia, Pennsylvania 19105
    (check telephone directory for local distributors)

31. Science Associates, Inc.
    Box 230, 230 Nassau Street
    Princeton, New Jersey 08540
    (609-924-4470)

32. Solar-Screen Company
    53-11 105th Street
    Corona, New York 11368
    (212-592-8223)

33. TALAS
    Technical Library Service, Inc.
    213 West 35th Street
    New York, New York 10001-1996
    (212-736-7744)

34. Taylor Instrument Company
    Consumer Products Division
    Sybron Corporation
    Arden, North Carolina 28704

35. 3M
    Film and Allied Products Division
    3M Center
    St. Paul, Minnesota 55101

36. University Products
    P.O. Box 101
    South Canal Street
    Holyoke, Massachusetts 01041
    (413-532-9431)

37. Vacudyne Altair
    375 E. Joe Orr Road
    Chicago Heights, Illinois 60411
    (312-757-5200)

38. Verd-A-Ray Corporation
    615 Front Street
    Toledo, Ohio 43605
    (419-691-5751)

39. Washi No Mise
    R.D. #2
    Baltimore Pike
    Kennitt Square, Pennsylvania 19348

40. Wei T'o Associates, Inc.
    P.O. Drawer 40
    21750 Main Street, Unit 27
    Matteson, Illinois 60443
    (312-747-6660)

Appendix G
Regional Conservation Centers

Non-profit regional conservation centers only are included in this list. They are briefly described as to focus and range of services offered. Many state archives and libraries operate conservation laboratories and undertake modest amounts of work for institutions within their state. Inquiries should be directed to the appropriate state agency. Information on private paper, book, and photographic conservators may be sought from the American Institute for Conservation and the Guild of Book Workers (see Appendix H for addresses).

Balboa Art Conservation Center
P.O. Box 3755
San Diego, California 92103
(619-236-9702)

Treatment services for paintings, works of art on paper, and archival materials. A discount on the hourly service rate is provided to member organizations. Work from non-member, non-profit organizations is accepted at a higher hourly rate. Offers consulting services and educational programs, including lectures, tours, and workshops.

Conservation Center for Art and Historic Artifacts
260 South Broad Street
Philadelphia, Pennsylvania 19102
(215-545-0613)

Conservation facility specializing in works of art on paper and archival and manuscript materials. Conservation surveys and consultations available to member institutions.

Northeast Document Conservation Center
Abbot Hall, School Street
Andover, Massachusetts 01810
(617-470-1010)

Services include a paper conservation workshop for the treatment of books, archival materials, and works of art on paper. Conservation bookbinding and microfilm and photographic copying services are available, as well as seminars, workshops, consulting services, and internships. Emergency disaster assistance provided. Fees charged on an at-cost basis to non-profit institutions in the region served by the Center; others (including those outside the region) may use the Center's services at slightly higher rates.

Pacific Regional Conservation Center
Bishop Museum
P.O. Box 9000 A
Honolulu, Hawaii 96819
(808-847-3511)

Treatment center for works of art on paper, library and archival materials, and ethnographical objects. Work undertaken for non-members on a time-available basis and at a slightly higher rate. Consultation services for Hawaii and the Pacific region.

Rocky Mountain Regional Conservation Center
University of Denver
2420 South University Boulevard
Denver, Colorado 80208
(303-753-3218)

Treatment facility for paintings, paper, textiles, and three-dimensional objects, including documents and books. Services available to non-members, though members receive a preferred hourly rate. Consulting and emergency services available.

Texas Conservation Center
Panhandle-Plains Historical Museum
Box 967, W.T. Station
Canyon, Texas 79016
(806-655-7191)

Treatment services for all types of art and artifacts, including books, works of art on paper, archival materials, paintings, textiles, ceramics, and ethnographical materials. On-site consultations, workshops, and internships available. Services provided to institutions, individuals, and government agencies both in and out of Texas. Fee structure based on labor and material costs.

The Upper Midwest Conservation Association
Minneapolis Institute of Arts
2400 Third Avenue South
Minneapolis, Minnesota 55404
(612-870-3120)

Conservation services for the treatment of works of art, cultural artifacts, furniture, textiles, archival documents, and photographs. Consultation services, on-site surveys, and workshops available. Membership is open to non-profit institutions that own or have custody of works of art or objects of cultural significance. Services to non-members are contracted at a slightly higher rate than to members.

Appendix H
Conservation Organizations

The following professional organizations, societies, and institutions are involved in various aspects of conservation, ranging from educational activities and publishing through research. Major program emphases are briefly described.

American Association for State and Local History
708 Berry Road
Nashville, Tennessee 37204
(615-383-5991)

Extensive publishing program includes books on preservation of record materials and historical artifacts. Also publishes *History News* (which includes the column "Conserva-tips") and series of technical leaflets, many of which are on conservation topics. Slide/tape training programs on conservation of historic houses and museum topics. Seminars, independent study courses, and annual meetings.

American Association of Museums
1055 Thomas Jefferson Street, NW
Washington, DC 20007
(202-338-5300)

Annual meeting sessions often address conservation issues. Publishes *Museum News* (reprints of conservation articles are available) as well as books on such topics as the environment, security, and exhibits.

American Institute for Conservation of Historic and Artistic Works (AIC)
The Klingle Mansion
3545 Williamsburg Lane, NW
Washington, D.C. 20008
(202-364-1036)

Members include conservators, conservation scientists, librarians, archivists, and curators of cultural property. Has adopted a Code of Ethics and Standards of Practice (reprinted in *Conservation Treatment Facilities in the United States*, published by the National Conservation Advisory Council in 1980; see bibliography for full citation). Publishes *Journal of the American Institute for Conservation* and quarterly newsletter; annual meetings include sessions organized by Book and Paper and Photographic Materials Specialty Groups.

American Library Association
50 East Huron Street
Chicago, Illinois 60611
(312-944-6780)

Preservation of Library Materials Section of the Resources and Technical Services Division coordinates a number of committees and activities, including publication of the *Preservation Education Directory*. Books on conservation topics have been published under the auspices of the Library Technology Program.

American National Standards Institute (ANSI)
1430 Broadway
New York, New York 10018
(212-354-3300)

Coordinates the development of national standards through consensus. Of special interest are standards relating to the storage and processing of photographic film. Complete list of published standards available.

Center for Occupational Hazards
5 Beekman Street
New York, New York 10038
(212-227-6220)

The Art Hazards Information Center, a project of the Center for Occupational Hazards, will answer inquiries on the hazards of materials used in the arts and conservation and suitable precautions. Offers courses and conferences; publication program includes newsletter, *Art Hazards News*.

Guild of Book Workers (GBW)
663 Fifth Avenue
New York, New York 10022
(212-757-6454)

Primarily educational in focus, the GBW provides a forum for individuals working in the hand book arts: bookbinding, calligraphy, paper decorating, etc. Sponsors workshops and seminars; publishes *Journal* and quarterly newsletter. *Opportunities for Study in Hand Bookbinding and Calligraphy* is available from the GBW office.

Institute of Paper Conservation
P.O. Box 17
London WC1N 2PE England

Publishes an annual journal, *The Paper Conservator*, and a newsletter, *Paper Conservation News*.

International Institute for Conservation of Historic and Artistic Works (IIC)
6 Buckingham Street
Loncon WC2N 6BA England

Organization composed primarily of professional conservators concerned with preservation of cultural and historical artifacts broadly defined. Publications include a quarterly journal, *Studies in Conservation*, and biennial *Art and Archeology Technical Abstracts*.

Library of Congress
Preservation Office
Washington, D.C. 20540
(202-287-5213)

The Preservation Office is organized under the following units: Binding, Collections Maintenance, Preservation Microfilming, Research and Testing, Restoration, and the National Preservation Program. Will respond briefly to technical inquiries. Publishes a series of "Preservation Leaflets" plus a growing number of books and pamphlets (see bibliography).

National Archives and Records Service
Preservation Policy and Services Division
Washington, D.C. 20408
(202-523-3159)

The National Archives is developing conservation survey and sampling techniques that will have a broad impact on archival conservation. The Document Conservation Laboratory is supported by an auxiliary testing lab. Issues occasional publications, and will respond to technical inquiries.

National Fire Protection Association
470 Atlantic Avenue
Boston, Massachusetts 02210
(617-482-8755)

Extensive publication program focusing on fire prevention and protection; publishes National Fire Code.

National Institute for the Conservation of Cultural Property (NIC)
Arts and Industries Building — 2225
Smithsonian Institution
Washington, D.C. 20560
(202-357-2295)

Formerly National Conservation Advisory Council (NCAC). Forum for the development of a national policy for preserving the cultural heritage of the United States. All fields of conservation are represented in the NIC; of special interest is the Libraries and Archives Committee, which issued a report in 1978 (*National Needs in Libraries and Archives Conservation*), and which currently is working to develop standards for environmental conditions for the storage of paper-based library and archives holdings.

Society of American Archivists
330 South Wells Street, Suite 810
Chicago, Illinois 60606
(312-922-0140)

Offers conservation workshops and consultant services. Conservation Section provides focus for concerns relating to archival conservation. Annual meetings include sessions on conservation and conservation tours and demonstrations. Publishes quarterly journal, *American Archivist,* and bimonthly newsletter.

Western Conservation Congress (WCC)
10200 West 20th Avenue
Lakewood, Colorado 80215
(303-238-8411)

Organized in 1980 as an outgrowth of the Western States Materials Conservation Project. State chapters are being formed in the twenty states composing the membership of the Western Council of State Libraries. Aims are to foster interest in conservation, to provide an information clearinghouse, and to offer training opportunities through workshops.

Appendix I
Funding Sources for Conservation

A number of federal, state, and local agencies and foundations, in both the public and private sectors, grant funds to support conservation activities. Funding guidelines and requirements vary from agency to agency, and over time, funding priorities alter within agencies. In the past, monies have been granted to support research, training, the establishment of conservation laboratories, and preservation microfilming, as well as physical treatment of intrinsically valuable archival collections. Generally, successful funding applications are on behalf of collections of national significance in a given field or discipline, and the sponsoring institution demonstrates some degree of commitment and ongoing support of conservation program activities.

The following is a brief list of public and private funding agencies that operate on a national level and have been known to grant monies for conservation-related projects. Inquiries regarding areas of interest, funding priorities, application procedures, and similar provisions should be directed to the individual agencies.

Council on Library Resources
1785 Massachusetts Avenue, NW
Washington, DC 20036
(202-483-7474)

The Ford Foundation
320 East 43rd Street
New York, NY 10017
(212-573-5000)

The Andrew W. Mellon Foundation
140 East 62nd Street
New York, NY 10021
(212-838-8400)

National Endowment for the Arts
2401 E Street, NW
Washington, DC 20506
(202-634-6369)

National Endowment for the Humanities
Research Resources Program
Old Post Office
1100 Pennsylvania Avenue, NW
Washington, DC 20506
(202-786-0200)

National Historical Publications and Records Commission
National Archives and Records Service
Washington, DC 20408
(202-724-1616)

National Museum Act
Arts and Industries Building
Smithsonian Institution
Washington, DC 20560
(202-357-2257)

Further information on federal grant-giving organizations may be obtained from *Cultural Directory to Federal Funds and Services for the Arts and Humanities,* Linda C. Coe, Rebecca Denney, and Anne Rogers, comps. (Federal Council on the Arts and Humanities. Washington, DC: Smithsonian Institution Press, 1980.)

In addition, local foundations should not be overlooked as a source of grant money. They may be encouraged to support archival repositories in their locality, especially if there are institutional ties or if the collecting focus of the archives holds special significance to the foundation. A useful guide in locating private philanthropic organizations is *The Foundation Directory,* New York: Columbia University Press. 7th edition, 1979. Frequently updated.

Acknowledgements

This manual was prepared as one phase of the Basic Archival Conservation Program. Other aspects of the Program included a series of conservation workshops and a consultant service. A number of people worked together to extend knowledge of archival conservation, and thereby helped to ensure the success of the Program. I am grateful to my colleagues who served as workshop instructors and/or consultants for their insights and consistent willingness to share their expertise: George M. Cunha, Kenneth W. Duckett, Judith Fortson-Jones, Edward R. Gilbert, Margery S. Long, Howard P. Lowell, Mildred O'Connell, and Gloria D. Scott.

I am also grateful to members of the Basic Archival Conservation Program Advisory Committee who were uniformly supportive and generous in their assistance: Shonnie Finnegan, Edward R. Gilbert, Mary Todd Glaser, Howard P. Lowell, and William L. McDowell, Jr.

Edward R. Gilbert, Technical Advisor to the Program, read the entire manual and made many helpful suggestions and additions. His sound advice and guidance have been a valued resource throughout the Program.

The following individuals provided counsel during various stages of the preparation of the manual: Terry Abraham, Mary Ann Bamberger, Paul N. Banks, David Horn, Judith Fortson-Jones, Mary Lynn McCree, Richard D. Smith, and Virginia Stewart. I am most appreciative of their help. SAA staff members provided a good measure of encouragement during the writing of the manual. I am especially grateful for the support provided by Ann Morgan Campbell and the technical capability of Deborah Risteen in producing the manual. Special thanks are also due Sylvia Burck and Linda Ziemer who ably managed many phases of the Program.

Pamela Spitzmueller's drawings add immeasurably to the instruction sheets for basic conservation procedures. I am grateful both for her comments on the written instructions and her artistic ability in interpreting them.

Finally, I am indebted to two special teachers. Philip P. Mason taught me archival theory and practice, and Bill Anthony taught me bookbinding and the proper approach to the craft. Both instilled in me great enthusiasm and love of the work, which I hope is conveyed in this manual.

Mary Lynn Ritzenthaler ✤